T0298470

RESOURCES FOR THE FUTURE LIBRARY COLLECTION
ENVIRONMENTAL AND RESOURCE ECONOMICS

Volume 2

Scarcity and Growth
The Economics of Natural Resource Availability

Full list of titles in the set
Environmental and Resource Economics

Scarcity and Growth
The Economics of Natural Resource Availability

Harold J. Barnett and Chandler Morse

RFF PRESS
RESOURCES FOR THE FUTURE

Washington, DC • London

First published in 1963 by The Johns Hopkins University Press for Resources for the Future

This edition first published in 2011 by RFF Press, an imprint of Earthscan

Earthscan LLC, 1616 P Street, NW, Washington, DC 20036, USA
Earthscan Ltd, Dunstan House, 14a St Cross Street, London EC1N 8XA, UK
Earthscan publishes in association with the International Institute for Environment and Development

For more information on RFF Press and Earthscan publications, see www. rffpress.org and www.earthscan.co.uk or write to earthinfo@earthscan.co.uk

ISBN: 978-1-61726-031-5 (Volume 2)
ISBN: 978-1-61726-003-2 (Environmental and Resource Economics set)
ISBN: 978-1-61726-000-1 (Resources for the Future Library Collection)

A catalogue record for this book is available from the British Library

Publisher's note

The publisher has made every effort to ensure the quality of this reprint, but points out that some imperfections in the original copies may be apparent.

At Earthscan we strive to minimize our environmental impacts and carbon footprint through reducing waste, recycling and offsetting our CO_2 emissions, including those created through publication of this book. For more details of our environmental policy, see www.earthscan.co.uk.

SCARCITY AND GROWTH

The Economics of Natural Resource Availability

SCARCITY
and GROWTH

The Economics of
Natural Resource Availability

BY HAROLD J. BARNETT AND CHANDLER MORSE

PUBLISHED FOR Resources for the Future, Inc.
BY The Johns Hopkins Press, BALTIMORE

Copyright © 1963, The Johns Hopkins Press, Baltimore, Md. 21218
LIBRARY OF CONGRESS CATALOG CARD NUMBER 63-9742
MANUFACTURED IN THE UNITED STATES OF AMERICA
Distributed in Great Britain by Oxford University Press, London
Originally published, 1963
Johns Hopkins Paperbacks edition, 1965
Second printing, 1967

FOREWORD

No problem is of deeper concern to mankind than that of coming to terms with the natural environment so that it will support a reasonably satisfying way of life. With the spread of modern science and technology during the past century and a half the problem has changed somewhat, at least for the economically more advanced areas of the world where the pressure of population on the resource base has been reduced. In such countries, and pre-eminently in the United States, there is no present threat of general resource scarcity—indeed, for basic agricultural products there is glut—but the age-old goal of winning a higher level of living from the soil, the water, and the subsoil minerals continues to call forth the enterprise and labor of large numbers of people as well as to tax, at times, the ingenuity of policy-makers. Even though technological innovation and managerial skill appear to assure Americans of adequate quantities of raw materials, the prospect of qualitative deterioration of the environment—in its livability and its aesthetic appeal—must concern us as a problem of the first rank.

Harold J. Barnett and Chandler Morse have addressed the "man/land" or the "population/resource" problem afresh, in terms of the latest statistical information and modern analytical tools. They have re-examined the propositions propounded by Malthus, Ricardo, and John Stuart Mill; and they have thought deeply about the roots of the American Conservation Movement associated with Theodore Roosevelt and Gifford Pinchot as these roots may be traced back into Darwinism and the speculations of George Marsh. They have emerged with a clearer view of where the essence of the problem is now to be found and what it means for people today.

It is not inaccurate to say this book is a reformulation of the theories of Malthus and his immediate associates and successors in the nineteenth-century stream of English classical economics. But it is not what has come to be called a Neo-Malthusian adaptation; the great forces it deals with are the same, but the implications of the reformulation are quite different. And the speculations it offers about the future may well change profoundly the intellectual content and the very objectives of conservation for the balance of this century. Their findings, though tested primarily in terms of the statistical record of American economic growth, will have relevance to the less developed countries as these countries succeed in harnessing more advanced technology to the task of economic development.

In this book the authors make telling use of the historical statistics presented in *Trends in Natural Resource Commodities: Statistics of Prices, Output, Consumption, Foreign Trade, and Employment in the United States, 1870–1957,* by Neal Potter and Francis T. Christy, Jr. (The Johns Hopkins Press for Resources for the Future, Inc., 1962), as the empirical support for their propositions. In fact, the two books were conceived at about the same time as the two parts of a theoretical-empirical combination. This book is also related to the forthcoming RFF study, *Resources in America's Future* (also Johns Hopkins Press), in which trends of resource demand and supply, projected to the year 2000, give further support to some of the main findings of the Barnett-Morse book.

This study was begun and largely carried out while Mr. Barnett was on the full-time staff of Resources for the Future. Mr. Barnett, subsequently professor of economics at Wayne State University, recently accepted the chairmanship of the department of economics at Washington University, St. Louis. Mr. Morse, professor of economics at Cornell University, has been associated with Resources for the Future on a part-time basis.

Joseph L. Fisher
President, Resources for the Future

December 1962

ACKNOWLEDGMENTS

The authors of this fully collaborative work are deeply indebted to colleagues who assisted during our exploration and study, and to reviewers who examined draft material and made criticisms and suggestions. All have left a mark but none need acknowledge responsibility for either the form or the content of the final product.

Our colleagues Neal Potter and Francis T. Christy, Jr., in their comparison study, *Trends in Natural Resource Commodities,* provided the bulk of basic data used in our statistical analysis. They also undertook special processing and supervision of chart work in order to up-date the numerous tables and charts in our Part III. Two other colleagues, working as research assistants, also rendered exceptional help. Katherine Dolfis Warden, assisting Barnett in Washington, did a large amount of statistical work and editorial checking during the period of the study. Wolfgang Schoellkopf (now at Princeton), assisting Morse in Ithaca, assisted in developing the theory chapters of Part II and the related charts.

Our other Resources for the Future colleagues also contributed to the study, directly in their suggestions or indirectly by their own research and in numerous discussions. At different times, Paul Cootner (now at MIT), Henry Jarrett, Herbert Mohring (now at the University of Minnesota), Richard Muth (now at the University of Chicago), and Harvey Perloff helped us over difficult places in the course of our analysis. Many other RFF colleagues were also generous in review and suggestions.

The complete manuscript was reviewed by Simon Kuznets of Harvard University and Anthony Scott of the University of British Columbia. Their trenchant criticisms and helpful suggestions enabled us to shorten an overlong manuscript and to improve it in many other respects. Our obligation (and the reader's) to Professors Kuznets and Scott for helping to make the book as a whole readable and useful is a substantial one.

We also imposed heavily on a large number of other persons, both within academic circles and outside, for review of particular chapters. We wish to express appreciation for comments to:

Hugh H. Bennett, formerly of the Soil Conservation Service of the U.S. Department of Agriculture (deceased); Yale Brozen, University of Chicago; C. H. Burgess, Kennecott Copper Corp.; Ansley J. Coale, Princeton University; Lyle E. Craine, University of Michigan; Sir Charles Galton Darwin, Cambridge, England; Ira T. Ellis, Dupont Company; J. K. Galbraith, Harvard University; Bela Gold, University of Pittsburgh; C. B. Goodhart, Cambridge University; Luther Gulick, Institute of Public Administration; D. Hamberg, University of Buffalo; Lawrence S. Hamilton, Cornell University; Arnold C. Harberger, University of Chicago; George H. Hildebrand, Cornell University; Jack Hirshleifer, University of California at Los Angeles; E. M. Hoover, University of Pittsburgh; Harold Hotelling, University of North Carolina; J. M. Hughes, U.S. Department of Agriculture; John Ise, University of Kansas; Alfred E. Kahn, Cornell University; Charles P. Kindleberger, Massachusetts Institute of Technology; Edward S. Mason, Harvard University; Richard R. Nelson, Council of Economic Advisers; Samuel H. Ordway, The Conservation Foundation; Fairfield Osborn, The Conservation Foundation; Frederick Osborn, Population Council; William N. Parker, University of North Carolina; T. W. Schultz, University of Chicago; Joseph J. Spengler, Duke University; George Stigler, University of Chicago; Arthur W. Stuart, Mine, Mill, and Smelter Workers; J. Vanek, Harvard University; William Vickrey, Columbia University; Henry H. Villard, The Ford Foundation; Jacob Viner, Princeton University; Peter Vukasin, Harpur College; R. C. Weigel, Dupont Company; Norman Wengert, Wayne State University; W. S. Woytinsky, Washington, D.C. (deceased); Erich W. Zimmerman, University of Texas.

We express sincere thanks to our editors, Henry Jarrett and Virginia Parker, whose interest was exceeded only by their contribution.

Finally, and particularly now that it is completed, we are grateful for the opportunity to have engaged in this intellectual adventure. To the two people who gave unfailing encouragement—Reuben G. Gustavson and Joseph L. Fisher—we tender a special thanks.

Harold J. Barnett
Chandler Morse

December 1962

CONTENTS

PART IV. WELFARE IN A PROGRESSIVE WORLD

LIST OF TABLES

LIST OF FIGURES

Chapter 1

SCARCITY AND GROWTH:
A SUMMARY VIEW

MAN's relationship to the natural environment, and nature's influence upon the course and quality of human life, are among the oldest topics of speculation of which we are aware. Myth, folktale, and fable; custom, institution, and law; philosophy, science, and technology—all, as far back as records extend, attest to an abiding interest in these concerns.

The Doctrine of Increasing Natural Resource Scarcity

The past two centuries—the period of industrial revolution, emergence of science, and population explosion—have witnessed a great broadening and deepening of interest in natural resources. An influential expression of this growing interest was that of British classical economics, early in the nineteenth century, with its doctrine that an inherently limited availability of natural resources sets an upper bound to economic growth and welfare. Later, there was the Conservation Movement in the United States, which took shape around the turn of the present century. Arising out of concern over natural resource scarcity and a consequent endeavor to formulate policies for the use of the extensive public domain, this movement provided broad, vigorous, and influential expression and political leadership. The interests, but not the vitality, of the Conservation Movement, survive in a vast current literature of scientists, engineers, social analysts, educators, journalists, businessmen, public officials, and adherents of a wide variety of academic disciplines. The occurrence and economic consequences of natural resource scarcity, and their social

1

and policy implications, run like strong threads through the variegated fabric of contemporary public concern over natural resources. The doctrine of increasing scarcity and its effects has achieved remarkable viability.

The classical economists—particularly Malthus, Ricardo, and Mill —predicted that scarcity of natural resources would lead to eventually diminishing social returns to economic effort, with retardation and eventual cessation of economic growth. Indeed, classical economic theory acquired its essential character, and for economics its reputation as the "dismal science," from this basic premise. In a somewhat different formulation, the scarcity idea also entered the theory of natural selection when Darwin, acknowledging a debt to Malthus, saw competition for limited means of survival as the determinant of biological evolution.

The Conservation Movement accepted the scarcity premise as valid for an unregulated private enterprise society. But, rejecting laissez faire, at least so far as activities connected with natural resources were concerned, they believed that the trend of social welfare over time could be influenced by the extent to which men conserved and managed resources with an eye to the welfare of future generations. The leaders of the Conservation Movement proposed that society, taking thought for the consequences of its actions, should forestall the effects of increasing scarcity by employing criteria of physical and administrative—not economic—efficiency. They argued that government intervention could improve on the untrammeled processes of private decision making with respect to natural resources, and that public policies should be devised with this end in view. Their willingness to employ public power as a check on business freedom, signifying as it did a certain disillusionment with the principles of laissez faire, made the Conservation Movement something of a catch-all for interventionist ideas of all kinds. This helps to explain its many-sided character. But the core of the Movement was concern for the effect of natural resources, and especially natural resource policy and administration, on the trend of social welfare in a world subject to increasing resource scarcity.

Our principal concern is with economic doctrines of increasing natural resource scarcity and diminishing returns, and their relevance in the modern world. This reflects a professional bias, but also a conviction that serious consideration of the social, and more qualitative, aspects of the natural resource problem must be secondary—that is, must follow understanding of the more quantitative economic aspects. For, if growth and welfare are inescapably subject to an economic law of diminishing returns, the necessary social policies and the moral and human implications are surely different than if they are not. Alternatively, if there is reason to believe that man's ingenuity and wisdom offer opportunities to avoid natural resource scarcity and its effects, then the means for such escapes and their moral and human implications become the center of attention.

The problem we treat, it will be apparent, lies in the realm of historical growth economics, not of static efficiency economics. The latter enters our analysis on occasion, but only in a subsidiary fashion. Our framework is that of the classical economists in their theorizing about the trend of output per capita over the long term. Our main effort, therefore, is directed to a thorough examination of the conceptual and empirical foundations of the doctrine of increasing natural resource scarcity and its effects. Part II conducts this inquiry in a classical framework of unchanging sociotechnical conditions. Part III admits sociotechnical change into the analysis.

A World Without Progress

We take as our starting point for examination of scarcity doctrine a resource situation which we call "Utopian." In this hypothetical situation, natural resources are freely available without limit and with no change in quality—they do not retard growth. The social production process is one of constant returns to scale. Technological and social progress are ruled out. Under these conditions, returns per unit of input do not diminish. The labor-capital cost of a unit of output remains constant as population (labor) increases and capital accumulates. Nor is growth explosive; the rates of growth of labor and capital through time are taken as predetermined, and resources are used only up to the point at which output is a maximum for the given amounts of the complementary inputs. Hence, some natural resources remain unused, though freely available, until the growth process provides the population and capital accumulation required to make them productive. The time shape of the growth path is determined by the rates of growth of labor and capital; in the sense that natural resource availability is unlimited, natural resources exert no influence on the rate or shape of growth.

The Malthusian and Ricardian versions of scarcity are introduced in this basic model. For the former case, we assume that there is an absolute limit to resources, beyond which they cease to be available. The Malthusian case is thus like the Utopian up to the limit of resources. Thereafter, the increasing intensity of natural resource use entails a steady increase in labor-capital cost per unit of output.

For the Ricardian case, we assume that resources are unlimited in quantity, but not homogeneous. The Ricardian case rests on the proposition that, as growth proceeds, it draws upon incremental resources with physical or locational characteristics different from the resources already employed. But this, in itself, does not imply diminishing returns, for such alterations need not cause costs to increase steadily over time. An additional postulate, that society possesses both the knowledge and the will to use resources in order of declining economic quality—that is, in an order which results in increasing cost per unit of output—is needed.

The foregoing conditions (together with some additional specifications of detail) are sufficient to produce diminishing returns in both the Malthusian and Ricardian cases. These initial conditions, however, are only a precisely defined starting point for our analysis. Having been specified, they are systematically modified in ways that bring them closer to reality, and the effects on diminishing returns are observed.

The first step toward greater reality is to recognize that the stock of resources is not constant, even when discovery and technological progress are ruled out. Resources are depleted through use, destroyed by careless or unnecessary action, and otherwise extinguished. This has the effect of strengthening the case for diminishing returns, either by hastening the approach toward the Malthusian limit, or by reducing the available amounts of better resources faster than inferior resources in the Ricardian case.

A second modification of the original conditions is to recognize that social output consists of many products, that natural resources are exceedingly varied, and that labor and capital inputs differ widely in kind and quality. Consequently, as differential resource scarcities lead to changes in relative costs, there are opportunities to make economically rational substitutions that will ameliorate and, in some cases, even forestall the appearance of diminishing returns. Substitutions that ameliorate resource extinction—increased recovery and use of scrap, for example—also are possible. Substitution possibilities are increased as the production process becomes more complex, and are more likely to be effective if decisions concerning production are guided by economic rationality. They, therefore, are more important in advanced industrial countries than in less developed areas.

Third, we observe that the structural characteristics of a society can have an important bearing on the prospects for diminishing returns. If capital grows at a faster rate than labor, as it has in the industrialized countries, output per unit of labor (or even per unit of labor plus capital) will not necessarily fall merely because the input of natural resources cannot be increased, or because the economic quality of resources declines. More needs to be specified about the character of the social production process when the ratio of capital to labor is variable. Similarly, if the social production process yields increasing returns to scale during long-term growth—and it is not legitimate simply to presume that it cannot—there can be no assurance that a postulated increase in natural resource scarcity will produce diminishing returns. More information is needed concerning the relative strengths of the opposing forces. Furthermore, it is clear that the composition of output changes as output per capita increases. To the extent that this takes the form of a substitution of resource-light goods and services for those that make relatively heavy drafts on the resource base, this also ameliorates the force of increasing resource scarcity.

A fourth modification concerns the requirement of the Ricardian hypothesis that resources be used in order of declining economic quality. Even under the assumption of constant technology, it is rather much to expect that society will never be surprised by discoveries of hitherto unknown resources, especially as the growth of population carries men into regions not previously settled or systematically explored. Moreover, the growth and spread of population, by altering the location of resources relative to markets, will modify the order of economic use, possibly to the extent of reducing current costs below those prevalent at an earlier time. Also, a concern for the future sometimes leads to the adoption of public policies and institutional arrangements calculated to force inferior resources to be used before superior ones. Then, there is the circumstance that certain types of resources occur in broad plateaus so that costs remain approximately constant for extended periods of growth instead of increasing as required by the hypothesis. And, finally, there is the possibility that ecological unbalance—a concern of the American Conservationists—creates, as well as destroys, resources, and that the gain, as in the case of river valleys and deltas, may be greater than the loss.

None of the foregoing modifications of our initial conditions does material violence to the more general tenets of classical econòmic theory. Even so, doubts are raised concerning the certainty that natural resource scarcity and diminishing returns will occur in a growing, yet essentially classical, world. Questions arise concerning (1) the validity and significance of the Malthusian and Ricardian hypotheses of increasing natural resource scarcity, and (2) the probability that increasing scarcity, if present, will lead to diminishing returns in the social production process as a whole.

Malthusian scarcity, no doubt, has characterized many relatively primitive societies which possessed limited knowledge and skill. They not only failed to develop cultural taboos which stabilized population but also were able to extract only a small proportion of the services available in their natural environment. Thus, the limits of their resources were quickly reached. But such societies would also have to be relatively isolated, for otherwise cultural diffusion, migration, and interregional trade would offer the possibility of progressive extension of the resource limit. Under primitive conditions of isolation a relevant question is whether it is the limited availability of natural resources or the limited stock of knowledge that produces diminishing returns and inhibits economic growth.

The Ricardian hypothesis of declining economic quality of resources appears to us to be broadly relevant in a world of sociotechnical constancy. It cannot be presumed to operate with certainty and continuity, yet a tendency to recurrent upward movement in the cost of output of the extractive sector would seem more probable than a constant or declining trend. During selected historical phases of growth, however, the hypothesis could be invalid.

To recognize the probable occurrence of increasing resource scarcity is not to say that diminishing returns in social output are equally likely. Substitutions, increases in the ratio of capital to labor, and perhaps the realization of economies of scale in the social production process as a whole—all weaken the effect of increasing scarcity. The unit cost of aggregate social output, therefore, may remain constant or decrease even if the unit cost of extractive output rises continuously. Acknowledgment of the probable validity of the scarcity hypothesis in a classical world thus does not imply belief in the necessary occurrence of diminishing returns, especially for complex and flexible industrial societies.

Resources in a Progressive World

The assumption of sociotechnical constancy, to which we adhere throughout the analysis of Part II, is particularly unrealistic. Accordingly, this constraint is removed in Part III. But it then becomes virtually impossible to postulate a realistic set of conditions that would yield either generally increasing natural resource scarcity or diminishing returns in the social production process as a whole.

Recognition of the possibility of technological progress clearly cuts the ground from under the concept of Malthusian scarcity. Resources can only be defined in terms of known technology. Half a century ago the air was for breathing and burning; now it is also a natural resource of the chemical industry. Two decades ago Vermont granite was only building and tombstone material; now it is a potential fuel, each ton of which has a usable energy content (uranium) equal to 150 tons of coal. The notion of an absolute limit to natural resource availability is untenable when the definition of resources changes drastically and unpredictably over time.

What technological progress does to the Ricardian scarcity hypothesis is less clear. We take account of two possibilities. One—which we call the strong hypothesis—is that the economic quality of resources undergoes decline despite the occurrence of technological progress. We cannot, unfortunately, test this hypothesis directly by measuring changes in the economic quality of resources—that is, in natural resource scarcity. However, we can measure changes in the cost of extractive output, an imperfect but reasonably acceptable stand-in for natural resources themselves. When this is done for the United States for the period 1870–1957, the indexes (1929 = 100) of labor-capital input per unit of extractive output [1] are as follows:

	Total extractive	Agriculture	Minerals	Forestry
1870–1900	134	132	210	59
1919	122	114	164	106
1957	60	61	47	90

The evidence mainly shows increasing, not diminishing, returns. The cost per unit of total extractive product fell by half during the period. Of agriculture and minerals—the two major components, which account for 90 per cent of the total—the latter fell even more. Only forestry gives evidence of diminishing returns; cost per unit of product rose from the Civil War to World War I. But since World War I, when an aggravation of scarcity due to further economic growth might have been expected, diminishing returns have given way to approximately constant (or slightly increasing) returns.

On the whole, our strong hypothesis of natural resource scarcity fails. True, the increase in the absolute cost of forest products can be taken as evidence tending to confirm the validity of the Ricardian hypothesis in this particular sector. During the period up to 1919, the exhaustion of the better and more accessible stands of trees led to increasing costs. In the subsequent three decades, however, the rise in costs had begun to produce three effects: an introduction of cost-reducing innovations, conversion of wood wastes into usable products, and a shift to wood substitutes. The first and second of these contributed primarily to the observed stabilization in unit costs; the third helped to moderate the effect of the previous rise in costs on the rest of the economy.

Our second—and weaker—formulation of the Ricardian hypothesis is that, in the extractive sector, the decline in resource quality will partly nullify the effect of economy-wide technological advance; and that costs of a unit of extractive goods will, therefore, rise relative to unit costs of nonextractive goods. The evidence—again for the United

[1] Data from Chapter 8.

States, 1870–1957, and using indexes (1929 = 100) of labor-capital input per unit of output [2]—is as follows:

	Total extractive goods relative to nonextractive goods	Agricultural goods relative to nonextractive goods	Minerals relative to nonextractive goods	Forest products relative to nonextractive goods
1870–1900	99	97	154	37
1919	103	97	139	84
1957	87	89	68	130

Increase in natural resource scarcity should, according to the weak hypothesis, prevent the cost of extractive output from falling as much as that of nonextractive output. But, again with the exception of forestry, this did not occur. Relative unit costs of total extractive goods, and of agricultural goods, have been constant, and those of minerals have fallen; those of forestry alone have risen.

Developments like these are to be anticipated. We may expect that particular extractive products will undergo cost increases from time to time. But we may also expect that substitutes will make their appearance (as in the case of fuel and lighting), and that cost-reducing innovations will begin to put in an appearance (as in production of food grains). Increasing costs for particular extractive products, therefore, do not signify increasing costs for extractive output as a whole, let alone for the aggregate of all goods and services. Either costs are brought down, or the product market is lost as costs rise and substitutes appear, or both developments occur.

These developments, it is important to realize, are not essentially fortuitous. At one time they were, but important changes have occurred in man's knowledge of the physical universe over the past two centuries, changes which have built technological advance into the social processes of the modern world. A major proportion of final output in Malthus' time represented mechanically transformed products derived initially from a heavily agricultural, and still somewhat primitive, extractive sector. Today, chemical processes and molecular transformation—not to say atomic—have greatly broadened the re-

[2] Data from Chapter 9.

source base. Such ubiquitous materials as sea water, clays, rocks, sands, and air have already become economic resources to some degree, and constitute major plateaus of virtually constant physical properties and—under the prodding of continual research and development —increasing economic quality.

The scientific age differs in kind, and not only in degree, from the preceding mechanical age. Not only ingenuity but, increasingly, understanding; not luck but systematic investigation, are turning the tables on nature, making her subservient to man. And the signals that channel research effort, now in one direction, now in another—that determine innovational priorities—are usually the problems calling loudest to be solved. Sometimes the signals are political and social. More often, in a private enterprise society, they are market forces. Changes in relative costs, shifts of demand, the wish to develop broader markets—all aspects of growth—create problems which then generate solutions. Technological progress is no longer a mere by-product of man's efforts to win a decent living; it is an inseparable, organic component of that process.

Thus, the increasing scarcity of particular resources fosters discovery or development of alternative resources, not only equal in economic quality but often superior to those replaced. Few components of the earth's crust, including farm land, are so specific as to defy economic replacement, or so resistant to technological advance as to be incapable of eventually yielding extractive products at constant or declining cost. When coal, petroleum, hydroelectric power, and the atomic nucleus replace wood, peat, and dung as sources of energy; when aluminum yields its secrets to technology and is made to exist, as never before, in the form of metal; when the iron in taconite, once held there inseparably, becomes competitive with that in traditional ores—when all this happens, can we say that we have been forced to shift from resources of higher to those of lower economic quality?

We think not; the contrary is true. And we doubt that it is proper, in long-term, empirical growth analysis, to ask what would have happened to the economic quality of natural resources in the absence of technological progress. For the technological progress that has occurred was a necessary condition for the growth that has occurred, and if the former is ruled out the latter cannot appropriately be taken as a given fact. The strength of the demand-pull on the resource base, therefore, and the resources that would have been used in the absence of progress, are not meaningfully determinate. Hence, we are unable to make a quantitative statement about what would have happened to the cost of extractive output in the absence of sociotechnical change, beyond the analysis of our highly constrained classical models. Besides, our curiosity about a stagnant world is not very pressing, given the rapid change of the one we live in. Under the circumstances, it is more interesting and useful to reformulate our views concerning the influence of natural resources so that they will fit the changing world.

Welfare in a Progressive World

A reformulated hypothesis for the modern world must recognize that the exceedingly varied natural resource environment imposes a multitude of constraints—social no less than physical—upon the processes of economic growth. This presents expansionist man with a never-ending stream of ever-changing problems. But modern solutions to particular problems seldom entail increasing costs. Advances in fundamental science have made it possible to take advantage of the uniformity of energy/matter—a uniformity that makes it feasible, without preassignable limit, to escape the quantitative constraints imposed by the character of the earth's crust. A limit may exist, but it can be neither defined nor specified in economic terms. Flexibility, not rigidity, characterizes the relationship of modern man to the physical universe in which he lives. Nature imposes particular scarcities, not an inescapable general scarcity. Man is therefore able, and free, to choose among an indefinitely large number of alternatives. There is no reason to believe that these alternatives will eventually reduce to one that entails increasing cost—that it must sometime prove impossible to escape diminishing quantitative returns. Science, by making the resource base more homogeneous, erases the restrictions once thought to reside in the lack of homogeneity. In a neo-Ricardian world, it seems, the particular resources with which one starts increasingly become a matter of indifference. The reservation of particular resources for later use, therefore, may contribute little to the welfare of future generations. The social heritage consists far more of knowledge, equipment, institutions, and far less of natural resources, than it once did. Resource reservation, by limiting output, and thereby research, education, and investment, might even diminish the value of the social heritage.

Population growth constitutes a special problem. Living space on, or effectively near, the earth's surface is limited. But if living space is the ultimate limiting factor, the notion of Malthusian scarcity is no longer what it was a century and a half ago. The space limitation seems more likely to become manifest in crowded living conditions, a changed environment, an altered quality of life, than as increasing unit costs. For this reason, man may eventually undertake to limit his numbers, not by the operation of positive Malthusian checks but voluntarily, to avoid the qualitative effects of overcrowding—or, more immediately, in the less developed nations, to improve their prospects of increasing capital per head and the rate of growth of output relative to population. Malthusian scarcity would thus be transformed from a problem of subsistence, the lower limit of man's survival, to one concerned with the quality of life, with raising the upper limit to man's total welfare.

And this, in effect, is also true of Ricardian scarcity. For if the increasing scarcity of particular resources generates quantitatively adequate antidotes to the increasing scarcity of resources in general, the cost aspect of potential diminishing returns ceases to be of dominant interest. With many alternatives from which to choose, the criteria of choice become a central concern, for it is these criteria, and the effectiveness of man's decision-making procedures, that will mainly affect the shape of total welfare over time.

This is a problem that, in an intuitive way, concerns contemporary conservationists. To an increasing extent, as they partly realize, the problems of natural resources are qualitative. The difficult questions now are not whether physical and economic problems can be solved, but which problems to solve and how to solve them. The kinds and qualities of changes in the environment, in the social production process, and in commodities; the composition and the allocation of benefits and costs; the standards and the procedures by which alternatives are to be evaluated—these, rather than the cost of an increment to the pre-existing product mix, have become of increasing concern. As man extends his mastery over output and its cost, it is inevitable that these social problems will acquire increased significance and receive greater attention. Whether the attention they receive will suffice to assure continuing improvement in the quality of life is now the open question.

PART I

THE DOCTRINE OF INCREASING
NATURAL RESOURCE SCARCITY

Chapter 2

CONTEMPORARY VIEWS ON THE
SOCIAL ASPECTS OF NATURAL RESOURCES

MOST contemporary literature on natural resources lies in the realm of physical science. Each of several dozen biological and earth sciences—aspects of geology, biology, hydrology, mineralogy, agronomy, oceanography, geography, and so on, deals with a defined sector or dimension of the natural universe. Each is concerned with improving knowledge and understanding of nature, without primary regard for the relation of such knowledge to social welfare and progress. Publications in these fields—inquiries in which nature, and not man, is the primary subject—are excluded from consideration here.

Our study is concerned with the social aspects of natural resources, not with nature as a purely physical phenomenon. The defect of so narrowing the inquiry is recognized. There is no precise way to determine which of the findings of biological and earth science studies do, and which do not, carry implications for man's social life and welfare.

While we try to exclude scientific subject matter of purely physical import, we give considerable attention to some writings of natural scientists. Their concern for social welfare is not less than that of political analysts, economists, or public administrators; their knowledge of the physical environment is greater; and they have been prone to express political, economic, and social views on the relation of natural resources to social welfare. Such expressions venture beyond the authors' scientific specialties into the more amorphous and difficult area of social analysis, sometimes without adequate awareness of the differences between natural and social science. Nevertheless, since these views often have influenced public opinion, and some have made noteworthy contributions in the area of our interest, we give them appropriate attention.

17

Interest in the social problem of the relation of natural resources to man's welfare is impressively extensive. The *Conservation Yearbook* identifies more than 500 private and public bodies in the United States concerned with the conservation of natural resources, and this is not meant to be a complete list of agencies interested in the social aspects of natural resources. There are about 70 land-grant colleges in the United States. Each has one or more faculty groups for instruction, research, or demonstration in the social aspects of natural resources. Two departments of the federal government, Agriculture and Interior, are mainly focused upon the social aspects of natural resources. A variety of other federal agencies—the Atomic Energy Commission, the Federal Power Commission, and the Army Corps of Engineers, for example—also share this interest. More than $6 billion of the 1958 federal budget—about 15 per cent of nonmilitary allocations—was concerned with agriculture and other natural resources (excluding atomic energy).

Modern literature on social aspects of natural resources is impressive—in volume, range of coverage, and complexity of analysis. A number of scholarly journals, excluding those in the natural sciences, are devoted to natural resource topics. In a recent United Nations bibliography on *The Determinants and Consequences of Population Trends,* a considerable portion of the 2,500 entries concerns natural resources. The Gifford Pinchot collection in the Library of Congress is said to include about a million papers. And while this includes numerous purely physical studies and items not dealing with natural resources, it also exludes many social studies of natural resources which were not available when Pinchot's collection was made. As another indication of the extent of interest in the subject, the 1948 register of the American Economics Association lists about 150 economists who specified land economics as their primary interest, and several times that number who named land economics as their second or third major interest.

The remainder of this chapter is a reconnaissance or sampling of statements by public officials and expressions of the diverse views on social aspects of natural resources currently found in professional and other serious literature. After starting with a brief reminder of public policy which has prevailed in recent decades, we report on contemporary thought in several groups—naturalism and its ethics and aesthetics, ecology, demography, political science, and economics. This structure falls far short of being a scientific classification. The headings were shaped by the relative emphasis of the various writers as we understand them. We have found that such identification of emphasis conveys useful insights into what the authors view as fundamental and what secondary.

In general, we believe that there has been inadequate communication among authors in the various disciplines writing on social aspects of natural resources. As a result, each group "knows" *on its own premises* that the other is wrong. For example, conservationists and economists use different premises concerning individual consumer sovereignty, and much of their disagreement flows from this. Purposely, this chapter is purely descriptive; we have attempted to be neutral, to reserve for later chapters our own appraisal and analysis. Our hope is that, as a result, this chapter may be useful in improving communication, even if not in reducing disagreement, and in providing a setting in which various disciplinary contributions can be viewed within the complex matrix of resource questions and problems.

Expressions of Public Policy

Throughout this century, the federal government has become increasingly aware of, and involved in, natural resource policy and management. Established public policy of the United States is based on the view that natural resources play a significant role in the nation's welfare. Recurrently, each four years, the platforms of both the Republican and Democratic parties reiterate this view; and the same theme, running through policy statements of presidents representing both parties, has given added force to platform pledges.

The general approach of former Presidents Eisenhower, Truman, and Franklin D. Roosevelt, and that of President Kennedy, has seemed to have its roots in the kind of thinking expressed in an address to Congress by President Roosevelt in 1935 on the role of natural resources in social welfare—the problems and the need for government intervention.[1] He deplored the "havoc" which had been wrought

---

[1] *Franklin D. Roosevelt and Conservation, 1911–1945* (Hyde Park: Franklin D. Roosevelt Library, 1957), Vol. I, pp. 341–42.

on the abundant resources found by early settlers on the American continent—havoc which had continued up to his generation. Science, he noted, had taught us not only "where and how we have violated nature's immutable laws" but also "how we can commence to repair the havoc." And stressing that "the throwing out of balance of the resources of nature throws out of balance also the lives of men," he warned of "even greater evils that will attend our children unless we act."

The stress placed on resources and on learning how better to organize their use is indicated also by the number of special presidential committees and commissions appointed during the last few decades to make intensive studies of over-all resources policy or special aspects of the problem.

During President Eisenhower's administration, a statement by industrialist Meyer Kestnbaum, chairman of a presidential advisory group, is a convenient summary of general policy of the time:

> Natural resources are the foundation of the material prosperity of the Nation—both present and future. Their wise use is therefore the concern not only of all the people but of all levels of government.[2]

Among other study groups under President Eisenhower, the Presidential Advisory Committee on Water Resources Policy looked into the "generally acute" water problem and concluded that the basic elements of policy were clear.[3]

The reports of two widely publicized commissions dealt with the nation's resources during the Truman administration. The President's Materials Policy Commission—popularly known as the Paley Commission—was set up to inquire "into all major aspects of the problem of assuring an adequate supply of production materials for our long-range needs and to make recommendations which will assist me

---

[2] U.S. Commission on Intergovernmental Relations, *Study Committee Report on Natural Resources and Conservation* (Washington: GPO, 1955), p. 6.
[3] It "must look toward an adequate water supply for our people, prevent waste of water, provide for a greater reuse of water, reduce water pollution to the lowest practicable level, provide means for the useful and equitable distribution of available water supply, and take steps to check the destructive forces of water which threaten to injure or destroy land, property, and human life." Presidential Advisory Committee on Water Resources Policy, *Water Resources Policy* (Washington: GPO, 1955), p. 1.

[President Truman] in formulating a comprehensive policy on such materials." [4] The resulting voluminous report opened with a statement that "even a casual assessment" of the needs of the free world in the years ahead "would show many causes for concern."

Earlier, a task force of the bipartisan Commission on Organization of the Executive Branch of the Government (generally known as the Hoover Commission) had reported to President Truman and the Congress in a statement on natural resources policy. Noting how crucial natural resources are for the nation's future, the task force stated its belief that

> . . . Federal activities in this field must therefore be studied in the full light of the part which these resources play in our whole manner of life . . . our country has reached a point in its development that calls for a new concept of the relation of natural resources to its economy.

> . . . To meet the needs of the future and to promote more orderly development and exploitation of the Nation's resources, as well as to guard the heritage of the people, the unification of the responsibilities and services of the Government dealing with such matters seems clearly called for.[5]

President Kennedy, for the present administration, has restated the government's continuing concern. In a special message to Congress on natural resources, he opened with the following words:

> From the beginning of civilization, every nation's basic wealth and progress has stemmed in large measure from its natural resources. This nation has been, and is now, especially fortunate in the blessings we have inherited. Our entire society rests upon— and is dependent upon—our water, our land, our forests and our minerals. How we use these resources influences our health, security, economy, and well-being.[6]

In each of the recent administrations, the high-level pronouncements on natural resources reflect, and are reflected by, statements, instructions, attitudes, and actions at other levels in the federal gov-

---

[4] President's Materials Policy Commission, *Resources for Freedom*, Vol. I, "Foundations for Growth and Security" (Washington: GPO, 1952), p. iv.

[5] Commission on Organization of the Executive Branch of the Government, *Report on Natural Resources* (Washington: GPO, 1949), Appendix L, p. 1.

[6] February 23, 1961.

ernment. Thus, throughout government, the over-all concern for resources is universal, recurrent, and insistent. The theme seems to be composed of at least four major notes: (1) Natural resources exert a vital influence on social welfare and progress. (2) Viewed as an economic sector, natural resources—to a much higher degree than other sectors—involve governmental interests. (3) Viewed as a political sector, natural resources also heavily involve government interests. And (4) the significance of natural resources for social welfare flows in major part from the belief that natural resources are scarce and, furthermore, exhaustible, and that imprudent resource management endangers the welfare of future generations.

Views such as these, and those of the public in general, obviously rest both upon value judgments and premises and upon analyses and findings in the professional disciplines—in short, upon views such as those summarized in the remainder of this chapter.

Philosophical Naturalism

Much of the literature on natural resources and social welfare, although predominantly practical, has a strong undercurrent of philosophical naturalism. This underlying interest is not with the concrete and essentially economic concept of natural resources, but with a metaphysical, and often abstract, concept of "nature" that has its roots in classical philosophy. G. P. Adams has this to say of the classical approach:

> . . . In the development of Greek thought, nature has a meaning, one intimately associated with the idea of birth, growth, and life. It is this idea of birth and coming to life which is caught by the Latin *natura,* derived as it is from the stem which signifies "to be born." Nature is the mother of all things.[7]

With the passage of time, this deification of nature has undergone modification. Among other forces, it had to contend with a point of view—often called mechanistic or materialistic—to which the scientific revolution gave birth. Naturalistic philosophy has necessarily

[7] Adams, *Man and Metaphysics* (New York: Columbia University Press, 1948), p. 69.

changed under the impact of new outlooks. But it has not been abandoned in the modern era, and in some respects has been strengthened. To quote Adams again:

> A poor and impoverished nature, stripped down to such a skeleton as was pictured by the older mechanistic and materialistic theories, cannot accommodate the wealth of meanings which man possesses in his own life and experience. And so we set about to add to nature's contents and to the existence which is hers by right. We restore to her the qualities of sound and color, taste and smell. We let her have life, for all living forms have sprung from her, sustained by what she can give them, and by the give and take between living organisms and the habitat which surrounds them. We give nature organization. Everywhere, nature is replete with structure, system, and organization. . . . And finally we give her meanings and meaningful relations. . . . All these meanings in terms of which the life and organization, the structures and processes within nature are depicted, imply that there is more in nature than coexistences in space and sequences and supersessions in time. . . . Nature takes on not only such meanings as these, but in doing so, she becomes the scene in which values are achieved. . . . So nature can now house value and beauty, harmony and charm as well as meaning. There is purpose there, fruition, and achievement, together with frustration and defeat. There are active tendencies, leadings, and strivings. . . . How like the human world has nature become! The gap which had erstwhile divided man from nature has been filled. . . . We have learned to put into nature that which an older science and philosophy denied her, and all of man's mind and spirit is domesticated within nature. (Pp. 119–21.)

Man's symbiosis with nature, in this view, is both total and indivisible—spirit, mind, and physical sustenance. If, now, one can successively identify "nature" with "natural resources," natural resources with "conservation," and conservation with "economic policy," what are the consequences for conservation doctrine and economic policy? The question is not idle. Compare, for example, Adams' philosophical naturalism with the views expressed earlier by WJ McGee, who was identified by Pinchot as the "scientific brains of the conservation movement." Based on the perceptive article of Whitney

Cross,[8] in the following paragraph we paraphrase and quote from McGee's 1894 lecture, *The Earth the Home of Man,* which Cross has said contains the essence of McGee's wide-ranging speculations concerning man and nature.

The earth, McGee stated, is the home of all living things. More than being merely the home of life, the earth virtually created life. There is a continuum from inert and stable compounds through the more complex hydrocarbon compounds (which have a kind of instability very much like a lesser vitality) to life forms proper. But this development of life formed under the stimulus of environment is only half the picture. Living things from the very beginning have been modifying the earth's surface, so influencing its progression of form that the earth is the product of life energies as well as of more purely astrophysical phenomena. Man's intelligence is not different in kind, but only in degree, from the sensitivity of the simplest form of living matter. The end of man's conquest can be foreseen: man will transform minerals from the bowels of the earth, control bacteria, and obtain full management of the soil, to become "master fitted" to civilized life. As quoted by Cross, McGee closed his lecture this way:

> . . . mankind, offspring of mother earth, cradled and nursed through helpless infancy by things earthly, has been brought well toward maturity, and like the individual man, he is repaying the debt unconsciously assumed at the birth of his kind by transforming the face of nature, by making all things better than they were before, by aiding the good and destroying the bad among animals and plants, and by protecting the aged earth from the ravages of time and failing strength, even as the child protects his fleshly mother. Such are the relations of earth and man. (P. 159.)

CONSERVATION ETHICS

The affinity between pure naturalism and a more practical, but frankly ethical, view of the problem of man's relation to nature is apparent in much conservation literature.[9] So, too, are the implications of the ethical view for policy.

[8] Cross, "WJ McGee and the Ideas of Conservation," *The Historian,* Vol. 15 (Spring 1953), pp. 148–62.
[9] We recognize that the words "ethics" and "ethical" have different meanings

In his recent book, Samuel H. Ordway, lawyer and prominent conservationist, severely questions the American goal of "working, struggling, inventing, fighting, living *to create an ever higher level of living for all mankind.*" [10] Ordway wrote his book (according to its foreword) to present a "Theory of the Limit of Growth . . . influenced by a personal predilection for the old-fashioned luxuries of simplicity (like candlelight) as distinguished from modern engineering achievements (like neon), and synthetics." This predilection, he says, is related to a belief "that 'within foreseeable time' increasing consumption of resources can produce scarcities serious enough to destroy our American Dream of an ever-higher level of living, and with it our present culture." After stating that "our modern religion is growth," Ordway continues with a question:

> Could it be that there are ultimate limits of growth—material and economic and even spiritual—limits which may turn mankind, willy-nilly, away from faith in growth, to a better and a greater kind of human progress—without stagnation and decay? (P. 8.)

Ordway concludes that natural resources currently are involved in two reasons for changing the "basic philosophy, indeed religion of modern man. . . ." First, he says, because of scarce natural resources, there is a physical limit to an economic level of living. And, second, long before these physical limits force an understanding that unlimited material growth is unsound, we must prudently adopt natural resource conservation. Otherwise we shall, by rapacious appetite for natural resources, sacrifice the "Good Life"—spiritual values, the

---

for different persons. Our use of the terms in the following discussion is an attempt to characterize certain conservation views as having significant bearing upon one or another of the "ethical" premises of society. We conceive of individual consumer sovereignty, freedom to have children, freedom to destroy natural resources, among other actions, as ethical premises, related to a larger English and American ethos of individual freedom. In this sense, significant modification of any one of these freedoms—for whatever reason—would revise existing ethics. Thus, conservation views are not done full justice when they are appraised against the usual criteria of efficiency under conditions of individual consumer sovereignty. Since the conservation proposals are for ethical revisions—that is, for new value judgments—they can only be appraised on the basis of more inclusive criteria than those which derive from the wholly individualistic premises which are being challenged.

[10] Ordway, *Resources and the American Dream* (New York: Ronald Press, 1953), p. 6.

beauty and flavor of nature, independence and freedom of the individual, and national character.

Similar ethical views are held by other modern conservationists. One of the leading figures was Aldo Leopold.[11] Another is Paul B. Sears, botanist and conservationist, who suggests that natural resource problems require that an ethical re-evaluation of the American way of life be undertaken. "Underlying all technological aspects of conservation," he says, "is the need for a value system, generally accepted, that takes into account the limitations and possibilities of biological process," binding upon both society and the individual.[12]

In a contribution to the 1958 Resources for the Future Forum on Conservation,[13] Sears referred to similar ethical views by Fraser Darling and Albert Schweitzer.[14] And economist John Kenneth Galbraith —aware that conservationists, from concern over natural resource inadequacies, have long challenged the gargantuan resource appetites of advanced industrial economies—had this to say in support of their revolt:

> It is silly for grown men to concern themselves mightily with supplying an appetite and close their eyes to the obvious and obtrusive question of whether the appetite is excessive.[15]

Ordway, Sears, and Galbraith do not carry ethical argument as far as some proponents of conservation. These three concern themselves, at least directly, only with the relatively temperate question of per capita growth in consumption. Their challenge is to the propriety of individual decisions which permit insatiable individual appetites for goods. Ordway, for example, explicitly points to this force as more significant for raw material consumption than population growth. Other writers, notably William Vogt and Fairfield Osborn, have

[11] See Leopold, *Sand County Almanac* (New York: Oxford University Press, 1949).
[12] Committee on Use and Care of Natural Resources, *Present Needs for Research on the Use and Care of Natural Resources* (Washington: National Academy of Sciences—National Research Council, 1953), publication No. 288, p. 2.
[13] RFF Forum, *Perspectives on Conservation: Essays on America's Natural Resources*, Henry Jarrett, ed. (Baltimore: The Johns Hopkins Press for Resources for the Future, 1958).
[14] *Ibid.*, "Ethics, Aesthetics, and the Balance of Nature," p. 108.
[15] *Ibid.*, "How Much Should a Country Consume?", p. 98.

opened a much hotter ethical issue. They have proposed that it is population growth itself that must be reduced, eliminated, or reversed.

Vogt asserts that "unless population control and conservation are included, other means [to save the world] are certain to fail." [16] His argument is that "we must adjust our demand to the supply," which means either "accepting less per capita (lowering our living standards)" or "maintaining less people." From the premise that our civilization cannot survive "a *drastic* lowering of standards," he concludes that "we cannot escape the need for population *cuts*." (P. 265.) To the view of "experts" that populations will eventually level off and stabilize themselves, he replies, *"there is not time."* (P. 282.)

As indefatigably as Vogt, Osborn, president of the New York Zoological Society and past president of The Conservation Foundation, urges revision of society's ethics of individual decisions which permit unrestrained population growth, on the ground of dangerous natural resource scarcity. He closes one of his books with the warning that

> . . . now as we look, we can see the limits of the earth. . . . We must have faith that humanity will triumph in the end in reaching its incomparable destiny. But always in speculating regarding the ultimate, one is drawn inexorably to consideration of the immediate, of the first need of all needs, of the means toward the barest living, of the question of minimal survival—adequacy of food and of other essential resources.
>
> We are under the power of a timeless principle, exerting its influence relentlessly on a global scale. This principle . . . finds expression in a simple ratio wherein the numerator can be defined as "resources of the earth" and the denominator as "numbers of people." The numerator is *relatively* fixed and only partially subject to control by man. The denominator is subject . . . to control by man. If we are blind to this law, or delude ourselves into minimizing its power, of one thing we can be assured—the human race will enter into days of increasing trouble, conflict, and darkness.[17]

[16] William Vogt, *Road to Survival* (New York: William Sloan Associates, 1948), p. 264.

[17] Fairfield Osborn, *Limits of the Earth* (Boston: Little, Brown & Co., 1953), pp. 206–07.

Julian Huxley, commenting on another of Osborn's books,[18] points out that it "draws attention, in a forceful and compelling way, to one of the most urgent problems of our times. . . . A new ethical attitude is required, in which the proper conservation of the natural and human resources of every country is regarded as a moral duty." His comment crystallizes the conservationist appeal for revision of the prevailing ethics of private decisions concerning resource use and population reproduction.

CONSERVATION AESTHETICS

More widely accepted is the conservationists' view of the aesthetic value of nature. This attitude, directly derivative from philosophical naturalism, is primarily a plea for preserving natural beauty. Secondarily, it is a plea for a degree of social control of man's exploitation of natural resources in order to prevent aesthetic atrocities.

Sears, whose views on conservation ethics we have already noted, observes in his RFF essay, "Certainly, sound and satisfying design is integral to good conservation, . . ." And he expresses the opinion "that Sir Francis Younghusband, the British explorer, was quite right in his belief that there are only two kinds of landscape that are tolerable—one where man has never been; the other where he has achieved harmony." (Pp. 107–08.)

Luna D. Leopold, chief hydraulic engineer, U.S. Geological Survey, believes that the aesthetic contribution of natural resources to the quality of life should take precedence over its economic contribution. After calling attention to the special aesthetic and ethical values which warrant attention in conservation practices, Leopold continues:

> . . . We must be willing to stand up and assert that there are some things which we as a nation want, but which in purely economic terms would be described as valueless or sheer luxury. To preserve such values it may be necessary to decide a-priori that we want them and assign to them high priority without attempting to put a price tag on the benefit received. If we want a particular canyon, a rare species of bird, or a particular valley preserved because of its scenic beauty when threatened by some other use, strictly economic comparisons will seldom result in

[18] Osborn, *Our Plundered Planet* (Boston: Little, Brown & Co., 1948).

its preservation. The reason for this is that we have not found, and in my opinion we should stop looking for, ways of placing dollar value on scenery, on recreation, and on that intangible mental well-being which we associate with beauty. . . .[19]

Many of the writings which emphasize the aesthetic importance of natural resource preservation are themselves poetic expressions— notably those by Joseph Wood Krutch, Aldo Leopold, Russell Lord, and John H. Storer.[20] Some of their aesthetic views undoubtedly derive directly from their highly developed sensitivities. Storer, for example, closed his *Web of Life* [21] with the following stirring quotation from Alan Paton's *Cry, The Beloved Country:*

> The grass is rich and matted, you cannot see the soil. It holds the rain and the mist, and they seep into the ground, feeding the streams in every kloof. It is well tended, and not too many fires burn it, laying bare the soil. Stand unshod upon it, for the ground is holy being even as it came from the Creator. Keep it, guard it, care for it, for it keeps men, guards men, cares for men. Destroy it and man is destroyed.

The Ecological Viewpoint

The biological science of ecology has been defined "as the study of the relation of organisms or groups of organisms to their environment, or the science of the interrelations between living organisms and their environment." [22] There have been slight beginnings in recent years, however, in the parallel study of "human ecology," which includes specifically human relations and values. Where naturalism and conservation ethics and aesthetics leave off, and where human ecology, if it is further developed, would take over is difficult to tell from contemporary natural resource literature. Sears, with his strong feeling

---

[19] Luna D. Leopold, "Water and the Conservation Movement," an address at Chautauqua, New York, July 9, 1957.

[20] See, for example, Krutch, *The Desert Year* (New York: Sloane, 1952), and *The Measure of Man* (Indianapolis: Bobbs-Merrill, 1954); Aldo Leopold, *op. cit.;* Lord, *Behold Our Land* (Boston: Houghton-Mifflin, 1938), and *Forever the Land* (New York: Harper, 1950); and Storer, *The Web of Life* (New York: Signet Books, 1956; originally published, 1953).

[21] *Op. cit.,* p. 142.

[22] E. P. Odum, *Fundamentals of Ecology* (Philadelphia: W. B. Saunders, 1953), p. 3.

for ethics and aesthetics in conservation, for example, is a former president of the Ecological Society of America.

As conservation ethics and aesthetics, in significant degree, derive from metaphysical naturalism, so ecology, in a certain sense, also derives from naturalism. Ecological contributions on the social aspects of natural resources have flowed in an expanding stream from natural scientists who have no major connection with conservation organizations.[23] These socioecological studies by natural scientists are of three types: a large "pessimistic" category; a much smaller body of "optimistic" writings (denigrated as "cornucopian" by conservationists); and some literature having a middle-of-the-road viewpoint.

The pessimistic group has messages similar to those already quoted from such modern conservationists as Osborn and Vogt. One of the pessimists, Harrison S. Brown, a geochemist, observes in his *Challenge of Man's Future* that a "substantial fraction of humanity today is behaving . . . as if it were engaged in a contest to test nature's willingness to support humanity." He continues, "If it had its way, it would not rest content until the earth is covered completely and to a considerable depth with a writhing mass of human beings, much as a dead cow is covered with a pulsating mass of maggots." (P. 221.)

Darwin, in *The Next Million Years,* is even more pessimistic. Whereas Brown believes mankind can make an intelligent choice as to his numbers, Darwin believes that society as a whole will tend to breed without limit. Furthermore, he says, it is exactly the poorest intellectual stock that will breed at higher rates, with a resulting tendency of civilization relatively to sterilize its ablest citizens; the "weak" shall inherit the earth.

Two of America's leading medical scientists have expressed them-

---

[23] See, for example, Harrison S. Brown, *Challenge of Man's Future* (New York: Viking Press, 1954); Brown, James Bonner, and John Weir, *The Next Hundred Years* (New York: Viking Press, 1957); Charles Galton Darwin, *The Next Million Years* (London: R. Hart-Davis, 1952); George Thomson, *The Foreseeable Future* (Cambridge, England: Cambridge University Press, 1955); L. Dudley Stamp, *Land for Tomorrow, The Underdeveloped World* (Bloomington: Indiana University Press—The American Geographical Society, 1952); Kirtley F. Mather, *Enough and to Spare* (New York: Harper, 1944); Clifford Cook Furnas, *The Next Hundred Years* (New York: Reynal and Hitchcock, 1936) and "Tomorrow's Engineering Problems," address at the Meeting of the American Society of Civil Engineers, Buffalo, New York, June 1957; and Jacob Rosin and Max Eastman, *The Road to Abundance* (New York: McGraw-Hill, 1953).

selves forcefully on natural resource scarcity relative to human numbers and consumption. Dr. Allan Gregg, director emeritus of the Rockefeller Foundation's Medical Division, has queried, "Is man a biological cancer?"

> There is an alarming parallel between the growth of a cancer in the body of an organism and the growth of human populations in the earth's ecological economy. If this idea is valid, and if man is indeed hurrying off to such a macabre "summit," humanity should now face the question of an optimum population, not only in terms of politics and economics, but in terms of a more healthy relationship between the human species and other forms of life on the planet Earth.[24]

And Dr. A. J. Carlson, in an earthier simile, asserted that "if we breed like rabbits, in the long run we have to live and die like rabbits." [25]

Other scientists in the pessimistic group play the same theme on a less grand scale. Geologist Alan Bateman, presenting a view common to geologists and mineral specialists, stresses the inroads suffered by our domestic mineral reserves. "Our former bountiful mineral supplies of which we were justly proud now show serious depletion." [26]

Similar pessimistic human ecological views recur in the seven substantive volumes of the *United Nations Scientific Conference on the Conservation and Utilization of Resources* (1953); in the *Proceedings of the Inter-American Conference on Conservation of Renewable Natural Resources,* held in Denver in 1948 (Department of State publication 3382); and in the contributions of most other symposia on natural resources.

Not all physical scientists are so alarmed. Furnas, chancellor of the University of Buffalo and formerly head of the Research and Development area of the U.S. Department of Defense, finds problems but thinks they can be solved,[27] and that they are urgent enough to start on immediately.

[24] Gregg, "Hidden Hunger at the Summit," *Population Bulletin,* Vol. 11 (August 1955), p. 74.
[25] Carlson, "Science Versus Life," *Journal of the American Medical Association,* Vol. 157 (April 16, 1955), p. 1440.
[26] Bateman, "Our Future Dependence on Foreign Minerals," *The Annals,* Vol. 281 (May 1952), p. 25.
[27] *Op. cit.*

In the symposium, *The Fabulous Future,* none of the writers who treated natural resources seemed pessimistic concerning their adequacy for human welfare. Both John von Neumann and Crawford H. Greenewalt, then president of the DuPont Corporation, emphasized the importance of technological change. Von Neumann thought it likely that we would gradually "develop procedures more naturally and effectively adjusted to the new sources of energy, abandoning the conventional kinks and detours inherited from chemical-fuel processes." He foresaw a time, perhaps, within decades, when "energy may be free— just like the unmetered air—with coal and oil used mainly as raw materials for organic chemical synthesis, to which, as experience has shown, their properties are best suited." [28]

Greenewalt, in his contribution to the symposium, "The Slow, Steady Way of Progress," speculated that the errors of past prophets had been largely due to a habit of reasoning from their own limited social and technical experience and from their failure to

> . . . take into account the new technologies that were just over the horizon. Thomas Jefferson, for example, in announcing the Louisiana purchase, felt that the territory might be fully occupied after 25 generations—i.e., along about 2600 a.d. He could not have foreseen that the invention of the railroad and the steamboat would open it up to settlement within a few decades. Sir William Crookes,[29] a very distinguished scientist, in 1898 foretold starvation for the human race through diminishing supplies of nitrogen. As things stood in his day, that was perhaps a perfectly valid prediction; but what he did not foresee was that chemistry, through the fixation of nitrogen from the air, within a generation or so would remove the threat of starvation far into the future. (Pp. 99–100.)

Finding alarmist views in error, owing to their neglect of social and technical change, Greenewalt went on to suggest that the solution of our long-term energy problems, for food as well as power and fuel, will be found in solar energy. Russell C. Weigel, also of DuPont, initially affirmed serious materials problems and unfavorable unbalance

[28] Von Neumann, "Can We Survive Technology?", *The Fabulous Future* (New York: Dutton and Company, 1955), p. 37.

[29] The reference to Crookes perhaps does him injustice. He did foresee the possibility of artificial fixation of atmospheric nitrogen, and called on his fellow chemists for discovery of the means. See the biographical entry in *Encyclopedia Britannica,* 11th ed.

in the ratio of materials and population. But then he found solutions in plastics, which "will be available to satisfy a multitude of human needs as our natural resources are depleted." [30]

The optimistic and middle-of-the-road viewpoints are presented also in a number of book-length treatments published in the 1940's and 1950's. The scientists represented include Kirtley F. Mather (1944), L. Dudley Stamp (1952), Jacob Rosin and (nonscientist) Max Eastman (1953), and Sir George Thompson (1955)—all cited earlier—and F. G. Walton Smith and Henry Chapin (1954).[31]

Demography and Related Literature

There is no agreement as yet concerning the determinants of population growth and stagnation. Modern demography developed as a science by measuring population numbers, characteristics, and changes; by breaking down these variables into component parts; and by associating changes in the numbers and composition of a population with its biological characteristics. Demography has thus greatly enriched our knowledge of population growth. It is now recognized that in modern societies populations grow at less than biologically possible maximum rates; and that the net reproduction rate is an algebraic amalgam of complexly related factors determining fertility and death rates.

But "the study of population remains largely unstructured as to theory." [32] Demographers appreciate that social variables and conditions are important underlying determinants of population change; but the roles of such influences as level of income, religion, and urbanization on population growth over the long term are not well understood.[33] It is believed, too, that population growth plays a role in

[30] Weigel, address before the Commercial Chemical Development Association, New York City, March 28, 1957, p. 13.

[31] Smith and Chapin, *The Sun, the Sea, and Tomorrow—Potential Sources of Food and Minerals from the Sea* (New York: Charles Scribner, 1954).

[32] Joseph J. Spengler, "Population Theory," *A Survey of Contemporary Economics,* Bernard F. Haley, ed., Vol. II, for American Economic Association (Homewood, Ill.: Richard Irwin, 1952), p. 83.

[33] A stimulating study by Sydney H. Coontz, *Population Theories and the Economic Interpretation* (New York: Humanities Press, 1957), suggests that sociological factors are less important than the economic ones. And Harvey Leibenstein, in *Economic Backwardness and Economic Growth* (New York:

long-term economic growth, but this relationship also is not clearly comprehended. Finally, contemporary interrelations of natural resources and population growth are not viewed as central to demographic science, and are even less understood.

Nevertheless, demographers and associated social scientists, impressed with their observations of persistent population growth, as social philosophers speculate on matters beyond the narrow confines of what is firmly known in the demographic discipline. Many of them are pessimistic concerning the capability of natural resources to support contemporary rates of growth of population and consumption per capita. Joseph J. Spengler, scholar in demography, economics, and economic history, writes:

> Admittedly and happily, the average consumer has "never had it so good." Yet this progress has put us in a situation where the more we have, the more we want, and our demands on the resources which cannot be augmented by technological progress will soon result in large-scale scarcities and the prohibitive prices and costs which accompany scarcities. Hence the paradox we have already noted—that poverty suppresses, and the removal of poverty generates, manifestation of population pressure.[34]

Arnold Toynbee in a Voice of America broadcast put it this way: ". . . the problem of limiting the birth-rate will have to be faced. The alternative is starvation." [35] And Frederick Osborn writes:

> Perhaps there are still advantages to be gained by further increases in the number of people in the United States. Continued growth will make possible larger scale production, and encourage business to make new investments in productive enterprises. But this does not mean that individual consumers would benefit by being more numerous. It is doubtful that further growth would be a factor making for increase in the income of individuals. We are at the point in our population-resources ratio where pressure of larger numbers upon scarce natural resources lays a restraining hand on increases in per capita production, which can be offset

---

John Wiley, 1957), presents a brief theory of the relation between increased income per capita and fertility decline. Most theorizing about population growth, however, tends to be eclectic and historical.

[34] Spengler, "Population Threatens Prosperity," reprinted from *Harvard Business Review,* Vol. 34 (January–February 1956), p. 88.

[35] Excerpts given in *Population Bulletin,* Vol. 12 (November 1956).

only for a limited time by technical advances and the use of new capital.[36]

Some of the demographers' views are only moderately pessimistic; some are extreme—as indicated by comparisons of the following two quotations. The first is a moderate expression from the society of professional demographers:

All except the most pessimistic estimates of the amounts of land and other sources of food which could be brought into use, and of the possible increases in agricultural yields, imply that it would be technically possible to feed a very much larger population than the world now holds. Studies of the sources of energy and essential raw materials likewise imply that, with prudence in the use and conservation of these resources and ingenuity in devising substitutes for those which are in shortest supply, they could be made to meet the needs of a growing population for a long time to come. The increases in production that are actually likely to be achieved within the foreseeable future, however, are much smaller than those which are technically possible. Ignorance, greed, strife, superstition, and blind adherence to tradition prevent men from accomplishing the works which are in their power, even though the alternatives may be misery and starvation. It is, therefore, easily possible that the means of producing the necessities of life will not be increased as rapidly as population grows, and that the level of living of the world's peoples will be depressed as their numbers increase. Moreover, it is not sufficient to match population growth with an equal increase in the means of subsistence. Progress demands an expansion of production greater than the increase of world population, so that all nations can achieve a better living standard. It is quite possible that the growth of population will substantially retard progress in this direction in the world as a whole.[37]

The next quotation, one of the extreme views, is from Robert C. Cook, the editor of the widely distributed *Population Bulletin*. He says:

[36] Frederick Osborn, "Population: An International Dilemma," *A Summary of the Proceedings of the Conference Committee on Population Problems, 1956–1957* (Princeton: Princeton University Press, 1958), p. 72.

[37] *The Determinants and Consequences of Population Trends* (New York: United Nations, 1953), pp. 192–93.

This nineteenth-century refutation of the population crisis is still a part of most contemporary belief. Science has made enormous strides. Disease is increasingly held at bay; the productivity of soil is enhanced by the work of agricultural geneticists and power plants which produce fertilizers from the air. The man in the street sees no compelling reason to be apprehensive that the science which has served him so handsomely thus far will fail him in the future. . . . Some scientists of distinction in other fields but as unlettered in reading the book of life as any layman subscribe to the illusion that science, given a little time, will solve the problem of food supply forever.

Such a paradise is strictly for fools. It is not one in which those who look straight at the facts can believe. The scientists who have made the closest study of the population problem believe it the least. In 1950 a panel of a dozen population experts, after on-the-scene checks of some of the world's most serious danger points, confirmed Malthus. The proposed "cures" show no prospect of providing for those wants.[38]

In the same book, geneticist Cook foresees mounting dangers:

Next to the atom bomb, the most ominous force in the world today is uncontrolled fertility. Unbalanced and unchecked fertility is ravaging many lands like a hurricane or a tidal wave. . . . The scramble for bare subsistence by hordes of hungry people is tearing the fertile earth from the hillsides, destroying forests, and plunging millions of human beings into utter misery. Even when unchecked fertility has not impelled human beings to scramble for survival, what is happening today has other sinister effects. In the United States, England, and every Western country, misplaced and badly distributed human fertility is leaching away the inborn qualities of tomorrow's children. This biological "erosion" is insidious in its action. No barren, gullied hillsides meet the eye, but in the foreseeable end such erosion of the biological quality of the people may, after no great lapse of time, result in disaster. (P. 15.)

And, elsewhere in the book, he warns:

The world's growing population will force the use of marginal lands, which in general are extremely expensive to exploit. More

---

[38] Cook, *Human Fertility: The Modern Dilemma* (New York: Sloane, 1951), p. 295.

and more human energy will have to be devoted to the basic problem of producing food, and the standard of living, instead of going up, will remain at the subsistence level in the areas where it now stands at that, while the wealthier areas will find their standards of living declining. . . .

Since Malthus' day, the problem has actually become more acute rather than less acute. . . . (P. 296.)

There is also skepticism concerning such projections and generalizations. Irene Taeuber, a leading demographer, is quoted by Horace Belshaw as saying that "we cannot project demographic movements in Asian countries 'straight to catastrophe.' " [39] And zoologist C. B. Goodhart sees hope in the behavior of the population variable. First, he has found evidence of a negative correlation between economic advance and the biological conditions of population growth:

It is notorious that declining numbers are found not only in primitive peoples brought into contact with civilization, but also in many of the most advanced nations and classes, whose declining numbers certainly cannot be attributed to genetical selection by famine. It has been suggested that the conditions produced by civilization and a high standard of living may in themselves be unfavourable to fertility, and it is certainly true that the more or less stable population in northwestern Europe at the present time owes much to the introduction of artificial methods of family limitation which are only practicable in relatively advanced and prosperous communities. However, the universal rule of declining numbers in advanced civilizations dates back long before the discovery of artificial means of bringing it about, and we must not overlook the possibility that those qualities leading to success in many may have been genetically correlated with relatively low fecundity, and there are some a priori arguments in support of such a view.[40]

As a second reason for hope, Goodhart finds no support for the widely believed thesis that the intelligence and other inborn qualities of tomorrow's children are declining, due to misplaced human fertility.

---

[39] Belshaw, *Population Growth and Levels of Consumption* (London: Allen and Unwin, 1956), p. xxvii.

[40] Goodhart, "World Population Growth and Its Regulation by Natural Means," *Nature*, Vol. 178 (September 15, 1956), p. 562. Also see his articles in *The New Scientist*, December 12, 1957; *Advancement of Science*, London, 13 (1957); *Saertrykk av Naturen*, 1957; and *Eugenics Review*, 1955.

With respect to intelligence, Goodhart writes "the only objective test that has been made does not support [the thesis]. This is the remarkable experiment in which practically all the school children of 11–12 in Scotland were tested in 1932, with a repeat on the next generation in 1947. It was on a big enough scale to have shown the predicted fall in I.Q., but actually what it showed was a trifling and non-significant rise." [41] The gradual improvement in athletic records, increases in heights of sons over fathers, and increases in longevity are also at variance with the thesis, unless it is conceived in such way as to disallow the effects of favorable environmental influences which contribute to the outcome in each generation.

Political Science

The issues of public policy concerning natural resources—indicated by our earlier sampling of statements by public officials—have received penetrating, if not extensive, consideration from political scientists and administration specialists. Forced by the nature of the issues and their disciplines, this group of analysts has tended to use wide-angle lenses in consideration of natural resources and social welfare. Most of the literature in this category is devoted to historical descriptions, case studies, advice, and proposed solutions to problems of policy and administration. There is not much conceptual analysis of the direct relation of natural resources to social welfare. The writings contain, however, a good deal of important and interesting conceptual discussion on motivation for government involvement in natural resources, the political struggle for control of government's natural resource activities, and problems in devising public machinery and executing public management functions "in the public interest." There is thus an implicit concern with the influence of resources upon social welfare.

Norman Wengert has analyzed what he describes as "the way in which political processes operate with respect to natural resource questions." [42] One of his major conclusions is that U.S. policy on

[41] In a letter to us. For a published discussion see Goodhart, "The Inheritance of Intelligence" in *The New Scientist*, August 22, 1957, and in *Nature*, *op. cit.*

[42] Wengert, *Natural Resources and the Political Struggle*, in a pamphlet series,

natural resources must remain an arena of political struggle and controversy, that any neat solution will do violence to the pluralistic objectives of the national interest in natural resources. He sees group conflict and strife as "inevitable—even necessary and desirable." It is only through continuing struggle among a multiplicity of groups, that "a working definition of the public interest may be achieved." In his view:

> The public interest is not some objective principle handed down to mortals from above. It is what we, the public, believe and feel as a result of our experience, as a result of our collective judgments. This has been the basis of the political struggle over resource policy. (Pp. 67–68.)

Here, then, based on a review of experience with public problems concerning natural resources, is a generalization similar to the Dahl-Lindblom view that U.S. public policy and management decisions are properly a bargaining result of competing forces, analogous to the resultant in an economic market.[48]

Lyle Craine, similarly drawing on empirical studies, reaches several major conclusions which may have general application in public policy concerning natural resources. One of these is that criteria for economic behavior in such public resource activities as a water conservancy district simply cannot be lifted whole from private enterprise. The government may have deliberately entered into management of the natural resources in question in order to create social or public values beyond, or other than, those which are conventional in the economic calculus of private enterprise and individual consumer sovereignty. Craine illustrates the criteria and value questions in the Muskingum Watershed Conservancy District:

> . . . Today the District boasts of being self-supporting. Too often this claim is not understood for what it is—namely, that the District's operation of forestry, recreation, and farm and mineral leasing on the 65,000 acres to which it still holds title returns sufficient revenue to meet current operating expenses plus servicing recreation bonds which were sold to finance capital

Short Studies in Political Science (New York: Doubleday and Company, 1955), p. 1.
    [48] Robert A. Dahl and Charles E. Lindblom, *Politics, Economics, and Welfare* (New York: Harper, 1953).

improvements required for recreation developments. Such a claim gives no consideration to a proper cost allocation with respect to the $50,000,000 investment in the dams and reservoirs and an appropriate amortization charge with respect thereto. This "self-support" policy, moreover, has removed from the MWCD practically all concepts of a public service agency, except as its services can pay their way from collectible revenues.

The "self-support" policy has, in effect, given to the MWCD many of the colorations of a private rather than a public enterprise. Recreation services and forestry activities which have little prospect of being self-supporting are given scant attention.[44]

Craine's second major conclusion is that the public interest in river basin and watershed development cannot be fully satisfied by local agencies. The overlapping and interlocking interests of federal, state, and local governments and private groups, Craine believes, are simply too pervasive for a purely local agency to be appropriate. Society has had an "environmental management" function thrust upon it, for which social policies and operating machinery are still to be perfected. He continues:

> Inescapably, a larger jurisdiction which is able to identify sufficient benefits in local developments to justify its financial participation must ultimately also share the decisions in some proportion to its share of costs. Thus, a program of the scope of the MWCD's cannot be independently planned and executed by a local agency.

> Moreover, not only is local independence impossible, it is undesirable. In fact, independent operation by any level of government in drainage basin development is undesirable. Total and comprehensive drainage basin development will always demand the full contribution of each level of government. This suggests that the problem is not so much one of demarcating functions or areas within which each governmental agency can operate relatively independently, but rather one of devising organizational machinery which will facilitate the contribution of all governmental levels to the common endeavor.

[44] Craine, "The Muskingum Watershed Conservancy District: A Study of Local Control," reprinted from a symposium on water resources, *Law and Contemporary Problems,* Duke University Law School, Durham, North Carolina, 1957, pp. 401–02.

But approximate accord with Wengert's and Craine's generalizations apparently is not sufficient to provide a fully satisfactory solution. The Corps of Engineers, the major U.S. agency in water development projects, for example, operates on funds provided in the congressional arena of severe political contest. It does not apply private enterprise criteria and is not localized in its purview. Yet criticism of the Corps' "charter," objectives, organization, and operations is widespread among social scientists.

One focus of the criticism is an allegation that the Corps' primary motivation is extensive construction, and not social benefits or efficiency in the use of tax dollars. Arthur Maass, for example, has questioned whether the Corps' survey, planning, and recommendation activities are fully responsive to its responsibilities and obligations. Another major criticism is that the Corps has acquired a concentration of political and economic power which not only prevents efficient behavior, responsive to the public interest in water development, but which also is unhealthy for a democratic society. The late Secretary of the Interior, Harold L. Ickes, in the foreword to Maass' book was characteristically direct:

> One way to describe the Corps of Army Engineers would be to say that it is the most powerful and most pervasive lobby in Washington. The aristocrats who constitute it are our highest ruling class. . . . Within the fields that they have elected to occupy, they are the law—and therefore above the law. . . . Their record shows that they not only regard themselves as independent of the Secretary of the Army and the Secretary of Defense, but even of the President. . . .
>
> It is to be doubted whether any Federal agency in the history of this country has so wantonly wasted money on worthless projects as the Corps of Engineers.[45]

Ernest Griffith, formerly Director of the Legislative Reference Service, in his essay "Main Lines of Thought and Action" prepared for the RFF Forum on Conservation, cited earlier, noted not steady, but sustained, progress in national understanding and policies concerning the relation of natural resources to social welfare. Given as evidence are the federal government's assertion of a public-domain

[45] Arthur Maass, *Muddy Waters* (Cambridge: Harvard University Press, 1951), pp. ix and xii.

interest in waters and forests; and recognition by the cities of their interest in these natural resources. Griffith also found, contrary to many other observers, a unity of purpose among governmental agencies and private interests. He speaks of the progress as follows:

> The Federal Water Power Act was a landmark. For its day and age—a period of decline in the national ethos, of renewed predatory capitalism—it represented a real achievement. . . . Private and public interests were recognized—but the paramountcy of the national domain was established. . . .

> The next important act—and almost the only important act till the conservation explosion of Franklin Roosevelt's first term—was the Clarke-McNary Act of 1924. . . . There was a crystallization of issues, a forward move with most major forces in substantial agreement. Federal, state, and private interests found therein a basis for three-way co-operation in fire fighting. Reforestation was authorized on an unprecedented scale—in fact as a program. Provision was made for the further extension of national forests, especially when watershed values were at stake. Experiment stations were established. . . . All in all, our national forest policy had largely come of age. Henceforth its battles were to be largely administrative, or those that arose out of defending a status quo against encroachment. Perhaps the only really new and major strand subsequently to appear on the forest front lay in the growing realization that the stake of the city man in the forest was not merely the forest's role in conservation, but its facilities for his future recreation. (P. 10.)

Also in the RFF Forum report, Luther Gulick, president of the Institute of Public Administration, tried to relate natural resources to social welfare in a predominantly urban society. In "The City's Challenge in Resource Use," he employs what we have called the ecological approach, but with extensive elaboration of the multiple-use facets of natural resources, of the types of natural resource needs of a modern society, and of the interdependencies in his now enlarged ecological model:

> . . . We must assume that the new pattern of vast belts of urbanization is here to stay, and that we will see more and more of our people in these great urban complexes over the next generation.

. . . It is my thesis that urbanization in and of itself, as a pattern of life, increases the dependence of our culture on the natural resources, and that urbanization furthermore makes for a revised scale of conservation priorities. (P. 117.)

Gulick then identifies four matters as calling for priority action:

. . . Allocating water resources, eliminating flood dangers and water pollution, reserving open spaces, and controlling the general pattern of land use particularly around metropolitan regions and thruway interchanges. . . .

The controls . . . go to the root of our society and its structure of power. We are dealing with who gets what, when and how, to use Harold Lasswell's pragmatic definition of politics. What we are saying is that the growth of urbanism has now raised these resource matters to the level of imperative public interest. It is this which justifies and requires governmental action.

. . . Man occupies his habitat and can exist, can prosper, can multiply only as he fits the total environment. And when man modifies this environment with his clever hands and inventive brain, he introduces new equilibria, ever-changing like a kaleidoscope, the end results of which may be less hospitable to the human species than the "balance of nature" within which man started his long climb to knowledge and power.

While this precept of the life-balance system is for all of mankind, it is of special significance for metropolitan man now, not alone because of his more involved and heavier dependence on resources, but because his apparent detachment from nature leaves him aloof and insensitive to the life system of which he is forever a dependent part.

The shortage mankind needs to guard against is not the exhaustion of the limited resources on this small planet. The shortage to fear is the lack of brains, character, spirit, leadership, and political competence. The depletion of land, water, and other resources could bring the prodigal son back to his senses, but his salvation will be found only in cultural conversion and in the arts of politics. (Pp. 133–37.)

If we read the foregoing pronouncements aright, there is an affinity here to philosophical naturalism, but the premises are those of ecology, now broadened to take into account man's social as well as his biological attributes. The suggested therapeutic measures are those of a broadly conceived political process in which ethical, aesthetic, and administrative considerations all play their appropriate part. In view of man's increasing physical and social interdependence and his power to control nature, it was inevitable that he eventually should be exhorted to use this power with, in some sense, improved conscience and rationality.

Economic Views

Since our study later deals intensively with economic doctrine, here we only briefly and incompletely characterize economic views in order to round out the general purpose of this chapter. Furthermore, contemporary economic literature on the aggregate relation of natural resources to welfare and growth is not large, and this corresponds to the relatively small numbers of economists interested in this over-all relation. We pass over specialized economic activities, such as agricultural economics (marketing, farm management, demand analysis, and specific commodity studies); energy studies; minerals commodity investigations; and so on.

Focusing upon a future year a generation or so away, the economic views expressed in the five-volume report of the President's Materials Policy Commission [46] found three important features in the relationship of natural resources to welfare. Most important was the real cost of raw materials. Next were international relations, as influenced by trade in raw materials; and preparedness for war, as a function of domestic raw materials supplies and capacities. On these three questions, the Paley Commission findings—approximately reflecting the views of its participating economists—may be summarized as follows: (1) There is evidence of recent moderate increases in costs of raw materials, and prospects for further rises. But there is no serious threat to economic growth during the next generation, and the public policy remedies which are required do not involve drastic interventions in the private enterprise economy. (2) For reasons of mild but growing shortages of raw materials, and in the interests of improved international relations, foreign natural resources should be increasingly relied

[46] *Op. cit.*

upon as a source for U.S. consumption of raw materials. (3) Defense preparedness in raw materials can be achieved by stockpiles and other special measures.

In other places, Edward S. Mason, a member of the Paley Commission, has reached roughly the same conclusions as those in the report, except that he is less certain of future increases in the real cost of raw materials. Mason points to a degree of uniqueness of natural resources in economic welfare which stems from four characteristics. These are (1) short-term inelasticities of demand and supply for extractive products; (2) greater association of external economies and diseconomies with natural resource sectors than with other sectors; (3) a long tradition of government incentives for the stimulation of minerals exploration and development; and (4) a problem of time distribution in investment or disinvestment (destructive use) in natural resources.[47] Mason characterizes this fourth element as "conservation economics." In so doing, Mason—one of the contemporary economists who take a broad view of the social significance of natural resources—follows the usage of John Ise, S. V. Ciriacy-Wantrup, and Anthony Scott, who devote themselves primarily to "conservation economics" in the above specialized sense.[48]

Ise, like the conservationists discussed earlier, finds that the time distribution of destructive utilization of U.S. resources is dangerously biased toward present and near-term use, with a threat of poverty for future generations. Ciriacy-Wantrup does not subscribe to this strong belief. But he recognizes the uncertainty and danger that the time distribution of net disinvestment in resources may be skewed toward the present. Thus for the protection of future generations, he thinks national prudence perhaps requires public policies which will shift the time distribution somewhat. The bulk of his excellent book is a lengthy and exhaustive consideration of public policies relative to time distribution of resource investment and disinvestment. Scott is even less convinced of maldistribution through time than Ciriacy-Wantrup. But,

---

[47] See, for example, the RFF Forum, *op. cit.,* "The Political Economy of Resource Use," pp. 158–59.

[48] Ise, "The Theory of Value as Applied to Natural Resources," *American Economic Review,* Vol. 15 (June 1925); Ciriacy-Wantrup, *Resource Conservation–Economics and Policies* (Berkeley and Los Angeles: University of California Press, 1952); and Scott, *Natural Resources: The Economics of Conservation* (Toronto: University of Toronto Press, 1955).

finding that it is an important area of public interest, he also contributes excellent economic analyses of the implications and repercussions of public policies as related to time distribution.

Harold Hotelling and E. O. Heady also concentrate on "conservation economics" in the sense given above. Starting with an assumption of a given resource availability, Hotelling and Heady contribute usefully in a technical way to the question of whether, and why, the time distribution of resource use and investment under private enterprise conditions may be socially erroneous.[49] Hotelling concentrates on mineral resources, and Heady on agricultural land. Expectations and interest rates play a major part in Hotelling's analysis, while interest rates and divergences between social and private costs and benefits are major in Heady's.

Erich Zimmerman's monumental *World Resources and Industries* and his other writings are difficult to characterize in a few sentences. His is an institutional, descriptive, gestaltist, optimistic analysis. Perhaps the best summary is his own statement of basic beliefs concerning the relation of natural resources and economic welfare:

> Resources are highly dynamic functional concepts; they *are not, they become,* they evolve out of the triune interaction of nature, man, and culture, in which nature sets outer limits, but man and culture are largely responsible for the portion of physical totality that is made available for human use. The command over energy, especially inanimate energy, is the key to resource availability. And, finally, the world is not "a bundle of hay" but a living growing complex of matter and energy, *a process rather than a thing.* . . . The problem of resource adequacy is also one of social institutions, of governmental policies, of international relations. If the preceding discussion has led to any vital conclusion, it is the altogetherness of things. In this inextricable mesh of forces and conditions man appears as the responsible agent. The problem of resource adequacy for the ages to come will involve human wisdom more than limits set by nature.[50]

---

[49] Hotelling, "The Economics of Exhaustible Resources," *The Journal of Political Economy,* Vol. 39 (April 1931); Heady, "Efficiency in Public Soil-Conservation Programs," *The Journal of Political Economy,* Vol. 59 (February 1951), and "Some Fundamentals of Conservation Economics and Policy," *Journal of Farm Economics,* Vol. 32 (November 1950).

[50] Zimmerman, *World Resources and Industries* (rev. ed.; New York: Harper, 1951), pp. 814–15, 818.

Among other infrequent writings by contemporary economists on the general relation of natural resources to economic welfare, is a forceful article by Henry Villard in which he views and projects contemporary population growth rates with alarm.[51] Theodore W. Schultz, in a consideration of factors affecting economic development, lists natural resource limitation as an adverse influence. He refers to "the amount of land (the nonreproducible factors which always act as a drag on economic growth because of the element of diminishing returns which they give rise to as the other inputs are increased relative to these nonreproducible resources)." [52]

Horace Belshaw's excellent book on economic development has a section on the social production function in which the fixed land input is a retarding force.[53] There have been a number of "Malthusian trap models"—among them important contributions by Harvey Leibenstein, Richard R. Nelson, Kenneth Boulding, and Everett Hagen.[54] In these it is argued, among other things, that with a fixed land factor and high rates of population increase, stimuli resulting in increased incomes may ultimately generate more population instead of improved capital formation and productivity.

Finally, there are recurrent comments on dangers from resource limitations in economic writings concerned with the disparity between private and social costs and benefits. The following quotations are examples. The late A. C. Pigou, the leading expositor of the doctrine

[51] Villard, "Some Notes on Population and Living Levels," *The Review of Business and Economic Statistics*, Vol. 37 (May 1955). Also see his *Economic Development* (New York: Holt, Rinehart and Winston, 1959), Chapter 9 and Table 14-2.

[52] Schultz, *The Economic Test in Latin America* (Ithaca: Cornell University, 1956), pp. 19–20.

[53] *Op. cit.*, Part II.

[54] The term "Malthusian trap" has been used to characterize situations (or models of presumed situations) that are "trapped" in a vicious circle of subsistence: a small rise in income per capita above the subsistence level generates a rise in population which reduces income per capita to the former subsistence level. See especially Leibenstein, *Theory of Economic-Demographic Development* (Princeton: Princeton University Press, 1954) and also *Economic Backwardness and Economic Growth, op. cit.*; Nelson, "A Theory of the Low-Level Equilibrium Trap in Underdeveloped Economies," *American Economic Review*, Vol. 46 (December 1956); Boulding, "The Malthusian Model as a General System," *Social and Economic Studies*, Institute of Social and Economic Research, University College of the West Indies, Jamaica, British West Indies, Vol. 4 (September 1955); Hagen, "Population and Economic Growth," Center for International Studies, Massachusetts Institute of Technology, Hectograph C/58–14, September 1958.

that an efficiently operating laissez-faire economy may fail to maximize social benefits, states:

> . . . But there is wide agreement that the State should protect the interests of the future *in some degree* against the effects of our irrational discounting and of our preference for ourselves over our descendants. The whole movement for "conservation" in the United States is based on this conviction. It is the clear duty of Government, which is the trustee for unborn generations as well as for its present citizens, to watch over, and, if need be, by legislative enactment, to defend, the exhaustible natural resources of the country from rash and reckless spoliation.[55]

And the late Wesley C. Mitchell pressed strongly the same general point:

> A specter that has troubled men's minds more and more as the industrial revolution makes headway is the rapid depletion of natural resources. In 1865 W. Stanley Jevons pointed out that the fixed limits of coal deposits made it impossible that Great Britain should long maintain its current rate of increase in industrial output. Somewhat later Americans began to feel apprehensive about their supplies of lumber, natural gas, oil, and other minerals. Now we are becoming fearful about the loss of soil fertility through reckless methods of cultivation and erosion. The appalling wastes of natural resources that are going on seem due largely to the policy of handing over the nation's heritage to individuals to be exploited as they see fit. It appears that business planning takes, and must take, a relatively short period of time into account—a period that is but as a day in the life of the nation. What is rational on the basis of this short-run private view may be exceedingly unwise on the basis of long-run public interest.[56]

Conclusions

Our survey of literature dealing with the social aspects of natural resources has lead to three conclusions.

---

[55] Pigou, *Economics of Welfare* (London: Macmillan, 1946), pp. 29–30.
[56] Mitchell, *The Backward Art of Spending Money* (New York: Augustus M. Kelley, 1950), pp. 88–89.

1) There is a considerable body of thought on this subject which, at least for the time being, will be viewed as outside our concern. Philosophical naturalism—its ethics and aesthetics—and the problem of population control are surely important; but they are not within the scope of the present inquiry. Nor are we concerned with processes of resource policy determination and administration.

2) A very widespread and persistent source of interest in the social significance of natural resources derives from a concern for their economic adequacy. Stated another way, a major interest centers on the problem of natural resource scarcity and its economic effects. Whether this is the most important social feature of natural resources does not concern us. We take it as sufficient that an interest so persistent, vocal, agitated, and basic justifies detailed analysis of the economic doctrine of natural resource scarcity and effect. Our neglect of other social aspects of natural resources does not imply an undervaluation of the importance of such questions. But it does imply our belief that the subject of this study—the economics of natural resource scarcity—needs to be clarified before the other questions can be satisfactorily discussed.

3) Our final conclusion consists of simplified inferences concerning the content of the economic doctrine of natural resource scarcity. In economic terms, the belief seems to be that natural resources are scarce; that the scarcity increases with the passage of time; and that resource scarcity and its aggravation impair levels of living and economic growth. This set of simple and seemingly meaningful propositions epitomizes the dominant group views of layman and expert alike concerning the influence of natural resources upon economic welfare and economic growth. But in our view—contrary to much of the opinion surveyed—these propositions are neither self-evident nor easy to formulate in meaningful terms.

Our ultimate task then is to conduct a conceptual and, in a preliminary way, a quantitative appraisal of the meaning and accuracy of these economic propositions. In pursuit of this objective, a necessary prior task is to improve and amplify our understanding of received doctrine on the subject.

Two major bodies of historical literature and analysis will serve this purpose. The first basic source is the contribution of classical economics to the doctrine of natural resource scarcity—the potent writings of Malthus, Ricardo, and Mill. Much of the contemporary doctrine is a restatement of their "laws."

The second body of literature relates to what Samuel Hays has termed the "First American Conservation Movement," which took place during the period 1890–1920.[57] This important phenomenon in the nation's history appears to be the origin of much contemporary doctrine concerning resource scarcity and effect. Not only do today's views derive abundantly from the Conservation Movement, but many expressions of these views reiterate with nearly literal exactness arguments and positions that appeared repeatedly in the vast literature of that early Movement. These conservation ideas are taught currently in the public schools, are reflected in the platforms of both political parties, and motivate hundreds of private and public officials and organizations.

From both sources, we hope to find answers to important questions on contemporary views of the relation of natural resource scarcity to economic welfare—such questions as these: Where did the views come from? What are the details of the analytical structure—the premises, the logic, the reasoned conclusions? On what evidence are they based? What is the economic process whereby the premised physical parsimony of nature manifests itself as retarded economic growth and welfare?

[57] Samuel P. Hays, "The First American Conservation Movement, 1890–1920," unpublished Ph.D. dissertation, Harvard University Library, August 1952. This was revised and published subsequently under the title, *Conservation and the Gospel of Efficiency: The Progressive Conservation Movement, 1890–1920* (Cambridge: Harvard University Press, 1959).

Chapter 3

MALTHUS, RICARDO, AND MILL ON INCREASING NATURAL RESOURCE SCARCITY

MODERN views concerning the influence of natural resources on economic growth are variations on the scarcity doctrine developed by Thomas Malthus and David Ricardo in the first quarter of the nineteenth century and elaborated later by John Stuart Mill.[1] There were two basic versions of this doctrine. One, the Malthusian, rested on the assumption that the stock of agricultural land was absolutely limited; once this limit had been reached, continuing population growth would require increasing intensity of cultivation and, consequently, would bring about diminishing returns per capita. The other, or Ricardian, version viewed diminishing returns as a current phenomenon, reflecting decline in the quality of land as successive parcels were brought within the margin of profitable cultivation.

Mill made two contributions. He systematized, clarified, elaborated, and qualified the ideas of Malthus and Ricardo. And he extended the scope of natural resource scarcity and effect to living space and the quality of life, thus adding a new—though imperfectly developed—dimension to the earlier versions. Despite the trenchant qualifications found in Mill's discussion, the doctrine of diminishing returns per capita became embedded in economic theory as self-evident fact, requiring neither precise formulation nor analytical investigation. Instead, therefore, of being subjected to a process of continuing re-

---

[1] *An Essay on the Principle of Population,* where the ideas of Malthus considered here were developed, went through six editions, the first of which appeared in 1798 and the final revision in 1816. A further statement of the theory was written for the 1830 edition of the *Encyclopedia Britannica.* Ricardo's *Principles of Political Economy and Taxation* first came out in 1817, with revised editions in 1819 and 1821. Mill's *Principles of Political Economy* was published initially in 1848 and went through six subsequent revisions, the last appearing in 1871.

51

view and refinement, as happens to most scientific propositions of large scope, it became increasingly vague. It is not surprising, therefore, that when the doctrine is subjected to close examination it is found to be less easy than ordinarily thought to specify the conditions under which diminishing returns will inevitably occur in a society.

The Malthusian Growth Model

Malthus' famous *Essay on Population* [2] may be credited with having widely propagated the belief that natural resource scarcity impairs economic growth. His doctrine is based on presumed natural law. That natural resources are limited and population multiplies continuously, subject to a biological restriction, are taken as nature-given facts. In the absence of social preventive checks, population increases to the limits of subsistence. The limits of nature constitute scarcity. The dynamic tendency of population to press continually to the borders of subsistence is the driving force. The incompatibility of a finite amount of agricultural land with provision of subsistence to a continually increasing population entails an eventual decline in output per capita and cessation of growth. This is the economic scarcity effect.

With respect to natural resource scarcity, Malthus in his *Essay* stated this belief:

> The rate according to which the productions of the earth may be supposed to increase, it will not be so easy to determine. Of this, however, we may be perfectly certain, that the ratio of their increase in a limited territory must be of a totally different nature from the ratio of the increase of population. . . . Man is necessarily confined in room. When acre has been added to acre till all the fertile land is occupied, the yearly increase of food must depend upon the melioration of the land already in possession. This is a fund, which, from the nature of all soils, instead of increasing, must be gradually diminishing. (P. 4.)

[2] Thomas Malthus, *An Essay on Population* (reprint of 6th ed.; London: Ward, Lock and Company, 1826). Unless otherwise noted, this is the edition from which we quote.

With respect to the law of population growth, Malthus held that there is a

> . . . constant tendency in all animated life to increase beyond the nourishment prepared for it. (P. 2.) . . . Population invariably increases where the means of subsistence increase. . . . (P. 14.)

And he was so convinced of his doctrine that he stated:

> The main principle advanced is so incontrovertible, that, if I had confined myself merely to general views, I could have intrenched myself in an impregnable fortress. . . . (P. xxxvi.)

Malthus was not the originator of the doctrine that he propagated. Adam Smith, for example, had stated that "Every species of animals naturally multiplies to the means of their subsistence, and no species can ever multiply beyond it." [3] It is also possible to question whether Malthus was the origin of subsequent views on natural resource scarcity and effect. His *Essay* is far more an analysis of population than of natural resources, and natural resource scarcity and effect are more asserted than demonstrated. Moreover, Malthus apparently did not consider the problem of resource depletion, and therefore had nothing to say about the possibility of increasing scarcity and scarcity effect from resource destruction.

Whether or not we attribute to Malthus the origin of the doctrine that resource scarcity restrains economic growth, we must credit him with a clear, forceful, and persuasive generalized statement of this view. It is not necessary to decide whether the *Essay* was a work of youthful genius, as suggested by John Maynard Keynes, but there can be no doubt concerning its social significance. What is important to recognize is that from the *Essay* have flowed—sometimes directly and sometimes indirectly—potent ideas and major public policies on natural resource scarcity and effect.

An Essay on Population is far from a complete statement, like that in a modern economic model, of the relation of natural resources to economic growth. We, therefore, have found it useful to

---

[3] Smith, *Wealth of Nations* (Cannan ed.; New York: Modern Library, 1937), p. 79.

construct such a model. It does not, we believe, violate the intent of the *Essay*.

At an unsophisticated level of thought, it is sometimes taken for granted that fixity of natural resources and an expanding population—the two fundamental Malthusian postulates—suffice to produce diminishing returns, but this is incorrect. The Malthusian model requires four sets of specifications. These concern the (1) time horizon and trend of population, (2) availability of natural resources, (3) technology and institutions, and (4) production process.

TIME AND POPULATION

The specification concerning the time horizon is important. If the time assumed to be spanned by the model is extremely long, the entire outcome depends on whether or not the rate of population growth is greater than zero. If the rate of growth is zero or less, no ineluctable force drives society toward diminishing returns. But if population growth is positive and persistent, then, given sufficient time, no matter how small the growth rate, there is trouble ahead. At a rate of growth of only one-tenth of 1 per cent per annum, for example, population increases tenfold every 2,300 years. This would indicate a world population of 25 billion to 30 billion by the year 4300, and 2,500 billion, hardly a conceivable figure, by the year 9000. If population growth continues at a constant rate, it will only double in n years, but it will grow a thousandfold in $10n$ years, and a millionfold in $20n$ years.

Conversely, the time horizon need not be remote if the rate of annual population growth is sufficiently high. Malthus assumed a sustained rate of 3 per cent, close to what is now considered to be the biological maximum. On this basis, all horizons seem frighteningly near. Population is the crucial variable for periods longer than a few generations, since the number of people on the earth is doubled every quarter century or so. At this rate, world population at the end of only five centuries from now would be 6 to 7 quadrillion, 2.5 million times the figure for 1950, and its mass would be approaching that of the earth.

The alternative results of different annual growth rates for world population over the next hundred years are shown below (in billions):

Year	Rate = .03 (Malthus)	Rate = .016 (Present)	Rate = .001 (Hypothetical)
1950	2.5	2.5	2.50
1975	5.2	3.7	2.57
2000	11.0	5.5	2.63
2025	22.9	8.2	2.69
2050	48.0	12.2	2.77

In short, if one thinks, explicitly or implicitly, in terms of a population growth rate of 3 per cent, then Malthus was surely right. Population is the only strategic variable for periods of, say, 100 years or more. On the other hand, one might be inclined to project the present annual rate of world population increase—about half that of Malthus. Then population must be considered, but other elements may not be neglected, as they were by Malthus. Variables, such as changing social structure and technological development, change in the availability of natural resources, and the possibilities of a worldwide demographic transition, begin to acquire promising significance. If one assumes a rate of .001, then population growth becomes significant only after centuries and may be currently neglected.

NATURAL RESOURCE AVAILABILITY

The concept of limited economic availability of natural resources is not so simple as it appears at first sight. A fixed physical world, in itself, does not mean economic scarcity of resources. To be economically scarce, the amount of fixed natural resources must be small relative to the labor, capital, and sociotechnical knowledge available for putting the resources to work. From this, it follows that while a fixed world always contains a threat of scarce economic resources, the actual onset of scarcity depends also on other conditions. Thus, the physical properties of the natural environment are, for all practical purposes, given; but the economically useful properties of the natural environment depend on what is known, is wanted, and can be produced. Only when these are specified do selected segments of the environment acquire those additional social properties that convert them into natural resources in the economic sense of the term. So long, then, as natural resources in this sense are large enough to permit growth at constant output per capita, resource scarcity is not necessarily experienced. Indeed, whether such scarcity is imminent or not depends on many variable circumstances, and is not a nature-given fact.

So far as we can tell, Malthus' premise concerning the availability of natural resources derived directly from his observation that the world's agricultural lands were of limited physical extent. Malthus' *Essay* gave very little space to discussion of the natural resource variable in the social production process, beyond the implication that finite limits of agricultural land could be equated to economic scarcity of natural resources.

It may seem odd that Malthus failed to take serious account of variations in the quality of agricultural land, or to pay attention to natural resources other than land. But this was not important to him. His central concern was the inconsistency between his postulated high birth rate and what seemed to be an obvious limit to expansion of the means of subsistence. For his purposes, the differences in the quality of the land could be ignored. So, too, could the question of the availability of resources other than land.

These oversimplifications do not disturb us. The mark of good theory is not that it describes reality completely and faithfully in all respects, but that it captures the essence of that part of reality which is under consideration. It is, therefore, in a sense, inappropriate to ask whether Malthus believed his conditions to be complete and detailed descriptions of reality. Of course, he did not. The proper question is whether Malthus believed his theory and conditions to be accurate in their essentials for his growth model. And this he certainly did.

TECHNOLOGY AND INSTITUTIONS

Although the beginnings of the industrial revolution were clearly visible to Malthus, he assumed that technology and institutions were essentially unchanging—again, perhaps, because a population growth rate of 3 per cent dwarfed all other influences. Even today, with incomparably wider appreciation of the possibilities of technological advance, projection of population growth at the maximum sustainable rate for more than several generations stifles the imagination. To us, much of the significance of sociotechnological progress is that it provides both time and motivation for a reduction in fertility rates to match—and then more than match—the decline in mortality rates for which progress also has been responsible. Malthus, lacking the gift of prophecy, foresaw neither the demographic transition nor the scientific revolution. Constancy of the technological and social framework was thus a more legitimate abstraction for him than it is today.

THE PRODUCTION PROCESS

Even if the world satisfied the foregoing specifications of the Malthusian model, it would not follow that the social production process would be characterized by diminishing returns. At an elementary level of thought, it is sometimes taken for granted that "fixed" land and expanding population make diminishing returns inevitable. But this statement does not justify the hypothesis, which requires the introduction of additional postulates.

One possibility is to rely on the so-called law of variable proportions—the "law" that if a single input is increased indefinitely, all other inputs and conditions remaining constant, output per unit of the increasing input will eventually diminish. Given the Malthusian premise of fixed availability of land, this widely accepted principle is usually considered sufficient for the eventual appearance of diminishing returns. However, it is an improper inference. The law of variable proportions can be tested only for a limited range of cases—cases of homogeneous products (such as wheat) obtained with inputs of constant quality and unchanging methods. This is hardly the circumstance implied by the Malthusian dilemma, which allegedly applies to the economy as a whole, with all its shifting complexity. Moreover, the law of variable proportions holds only for increases in a single input, all others remaining constant, while the Malthusian natural resource premise holds one input constant and allows all others to increase. Even if "all others" is interpreted as consisting only of labor and capital, there is no support in either logic or experience for the assertion that, under these conditions, there must be diminishing returns to labor merely because land is constant. In order to justify diminishing returns to labor under these circumstances, it is necessary to specify that capital must not increase relative to labor sufficiently to offset the effects of the increasing ratio of labor to land. In fact, Malthus and his contemporaries and successors did make this additional assumption in a strong form—labor and capital were employed in "doses" of unvarying proportions, in effect reducing the two inputs to one.[4]

The Malthusian diminishing returns proposition, therefore, is neither simple nor self-evident. Conditions of the distinct types mentioned are individually necessary and, if appropriately specified, collectively sufficient to produce diminishing returns on the basis of the Malthusian increasing scarcity hypothesis. Moreover, there is not a unique set of required specifications. We have seen, for example, that the length of the requisite time horizon is inversely related to the postulated rate of population increase and positively related to the assumed abundance of currently unutilized resources. Also, the appropriateness of Malthus' neglect of resources other than agricultural land, and the possibilities of technological change and demographic transition, depend on the length of the time horizon. Numerous combinations of particular conditions of the four types are thus sufficient to produce the postulated Malthusian result. Conditions sufficient to produce the result can indeed be specified, but whether any of the combinations exists, or ever has existed, is a question of fact that must be investigated before the Malthusian hypothesis of increasing resource scarcity and effect can be accepted as a reasonable description of the shape of economic growth.

---

[4] See Mark Blaug, *Economic Theory in Retrospect* (Homewood, Ill.; Irwin, 1962), p. 72. Alfred Marshall's acceptance of the law of diminishing returns in agriculture (and of its eventual dominance over increasing returns in manufacturing) may have been due in part to insufficient exploration of the concept of a "dose" of labor and capital. Thus, he writes: ". . . Our law [of diminishing return] states that sooner or later (it being always supposed that there is meanwhile no change in the arts of cultivation) a point will be reached after which all further doses will obtain a less proportionate return than the preceding doses." (*Principles of Economics,* 8th ed.; London: Macmillan, 1920, p. 153). But then he refers in an appended "Note" (p. 171) to the "great variations in the relative amounts of labour and capital in a dose," without recognizing that this casts doubt upon the validity of the alleged "law."

Ricardo and Malthus Compared

At first glance, the Ricardian version of resource scarcity appears easier to justify than that of Malthus. We know that land varies in physical characteristics. It therefore seems plausible that it will vary in productivity, and that the better lands will be brought into use before the poorer ones. The view that growth will be accompanied by increasing real costs—that is, by diminishing returns to labor and capital—then seems to follow as a matter of course.

But differences in physical characteristics do not in themselves necessarily imply that costs will increase as resources with differing physical properties are brought into use. For this to occur, special conditions must be satisfied. There must be knowledge of the still unutilized resource base, not only of its extent and characteristics but also of its cost implications. Resources must then be used in order of increasing labor-capital cost of output—that is, in the order of declining economic quality. This means that the prevailing economic rationality must call for the use of resources in this order, and that no changes in technology or the product mix will bring about unforeseen modifications in resource requirements and use patterns. Finally, the rise in costs, implied by the foregoing conditions, must not be offset by increasing returns to scale in the social production process as a whole, or by improved productivity from changes in technology and institutions.

Thus, the proposition of Ricardian diminishing returns, like that of Malthus, also is neither simple nor self-evident. An important difference between them is that the Ricardian diminishing returns take effect from the outset, thus requiring no specification concerning the time horizon, and no assumption of an absolute limit to the availability of resources. The rate of population growth does not determine when Ricardian diminishing returns will set in, but only how long it will take for total output to rise and output per capita to fall to given levels.

Ricardo was by no means the first to observe that agricultural lands vary in fertility and proximity to markets. Differential economic quality has become associated with his name because he made it a central feature of a sophisticated analysis of natural resource scarcity and its economic effects. Thus, Ricardo's interest in natural resources differed from that of Malthus. Whereas Malthus evoked scarcity to lend point to a polemical, inexact, and untested population theory, Ricardo did so to explain the phenomenon and behavior of rent in a closely reasoned and very abstract theory of economic growth. Aware that land varied in quality, Malthus nevertheless focused upon the extensive limits of the earth, and found resource scarcity inherent in the finiteness of the globe. Aware of the extensive limits of the earth, Ricardo nevertheless focused upon the differential fertility of the individual parcels of land; and, assuming that the better lands would be used first, he found declining quality to be the cause of increasing resource scarcity.

Malthus and Ricardo would have charted the availability of agricultural land as indicated in the two panels of Figure 1, the ultimate

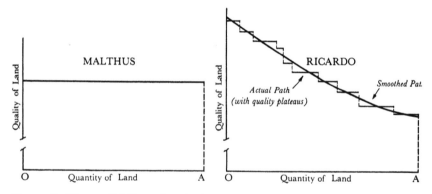

Figure 1. The availability of agricultural land: Malthus vs. Ricardo

limits of the earth being represented in each case by *OA*.

The effect of economic scarcity may be compared for the two formulations. In the classical manner, capital and labor are assumed to vary in doses of fixed proportions, so that, in reality, there are only two inputs—resources and labor-capital. The effects of increasing output—that is, of economic growth—are compared in Figure 2.

Panel 2-a shows that, in the Malthusian case, labor-capital cost per unit of output is constant until the limits of the earth are reached where all land is employed at *A*. From that point onward, cost per unit of output rises because of the intensive application of labor-capital and the assumed Malthusian conditions. Although natural resource availability was always limited in a physical sense, this limited availability does not constitute *economic scarcity*—that is, it is not an economic phenomenon—until all land is employed at *A*. Only then, do the limits acquire economic meaning and reality; only then, is there an economic scarcity effect.

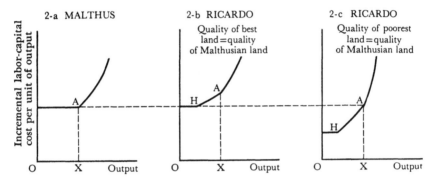

Figure 2. Malthusian and Ricardian economic scarcity effects

Panel 2-b shows Ricardian scarcity where the quality of the best land is the same as the homogeneous quality assumed by Malthus. Differing from Malthus, Ricardian scarcity effects are not postponed until the limits of the earth are reached at *A,* but begin to appear as soon as point *H* is reached, where fertility begins to decline as more land is brought into use. Ricardian labor-capital cost per unit of output is higher than Malthusian when all *A* units of land are employed. In both cases, the scarcity effect, once it appears, becomes stronger as output increases; but the severity or magnitude of the scarcity effect is greater in this particular Ricardian case, since scarcity appears before *A* is reached. The rate of increase in scarcity effect is also greater under the postulated conditions. In the Ricardian scheme, unlike the Malthusian, physical scarcity becomes economic scarcity, and produces economic scarcity effect, as soon as the initial small amount of the resource of highest quality is fully employed.

Ricardian scarcity effects also appear long before Malthusian even if it is assumed that the homogeneous Malthusian land is of the same quality as the poorest Ricardian land ever to be brought into use. Panel

2-c illustrates that the scarcity effect appears at H as soon as the highest-quality Ricardian land is fully employed. This is so even though Ricardian marginal land is still superior to Malthusian, and Ricardian labor-capital cost is lower.

It is useful to place one of the Ricardian curves under a magnifying glass. This is done in Figure 3, in which the neighborhood of point H

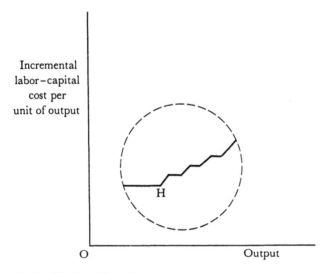

Figure 3. Detail of a Ricardian cost curve

(where it becomes necessary to use resources of poorer quality) is magnified. The chart illustrates the compatibility of the Ricardian view with the simpler Malthusian notion. At outputs below H, costs are constant for both hypotheses. Thereafter, a Ricardian stairway appears. Each riser on the stairway represents a Malthusian type of increasing cost due to the (temporary) constancy of the land input. That is, on the risers, the model is temporarily Malthusian, because land of the given qualities is all employed, and increases in output involve more intensive cultivation. But the intensive cultivation does not go on for long. Shortly, a point is reached where the marginal product of intensively employed labor-capital has fallen to that which could be obtained on the next lower grade of land still not used. It then becomes more economical to shift to this new plateau, where the marginal product for a time will be constant, than to proceed further with more intensive cultivation and declining marginal productivity of labor-capital. But eventually this quality of land is all in use, and again a Malthusian type of more intensive cultivation produces a further scarcity effect. Finally, all land is in use, and expansion of output becomes Malthusian.

The Ricardian view of economic resource scarcity and its effects, in one sense, is more pessimistic than the Malthusian view. In a lightly peopled world, Malthusian scarcity and its effects would not be immediately felt. Ultimately these would have to be faced; but the time might be distant. Before then, possibly, the "law" of population growth could undergo modification. Malthus' advice to adopt preventive checks might be followed, for example. Ricardo, however, grants virtually no period of grace, and partly closes off these possible escapes from scarcity. He views economic scarcity as a continuously operative force, and scarcity effect is virtually always present. The question is not whether scarcity and its effects can be avoided— this is impossible. Even cessation of population growth could only prevent existing scarcity from increasing further.

But there is an important sense in which a Ricardian model is more optimistic than that of Malthus. Perhaps because he implicitly doubted the significance of Malthus' ultimate limit, Ricardo never mentions it. Thus, there seems always to be for Ricardo a resort to additional, if lower-quality, resources. There is always another extensive margin, another plateau of lower quality, which will be reached before the increasing intensity of utilization of presently employed resources becomes intolerable. For purposes of comparison, we show in the figures an ultimate limit to the continuance of the Ricardian growth process, but this is not strictly correct. An absolute limit is perhaps conceivable in a Ricardian world but it is certainly not definable. Perhaps this is a further reason why Ricardo, with his penchant for exactitude, avoided committing himself on the issue.

While Malthus, in his *Essay,* was completely silent concerning minerals, Ricardo took mining into account. Since mines vary in fertility (Ricardo's term), the scarcity principle applicable to mining is identical with that devised for agricultural land. But Ricardo's views on mines were somewhat incidental in nature, introduced to complete the exposition of his theory of rent and of his views on the inability of gold to serve as an invariable measure of value. Having devised his scarcity formulation for agriculture, the dominant sector of the time, he then observed that it was also applicable to mining. He also noted that new mines could be discovered, that mining techniques could improve, and that depletion might force deeper diggings. Owing perhaps to preoccupation with the general concept of variations in natural fertility as a scarcity force (and their relation to the concept of rent), Ricardo did not speculate on whether minerals exhaustion—an economic scarcity phenomenon different from natural fertility gradations—might be significant. So far as variations in fertility and accessibility were concerned, mines and agricultural land were to him the same.[5]

Mill's Clarification and Extension of the Scarcity Doctrine

Mill elaborated upon the ideas of Malthus and Ricardo, viewing them in wider perspective, rendering them more representative of the world of the nineteenth century, endowing them with new dimensions that now seem strikingly relevant to the twentieth century. While accepting the basic Malthusian premise that population had the power and the tendency to increase geometrically, Mill observed that this power was seldom, if ever, used to the utmost. He also expressed doubts concerning the relevance and realism of Malthus' assumption that there was an absolute and foreseeable limit to the availability of agricultural land. More reasonable, he thought, was the Ricardian view that resources (including mines) underwent a persistent decline in economic quality as the consequence of growth.

MILL ON MALTHUSIAN SCARCITY

Initially, Mill accepts the Malthusian view of natural resource scarcity, the limits of the earth, as relevant for economic analysis. In

[5] Ricardo asserted categorically that "wherever I speak of the rent of land, I wish to be understood as speaking of that compensation which is paid to the owner of the land for the use of its original and indestructible powers." See David Ricardo, *Principles of Political Economy and Taxation* (Everyman ed.; London: 1926), p. 34. When he said (p. 46) that "this principle [of the rent of mines] is precisely the same as that which we have already laid down respecting land," he presumably thought it unnecessary to warn the reader that the rent of mines did not constitute payment (that is, a royalty), for exhaustion of the mineral content, especially as he had already implied this clearly. (P. 34.)

his *Principles,*[6] Chapter 12 (which is entitled "Of the Law of Increase of Production from Land") opens with the following passage:

Land differs from the other elements of production, labour and capital, in not being susceptible of indefinite increase. Its extent is limited. . . . It is also evident that the quantity of produce capable of being raised on any given piece of land is not indefinite. This limited quantity of land, and limited productiveness of it, are the real limits to the increase of production. (P. 176.)

Similarly, Mill affirms Malthusian doctrine on the tendency of population to increase. "The increase of labor," he writes, "is the increase of mankind; of population. On this subject the discussions excited by the *Essay* of Mr. Malthus have made the truth, though by no means universally admitted, yet so fully known. . . ." (P. 156.)

But on both scores—ultimate limits of the earth and the tendency of population to increase—Mill then significantly weakens the Malthusian formulations. In fact, all four of the crucial relationships in the Malthusian model are qualified. With respect to natural resource availability and the time horizon, Mill asserts that the ultimate bounds of the earth constitute neither immediate nor even, perhaps, moderate-term limits.

That they are the ultimate limits, must always have been clearly seen. But . . . the final barrier has never in any instance been reached; . . . there is no country in which all the land, capable of yielding food, is so highly cultivated that a larger produce could not (even without supposing any fresh advance in agricultural knowledge) be obtained from it and . . . a large portion of the earth's surface still remains entirely uncultivated; . . . (P. 176.)

Similarly, according to Mill's *Principles,* the capability of population increase is potential, not actual.

Its [population's] power of increase is indefinite, and the actual multiplication would be extraordinarily rapid, if the power were exercised to the utmost. It never is exercised to the utmost. (P. 157.)

And he goes on to say why:

[6] John Stuart Mill, *Principles of Political Economy* (Ashley ed.; London: Longmans, Green, 1929).

. . . the conduct of human creatures is more or less influenced by foresight of consequences, and by impulses superior to mere animal instincts: and they do not, therefore, propagate like swine, but are capable . . . of being withheld by prudence, or by the social affections, from giving existence to beings born only to misery and premature death. In proportion as mankind rise above the condition of the beast, population is restrained by the fear of want rather than by want itself. (Pp. 158–59.)

The emphasis here (and also in the chapter, "On the Probable Futurity of the Labouring Classes," especially Section 3) is on changes in intelligence, attitudes, and institutions; but we infer that Mill had rising per capita income and its consequences in mind as the major weapon against the Malthusian dilemma.

Finally, Mill recognizes that technology and institutions do vary, owing to what he calls (apologizing for the vagueness of the phrase) the "progress of civilization." And he shows the difference between a social production function and the production function applicable to a firm or industry. While he affirms strongly the applicability of the true law of diminishing returns to the latter, he weakens its applicability to the former.

MILL ON RICARDIAN SCARCITY

The major reason why the Malthusian extensive limits of the earth are not a controlling force, Mill believes, is because Ricardian scarcity comes into play long before these limits can be reached. Mill affirms in the *Principles* the validity of Ricardian natural resource scarcity and scarcity effect. More important than the limited extent of the earth is the still more limited extent of the more productive kinds of land. And Mill is greatly concerned lest it be thought that, because Malthus' ultimate limits have not been reached, scarcity is only a distant threat and not a current force. The commonly held belief that what we have here called natural resource scarcity effect is not being experienced is, in his view, "not only an error, but the most serious one, to be found in the whole field of political economy." (P. 176.) Increasing labor-capital cost per unit of output—the scarcity effect—he characterizes as the "general law of agricultural industry [which] is the most important proposition in political economy." (P. 177.)

Mill elaborated upon mining, which Ricardo had treated as an implicit aspect of the general proposition of resource use in order of declining fertility and accessibility. But in mining there is another feature which, Mill observed, makes the situation worse than in the case of land. Exhaustion of the richer mineral deposits sets in, so that, even in the absence of growth, it is not possible for society to obtain a constant yield at constant cost year after year. Moreover, even before a particular mine actually shows signs of exhaustion in terms of aggregate mineral content, the law of scarcity and effect applies, since "shafts must be sunk deeper, galleries driven farther . . . ," and so on. (P. 188.)

The American economist, H. C. Carey, was at least partially responsible for Mill's recognition of another qualification to Ricardo's views. Carey asserted that the real law of agricultural expansion is the very reverse of that stated by Ricardo and affirmed by Mill. He argued that agricultural land was not used in the order of best quality first. Rather, cultivation begins with poorer lands, and later extends to more fertile ones. The result is that expansion of agricultural output is carried on under conditions of increasing returns. The reason that settlers in a new country do not use the lands of greatest quality first is that river lowlands are unhealthy, or require considerable prior investment in clearance and drainage. Settlement, therefore, commences on lands that are high and less fertile. Only as population increases and wealth accumulates are the more fertile lands eventually brought into use.

Although Mill denies the general validity of Carey's views, he argues that Carey

> . . . has a good case against several of the highest authorities in political economy, who certainly did enunciate in too universal a manner the law which they laid down, not remarking that it is not true of the first cultivation in a newly settled country. (P. 181.)

But Mill does not find the exception to be very important [7] because

> . . . it is not pretended that the law of diminishing return was operative from the very beginning of society: and though some

[7] Anthony Scott has called our attention to an interesting demonstration that Carey's case was theoretically sound. See R. Turvey, "A Finnish Contribution to Rent Theory," *Economic Journal*, Vol. 65 (June 1955).

political economists may have believed it to have come into operation earlier than it does, it begins quite early enough to support the conclusions they founded on it. (Pp. 181–82.)

On the other hand, Mill remarks later in the *Principles* that "in the case of mines and of fisheries, the natural order of events is liable to be interrupted by the opening of a new mine or a new fishery, of superior quality to some of those already in use." (P. 475.)

An important qualification of Ricardian theory is Mill's argument that the principle of "progress" operates in opposition to diminishing returns. He asserts that this "antagonistic" principle includes progress of agricultural techniques and other knowledge, skill, and invention, which he details at length. These include improved processes such as rotation of crops; introduction of new articles of food; better knowledge of fertilizers; improvement in plant and animal breeds; reduction of agricultural waste; new forms of agricultural machines; improved roads, railways, canals, and other forms of transport; manufacturing improvements of all kinds; institutional progress; and so on. (P. 183.)

> There is, thus, no possible improvement in the arts of production which does not in one or another mode exercise an antagonistic influence to the law of diminishing return to agricultural labour. Nor is it only industrial improvements which have this effect. Improvements in government, and almost every kind of moral and social advancement, operate in the same manner. . . . We may say the same of improvement in education. (Pp. 186–87.)

The "antagonizing agency" of "progress of civilization" also applies, and with even greater force, in the minerals sector. Mining operations, Mill says, are more susceptible than agriculture to technological improvement. And another important counterbalance to the gradual depletion and eventual exhaustion of existing mines is "the discovery of new ones, equal or superior in richness." And finally, of no small importance, progress in manufactures tends to "preponderate greatly over the one cause which tends to diminish it: and the increase of production, called forth by the progress of society, takes place, not at an increasing, but at a continually diminishing proportional cost." (Pp. 185–86.)

Mill's final conclusion concerning the "law of increase of production from land"—his synthesis of Malthusian and Ricardian scarcity doctrine—is that

. . . all natural agents which are limited in quantity, are not only limited in their ultimate productive power, but long before that power is stretched to the utmost, they yield to any additional demands on progressively harder terms. This law may, however, be suspended, or temporarily controlled, by whatever adds to the general power of mankind over nature; and especially by any extension of their knowledge, and their consequent command, of the properties and powers of natural agents. (P. 188.)

MILL ON LIVING SPACE

Mill's reformist temperament is reflected in his extension of the application and meaning of natural resource scarcity and effect to the notion of living space—its quantity and its quality. Observations to the effect that land is used for purposes other than agriculture, and provides utilities in the form of beauty and convenience, were introduced in the *Principles* only incidentally (see, for example, pp. 475–76). But in his famous chapter, "Of the Stationary State," Mill expatiates upon the advantages of personal solitude and natural beauty:

A population may be too crowded, though all be amply supplied with food and raiment. It is not good for man to be kept perforce at all times in the presence of his species. A world from which solitude is extirpated is a very poor ideal. Solitude, in the sense of being often alone, is essential to any depth of meditation or of character; and solitude in the presence of natural beauty and grandeur, is the cradle of thoughts and aspirations which are not only good for the individual, but which society could ill do without. Nor is there much satisfaction in contemplating the world with nothing left to the spontaneous activity of nature; with every rood of land brought into cultivation, which is capable of growing food for human beings; every flowery waste or natural pasture ploughed up, all quadrupeds or birds which are not domesticated for man's use exterminated as his rivals for food, every hedgerow or superfluous tree rooted out, and scarcely a place left where a wild shrub or flower could grow without being eradicated as a weed in the name of improved agriculture. (P. 750.)

This extension by Mill of the doctrine of natural resource scarcity and effect is merely asserted. It is not analyzed at any length, but its implications are plain. Natural resources as a broadly defined idea of living space may become scarce. And this scarcity effect, no less than scarcity of tangible economic goods, can impair welfare. One aspect of such natural resource scarcity is rather narrow—sites for residences and other structures. Another is more general—the value to man of the totality of his natural and modified physical surroundings.

Mill's treatment of scarcity should be regarded more as a set of variations on the classical theme than as an original composition. He found it difficult to accept the traditional views as wholly accurate descriptions of the course of growth. Yet he found no grounds on which to deny the existence of an underlying "natural" tendency for population to increase and for returns to diminish in agriculture, and perhaps mining. He therefore could not deny that the "stationary state" was the probable outcome of the growth process. But he saw many actual and potential ameliorations in the possibilities of technological and social progress. He contented himself with the assertion that he could not "regard the stationary state of capital and wealth with the unaffected aversion so generally manifested towards it by political economists of the old school." (P. 748.)

In his elaborations upon the ideas of Malthus and Ricardo, Mill took account of, and lent credence to, nearly all the qualifications of scarcity doctrine that seem relevant today. But he was ambivalent, and his views were ahead of their time. He alluded to the possibility that "the increase of intelligence . . . must be attended with the corresponding growth of the good sense which manifests itself in provident habits of conduct, and that population, therefore, will bear a gradually diminishing ratio to capital and employment. . . ." (P. 759.) This, however, was more an adumbration than a reflection of the demographic transition. His recognition that discovery, and especially technical progress, importantly oppose the increase in natural resource scarcity and forestall the appearance of diminishing returns, rested (as it now appears to us) on a modest record of industrial achievement and involved a necessarily limited appraisal of potentialities. Mill asserted that "there is room in the world . . . for a great increase in population, supposing the arts of life to go on improving, and capital to increase," but because of the implications, he saw "very little reason for desiring it." (P. 750.) He was asking others to share his confidence in the evolutionary direction of the world by coupling a concern for the quality of human living with the classical concern over diminishing returns.

But his successors were not, on the whole, ready to share this confidence and this concern. This may have been because Mill, with characteristic modesty, regarded his contribution as an amplification and clarification of the work of his distinguished predecessors rather than a new departure. Perhaps for these reasons, it was easy for subsequent generations of economists generally to overlook the significance of his elaborations and observations, to maintain an emphasis on the simple and seemingly self-evident main line of traditional doctrine.[8] Part of what we say in the remainder of this volume might be regarded as a development of Mill's suggestive insights concerning natural resource scarcity—we shall have but little to say about population—in terms appropriate to the present state of economic theory and scientific knowledge.

[8] Marshall, *op. cit.*, for example, repeats most of Mill's points, but in less, rather than more (as we think would have been appropriate), forceful terms.

Chapter 4

THE CONSERVATION MOVEMENT

"CONSERVATION," a coined term, was a part of the "Progressive" political reform program at the turn of the century. It was also a major social movement underlying that program. Conservation doctrine,[1] it is true, began with a focus on natural resources. But in the quest for political support, the doctrine was broadened to include other Progressive social welfare ideas. In terms of ideas, Conservation ranged all the way from abstract metaphysics to practical everyday activity of the individual—it concerned all the various natural sciences, economics, political science, public administration, sociology, engineering, art, and public health.

The Political and Social Nature of the Movement

To look at the Conservation Movement as a set of social values, and a successful and practical political force derivative from these, clarifies some of its features which are difficult to understand. The internal contradictions of the Movement resulted from efforts to enhance its political appeal and to ally divergent groups and interests. Thus the Conservation Movement ultimately moved from natural resources to doctrine and policies on immigration, anti-industrialization, trust-busting, pure food laws, child labor, Anglo-Saxon supremacy, and so on. The clue as to how this happened is found in the fact that it was a successful political movement; architects and managers of a developing political program are rarely consistent in thought or action.

[1] In this chapter, unlike other chapters, we use the words "Conservation" or "Conservationist" with relation to the Conservation Movement of 1890–1920, unless we specifically indicate that we are referring to our contemporaries.

72

Further—like all successful political movements—the Conservation Movement was dominated by its leaders and flavored by their personalities, rather than intellectually led and constructed with scholarly rigor.

Despite the high personal ethics of Conservation leaders, power alliances, scare propaganda, and other political maneuvers were employed. For example, President Theodore Roosevelt put 75 million additional acres of forests under the control of the Forest Service between the time Congress passed a bill to revoke the President's authority to create new forest reserves and the time of his signature. National forests totaled about 45 million acres when Roosevelt became President, and had been increased to 75 million acres when, in congressional reaction against his exercise of executive power, the revocation bill was passed in 1907.[2] As another example, it was charged during a congressional investigation, but was not proved, that Gifford Pinchot, as Chief Forester, used money for conservation activities which was appropriated for other purposes. Since it was political, the Conservation Movement was opportunistic, expedient, and ready to compromise.

Conservation was thus the banner of a crusading political march led by one of the most able, vigorous, and successful presidents of our century, during and after his tenure of office, and much of the Conservation Movement's history and contributions can be understood in this light. Its political and social character explains its heterogeneous support and membership; its dynamism of subject matter, approach, and goals; and its later metamorphosis, senescence, and relative decline.

As it was a successful political and social movement in American national life, Conservation could not be revolutionary in its *immediate* impact. The American political fabric with its loose weave and flexible fibers, cannot be torn easily; instead, it is susceptible to gradual reshaping. In this gradual sense, Conservation could be, and was, revolutionary in part of its doctrine, and in its eventual influence upon American society. The doctrine of "conservation of nature" was an American part of a major revolution in thought throughout the West-

[2] See Samuel P. Hays, *Conservation and the Gospel of Efficiency: The Progressive Conservation Movement, 1890–1920* (Cambridge: Harvard University Press, 1959), p. 47.

ern world against the then dominant social philosophy of the fully self-regulating market economy. Marxism was another European part of that revolution in ideas. The same period, too, marked the beginning of the now somewhat successful revolution against the prevailing social views on labor. Resistance was arising to the idea that labor is merely a factor input to the production function in a purely competitive, laissez-faire economy, and that wages should properly be, according to natural law, the factor return from a laissez-faire distribution system. And as with labor, so with the "land" factor of classical economics. Conservationists rejected the idea that nature could be reduced to the classical market place concept of "land." It was more than this, they insisted.

Fifty years later, Karl Polanyi described the larger revolution of Western society against the self-regulating economy in a stimulating book. He never mentioned the Conservation Movement or any of its adherents. Yet, out of his general thesis on the revolution, he stated the essence of the Conservationists' rebellion against laissez faire in land with wonderful succinctness and accuracy:

> What we call Land is an element of nature inextricably interwoven with man's institutions. To isolate it and form a market out of it was perhaps the weirdest of all undertakings of our ancestors.
>
> Traditionally, land and labor are not separated; labor forms part of life, land remains part of nature, life and nature form an articulate whole. Land is thus tied up with organizations of kinship, neighborhood, craft, and creed—with tribe and temple, village, guild, and church. . . .
>
> The economic function is but one of the many vital functions of land. It invests man's life with stability; it is the site of his habitation; it is a condition of his physical safety; it is the landscape and the seasons. We might as well imagine his being born without hands and feet as carrying on his life without land. And yet to separate land from man and organize society in such a way as to satisfy the requirements of a real-estate market was a vital part of the utopian concept of a market economy.[8]

[8] Karl Polanyi, *The Great Transformation: The Political and Economic Origins of Our Time* (Boston: Beacon Press, 1957; originally published, 1944), p. 178.

The Conservation View of Scarcity

In the vast Conservation literature of the period 1890–1920, there is no rigorous economic analysis of what is natural resource economic scarcity. Nor is there analysis of nineteenth-century economic history which, in a scholarly way, identifies and measures natural resource economic scarcity and its economic effects. Rather, scarcity doctrine arises in a variety of ways out of more practical, less academic, writings. We summarize in the following pages the major meanings of scarcity found in Conservation literature.

INESCAPABLE SOURCES OF SCARCITY

In the doctrine of the Conservation Movement certain scarcities are inescapable—they cannot be avoided by even the wisest men. The limits of the nation are physical bounds. The facts of ecological interdependencies are physical. Man's weakening of the natural ecological optimum occurs as a result of the physical drains caused by his large numbers. Mineral depletion is a physical necessity in industrialized society.

Limits of Natural Resources.   The Conservation literature of the period 1890–1920 abounds with estimates and descriptions of physical natural resources and exhortations to amplify these estimates. One of the important practical contributions of the Conservation Movement, according to its leaders, was the inception of a program to take inventory of natural resource wealth in the United States. The historic 1908 Governors' Conference [4] and an Inland Waterways Conference were responsible for literally thousands of estimates of the physical quantities and characteristics of natural resources within the nation's boundaries. And the discussions continually emphasized that these quantitative estimates, and those proposed, would constitute an economically adequate representation of the nation's natural resource wealth. It is quite clear from the record that economic natural re-

[4] *Proceedings of a Conference of Governors, in the White House* (Washington: GPO, 1908), No. 48489.

source scarcity was equated with these estimates of finite physical resources within the nation.

We thus arrive at an important, first approximation of what the Conservation Movement meant by economic scarcity of resources. (And, by implication, we acquire insight into the meanings of contemporary views concerning resource scarcity, where these derive from Conservation teachings.) This doctrine of economic scarcity was, in major degree, starkly and simply that national resource wealth is limited to nature's physical magnitudes within the borders of the nation. Finite physical limits of natural resources, to the early Conservationists, constituted economic scarcity. This approach is clearly stated by Gifford Pinchot, who shared with President Theodore Roosevelt the leadership of the Movement.

> We have a limited supply of coal, and only a limited supply. Whether it is to last for a hundred or a hundred and fifty or a thousand years, the coal is limited in amount, unless through geological changes which we shall not live to see, there will never be any more of it than there is now. But coal is in a sense the vital essence of our civilization. If it can be preserved, if the life of the mines can be extended, if by preventing waste there can be more coal left in this country after we of this generation have made every needed use of this source of power, then we shall have deserved well of our descendants.[5]

Later in the same book, Pinchot said:

> *The five indispensably essential materials in our civilization are wood, water, coal, iron, and agricultural products.* . . . We have timber for less than thirty years at the present rate of cutting. The figures indicate that our demands upon the forest have increased twice as fast as our population. We have anthracite coal for but fifty years, and bituminous coal for less than two hundred. Our supplies of iron ore, mineral oil, and natural gas are being rapidly depleted, and many of the great fields are already exhausted. Mineral resources such as these when once gone are gone forever. (Pp. 123–24, italics added.)

The Conservationists' concepts of limits—and thereby, implicitly, economic scarcity—are multidimensional. In this sense, they are un-

    [5] Pinchot, *The Fight for Conservation* (New York: Doubleday, Page & Co., 1910), p. 43.

like the concepts of Malthus, and unlike the emphasis of the other classicists on agricultural land. Natural resources are specific in type, location, qualities, and relationships to one another. And economic scarcity in the sense of limited physical availability characterizes all the dimensions. Thus, one type of natural resource may be more scarce than another, one quality more scarce than another, and so on. The aggregate of all resources is clearly capable of being characterized by multidimensional scarcity magnitudes, by (say) a vector description. It is also conceivable that the aggregate of resources is susceptible to a more summary type of measurement and description, of fewer dimensions than the arraying of all types, locations, qualities, or other features.

Ecological Balance or Interdependence. The past few generations have learned (in part from the stimulus of the Conservation Movement and its educational efforts) that there are both small and large overlapping systems of interdependency among nature's biological organisms and its geological and atmospheric features. Forest watersheds, for example, play an important role in determining both the quality of water and the quantity available at different times in the water courses. In the absence of forests or other plant cover, surface runoff increases, soil is washed into water courses, flood peaks are higher, and so on. The conception of ecological balance has been widely presented in scholarly and popular literature.[6]

Additional meaning is thereby given to the concept of "limits" and the doctrine of economic scarcity by the Conservationists' emphasis on interdependence in nature. The metaphors of a chain as strong as its weakest link and of the war lost for want of a nail are suggestive and relevant. Quantities and qualities of individual natural resources physically depend one upon another. In a dynamic world, constraints on the over-all limits of natural resources are imposed by the idea of ecological equilibrium. This "scarcity" in no way depends upon man; it derives from physical interdependencies in nature. It would be true in a dynamic world, even if man did not in a substantial way modify nature.

[6] See, for example, E. P. Odum, *Fundamentals of Ecology* (Philadelphia: W. B. Saunders, 1953), and John H. Storer, *The Web of Life* (New York: Signet Books, 1956; originally published, 1953).

Ecological "Damage."   In the Conservationist view, stated extremely, nature without man was a world in optimal ecological balance. While this is overstatement, it properly emphasizes and implies an important element in Conservation doctrine. Nature's own ecological balance has intrinsic merit simply because of its high physical level—its "naturalness." The doctrine attaches positive cultural and social values to an ecological balance in which nature's biological systems are at high levels of physical output and activity, and fears or deplores radical departures from such ecological levels.

Of course, the urban and industrial activities of modern man, however prudent, and the manifold growth in his numbers extensively disturb natural ecological balances, destroy part of original nature, and significantly reduce the levels of some of nature's biological systems. The over-all ecological system is thus weakened. This relative physical debility is an additional dimension in the concept of economic scarcity of natural resources. The scarcity of limits, already tighter than the classicists had thought because of the constraint of balance, is aggravated by reduction and distortion of the more natural ecological balances, caused by civilized man's presence.

An example will be helpful. Civilized man appropriates land for cities and highways. Land is thus removed from the natural ecological system. Natural resource capacity is thus reduced. Civilized man also channels nature's processes to his own purposes. He eliminates forests and puts the Great Plains under the plow, and thereby changes nature's balance. Tree growth is reduced, buffalo and other wildlife disappear, soil is lost, and rivers silt. The point here is not poor management. It is that nature's ecological system once contained only several million inhabitants in the U.S. area who were more or less nomadic. Today, the United States has close to 200 million inhabitants and endless miles of concrete on land which once supported a profusion of plant and animal life.[7]

---

[7] The views of the Conservationists on ecological damage involved value judgments in favor of high-level ecological systems, but implied that these were "scientific" or "objective." Modern ecology would not support this position. And social scientists also reject it. In personal correspondence, Anthony Scott has stressed that nature is rarely in balance, and that the science of ecology does not posit a static balance as being normal: "The biologists were just as guilty as some older economists of taking the idea of equilibrium, turning it from an abstract point of reference to a state called 'normal' and then assailing all those who did not wish to have things made 'normal' as

Mineral Depletion. The economic scarcities caused by the limits of nature and the damage to biological systems are further subject to aggravation by modern man's destructive utilization of mineral resources. Fuel mineral resources once burned, are forever lost. Secondary metal recovery permits the repeated use of metallic minerals, but, even under the best of circumstances, metals are eventually dissipated by corrosion, wear, and other loss. This type of additional economic scarcity is thus a necessary consequence in a society which utilizes nonrenewable mineral resources. Of course, its degree is at man's discretion; the rate of such deterioration in resource availability can be moderated as society chooses to consume less of these natural resources.

WASTE AND WISE USE

All of the foregoing sources of economic scarcity operate even under conditions of wise resource use. But the extent of these inescapable scarcity forces is greatly aggravated by "waste." In Conservation literature, waste is given much attention as a source of economic scarcity of natural resources. This is not to say that waste is held to be more important than "limits" under conditions of "ecological interdependence" as an origin of scarcity. Waste is emphasized, rather, because limits have a nonactive, constraining character, whereas waste is an active element in the generation of scarcity. Waste has some similarities to the population and consumption pressures of large modern societies in causing "ecological damage" and "destroy-

---

soon as possible. . . . These writers often assume that an ecological balance actually existed when the population had only several million inhabitants. But why should nature have reached a balance at that time? Darwin suggests there never has been a balance since life began." Lyle Craine, discussing the lack of a single balance, in personal correspondence, said: "As I understand it, biologic communities can usually be found to behave according to some successional pattern. I think the ecologist merely says that the resource manager's job is to determine at what stage of succession man can receive his most desired products and services, and the ecologist can tell him how to encourage nature to hold her production at that point of 'succession' with a minimum of man's efforts. . . . For example, the study of silviculture is in itself the application of ecology to the growing of trees with the consequence that man is able to improve on nature. I have argued that our present concept of applying technology to river management is of the same variety. In short, we are searching for ways to improve the total services that can be rendered from the natural unit of the river."

ing mineral resources." Like these scarcity forces, waste depends upon man's decisions and activities. But unlike them, waste could be easily avoided by "wise use." Waste is man's foolishness in aggravating an already existing and ineluctable situation of natural resource scarcity. Waste is physical inefficiency in the use of resources. It results from ignorance or apathy of man in his individual and group behavior; from improper criteria built into the system of private property, consumer sovereignty, competition, and laissez faire; from inefficient government activity and inadequate government intervention in the economic sphere; and other causes.[8]

That "waste" or "unwise use" or "inefficient use" is a physical, not an economic or social, concept is demonstrated in the four types of waste or unwise use we have distilled from the Conservation literature. The first type results from not using resources in the proper order of priority; the second and third, from exploiting resources improperly; and the fourth, from unwise use of extractive or final products made from natural resources.

Destructive Use.   The first type of waste is the destructive use of a particular natural resource where it would be possible to obtain approximately the same kind of product or service in a less destructive way. For example, if arid grazing land is turned to crop production, with subsequent erosion, this is waste. It is wasteful to pollute streams. If hydropower dams are permitted to silt, with eventual reduction or total loss of their output, this is waste. If coal, oil, or gas, irreplaceable in nature, are used to generate electric power while undeveloped water power sites remain unexploited, this is waste. In this case, the mineral fuel once burned is forever lost; the hydropower, sensibly handled, would provide power practically in perpetuity. The use of oil or gas under boilers in place of coal is wasteful, since coal reserves are many times larger than those of oil and gas.

The list of examples can be greatly multiplied, by means of the following simple rules we have concocted of what Conservationists meant by "waste avoidance," "wise use," or "efficiency": (1) The regen-

---

[8] John Ise has observed that waste as defined in Conservation literature is often the result of competition, and that monopoly has done better. See the concluding chapter of his *The United States Oil Policy* (New Haven: Yale University Press, 1926). Also see his article, "The Theory of Value as Applied to Natural Resources," *American Economic Review,* Vol. 15 (June 1925).

erative capacity or potential of renewable resources (such as forests, grazing land, cropland, water) should not be physically damaged or destroyed. (2) Renewable resources should be used in place of minerals, insofar as physically possible. (3) Plentiful mineral resources should be used before less plentiful ones, insofar as physically possible.

These are not the rules of an economy guided by individual consumer sovereignty, either private or socialist. Such economies are, in principle, guided by cost minimization in the productive sectors and individual utility maximization and freedom of choice in the consumer sector. In Conservation doctrine, such societies are wasteful and generate unnecessary natural resource scarcity.

Underuse of Renewable Resources. The second type of waste is failure to procure the maximum of sustained physical yield of useful extractive products from nature's renewable resources. Whereas the first type of waste includes overexploitation of renewable resources to the point where their capacities are reduced, this type results from underexploitation. Crops, fish, livestock, timber, and hydropower should be produced to the limits of sustained physical yield from the respective resources. In two ways, it is wasteful to partake less than fully of nature's potential renewable bounty. If nature's perennial yield is not used, this is waste in an elemental sense, like leaving fruit to rot on the tree or vine. Further, if the renewable resources are not employed to produce the maximum of their sustained yield potential, then nonrenewable resources will tend to be drawn upon for man's voracious appetite. Mineral fuel resources will be tapped instead of hydropower, fuel wood, and solar energy; mineral resources for synthetic fibers, and plastics instead of natural fibers, hides, and rubber; iron ore reserves instead of timber. Thus failure to maximize sustained physical yield of useful extractive product generates natural resource scarcity too.

Mismanagement of Nonrenewable Resources. Wasteful management of nonrenewable resources results from failure to obtain the maximum yield of extractive product from the physical resources which are destroyed. Conservationists expressed doubt that the mineral resources in the earth should be tapped so rapidly. But, if a resource —say, an oil pool—is tapped and drawn upon without withdrawing ultimately the greatest possible volume of petroleum from the pool, then it is wasteful, and generates scarcity. It is wasteful to permit underground fires in coal mines; to use methods of coal and gas production that do not maximize the ratio of ultimately recoverable yield to underground deposit; to permit mines to flood while useful ore remains there. Again, this is a simple and straightforward notion. To conduct oil production in such ways as to make only 20 per cent of the pool recoverable, or coal mining so as to leave 50 per cent of the deposit underground and unrecoverable—this is mismanagement, waste, and it generates scarcity.

Wrong Use of Extractive and Final Products.   The wrong use of products yielded by natural resources contributes no less to scarcity than the unwise use of the resources themselves. Unless the maximum level of service is derived from extractive products, there is, indirectly, waste of the original natural resources. Gas, if withdrawn and not recycled back to the pool, should be used, not flared. Mineral fuels, if withdrawn from nature, should furnish useful heat; to burn them in furnaces of low thermal efficiency is wasteful. Metals were mined and timber cut to provide useful services; since they are physically recoverable as secondary materials and scrap, they must be so recovered and reused or there is waste. Common-sense analogies are not leaving food on the plate for the garbage can, or failing to make hash from leftovers. This is further extension to the utilization sphere of the principle of maximizing physical yield and minimizing physical destruction of natural resources.

Social and Economic Effects of Resource Scarcity

What, according to the doctrine of the Conservation Movement, are the consequences of natural resource scarcity? Given that availability of natural resources is limited; that nature is a system of ecological interdependence; that modern society is damaging to desirable ecological levels; that mineral resources are depleted; and that wasteful behavior aggravates scarcity—what are the social and economic implications?

SOCIAL EFFECTS

We begin by briefly identifying, according to Conservation literature of the period, some of the larger social implications: As the result of scarcity, major portions of the population are unnecessarily separated from livelihood on the land and close association with nature—with resulting evil social consequences. There is a reduction in the relative numbers of the most valuable citizen group, the independent farmer, and a weakening of agrarianism as the core of national life. There is damage to the ethical system. Values are perverted by crass materialism and urban pleasures. There is increased industrialism and urbanism, an undesirable development and a poor trade for the former agricultural society. The beauty and wonder of nature are increasingly lost to Americans now and also to their descendants. There is psychic damage—to the individual, the family, the community, and the nation.

Another quotation from Gifford Pinchot's *The Fight for Conservation* illustrates this view:

> The man on the farm is valuable to the Nation, like any other citizen, just in proportion to his intelligence, character, ability, and patriotism; but, unlike other citizens, also in proportion to his attachment to the soil. That is the principal spring of his steadiness, his sanity, his simplicity and directness, and many of his other desirable qualities. He is the first of home makers. . . . The nation that will lead the world will be a Nation of Homes. (Pp. 22–23.)

Other leaders of the Conservation Movement expressed similar views, as indicated by the following excerpts from Samuel Hays' *Conservation and the Gospel of Efficiency:*

> This new interest in conservation, which dominated the movement between 1908 and 1910, came primarily from middle- and upper-income urban dwellers. . . . Groups such as these viewed with alarm the way in which industrialism in a short space of 50 years, had altered American society; they looked upon conservation as an antidote to changes they resisted. The organization of industry into combinations and labor into unions, they feared, threatened the traditional, independent, self-made man. Sprawl-

ing urban monstrosities were replacing sobriety, honesty, and hard work with disease, immorality, and squalor. Political decisions no longer came as a result of reasonable action by intelligent men, but involved a crude power struggle dominated by privileged wealth and effective city machines. Religious values and personal morality were giving way to secular life and group action. Everywhere one saw ugly urban centers, the conspicuous consumption of huge fortunes, and a headlong worship of the almighty dollar. Traditional American virtues, so these discontented argued, were on the point of extinction. (Pp. 142–43.)[9]

ECONOMIC EFFECTS

In Conservation literature, the economic effects of scarcity may be differentiated in two groups: (1) those involving economic structure

[9] Hays continues his characterization of the views of the Conservation Movement with the help of direct quotations from literature of the period (*op. cit.,* pp. 143–45 *passim*):

> Conservation . . . was oriented toward the countryside, toward nature and the eternal values in nature, rather than toward the more artificial, materialistic, and socially unstable cities. Industrialization and urbanization . . . has spawned a "grovelling lust for material and commercial aggrandizement." [Mrs. Matthew T. Scott in *Proceedings, National Conservation Congress, 1910,* 272.] Urban dwellers had to turn elsewhere for the "regeneration of the spirit of man," and this they found in the wonders and beauties of nature which alone could "sustain life and make life worth sustaining." [Henry A. Baker in *Proceedings, National Conservation Congress, 1909,* 103.] An interest in rural life . . . also helped to draw many urban enthusiasts into the conservation crusade . . . "Man's inherent and ineradicable love for the soil is one of the strongest traits of human nature. . . . This is our natural taste, while the fascinations of town life are artificial. They do not satisfy our deeper feelings." [Thomas F. Walsh, "Humanitarian Aspect of National Irrigation," *Forestry and Irrigation* (Dec. 1902), 8, 505–509.] Fearing that mushrooming cities also threatened the United States with social disorder, many hoped to promote rural life as a stabilizing factor in society . . . "Stability of national character comes from firmness of foothold in the soil." [David Starr Jordan in *Maxwell's Talisman* (Sept. 1905), 5, 3.] . . . "We feel that it is for us, who are not wholly absorbed in business, to preserve ideals that are higher than business. . . ." [Scott, *Proceedings, 1910,* 270–277.] . . . In greater contact with nature one could renew his spiritual life . . . In a more general manner, many felt that the conservation movement aroused Americans from their materialistic lethargy to fight for higher ideals . . . "The moral tonic which the conservation movement has given to the entire country has perhaps been more effective for the general good of the American people than any one thing in our generation." [Alfred L. Baker to Pinchot, Dec. 27, 1910 (GP #1818).]

and organization of the nation; and (2) those involving productivity, cost, and price. Since the economic structural and organizational effects of scarcity are only one step removed from the social consequences above, they will be identified first.

Economic Structure.   The Conservationists believed that—except as remedial steps were taken by government and by improved behavior of the citizenry—monopoly would result from natural resource scarcity coupled with the high efficiency of the trust as a form of industrial organization. In turn, this would bring large unearned increments to monopolists, and maldistribution of income among the populace so severe as to be inconsistent with a democratic society. Powerful private interests would gradually gather natural resources and other wealth into relatively few hands, thus further strengthening their ability to create monopolies. Monopoly controls and pressures would be exerted—to force the sale of small landholdings, to increase and perpetuate the monopoly in other ways, to exploit consumers, to influence governmental activities in improper degree and even dominate political life.

From scarcity and monopoly control there would thus increasingly develop larger and larger profits—unearned increment—as the land and urban monopolies exerted their powers. The monopolistic tentacles would creep outward, to entrap and stifle all sectors of the economy. The eventual outcome would be severe maldistribution of land and property ownership, and of income.[10]

[10] In his Ph.D. dissertation ("The First American Conservation Movement, 1890–1920," Harvard University Library, August 1952), Hays characterizes Conservationist views on these matters as follows: "Monopolies and a permanent wage-earning class were threatening the American independent, self-made man. (P. 239.)

"Although industrialism was the cause of these new conditions, the trust and corporate wealth symbolized all that was evil in industrialism. The trust was not only the most effective type of industrial organization, but, because of its economic power, it could exert a strong influence in business, politics, and all aspects of American life. Due to their injustice toward the working classes, trusts were considered the primary cause of class consciousness, and the main contributing factor in impending socialism. Therefore, the main objective of progressives and crusaders in the conservation movement was effective trust control.

"The Roosevelt resource administrators interpreted the 'Trust' problem largely in terms of how corporations had interfered with their work. Business organizations which approved administration policies and which cooperated in them were 'good' trusts, but those which opposed them were 'bad.' 'Bad' trusts

Cost and Productivity.   Conservation literature viewed scarcity as a powerful force working to reduce labor productivity and to increase the real cost of all products. The growing economy would increasingly press upon already scarce resources. Destructive use of minerals would make them more scarce. Encroachment of cities and highways would further reduce available resources. And waste would be the final turn of the screw to grind the American society to poverty and misery. Output per worker would decline steadily. The real cost of commodities would rise steadily. Real income per capita would fall to subsistence levels.

Intellectual Antecedents of the Conservationists' Scarcity Doctrine

The Conservation Movement certainly was politically novel, ingenious, and effective. The Movement's sense of impending scarcity derived directly from a concern for the future of America's forests, dating back at least to the 1870's.[11] But antecedent to this, and exert-

---

were the speculators, private irrigation companies, livestock companies which cut down fences on the public domain, and others which interfered with the administration's attempt to rationalize the use and development of resources. Private corporations or individuals who were able to prevent the fullest development of a river by controlling some strategic site were 'bad' trusts. At the same time, the administration believed that any monopoly which, because of its control of production, the market, or patents, was able to prevent the most efficient and cheapest production and sale of goods was also a 'bad' trust." (Pp. 240–41.)

For examples of first-hand comments, see Gifford Pinchot, *Breaking New Ground* (New York: Harcourt, 1947); and the *Proceedings* of The White House Conference of Governors and the National Conservation Congress cited earlier; and Roy M. Robbins, *Our Landed Heritage* (Princeton: Princeton University Press, 1942).

[11] We are indebted to John Ise and Lawrence Hamilton for calling this to our attention. Ise notes that Carl Schurz, Secretary of the Interior under Hayes, was one of the first to be concerned, and that Cleveland, together with some of his Cabinet officers, and Benjamin Harrison were also interested. Hamilton, in personal correspondence, remarked: "Aside from the early local concern for 'place-convenience' scarcity, or for special species that were important for national security such as naval timbers, the first important 'timber famine' forecast was that of Secretary of Interior Carl Schurz in his annual report of 1877—forecasting only 20 years' supply. This was supported in the 1880 census and then picked up as the Movement took definite shape, and to my way of thinking was the jumping off point for the scarcity concept which involved not only timber but the other natural resources. This early scare of course was based on an inaccurate and incomplete inventory of the resource and as usual, the inability to forecast with any accuracy the technological changes which would take place."

ing a direct or indirect influence on the development of Conservation doctrine, were two streams of thought. One was the contribution of the classical economists—Malthus, Ricardo, and Mill—which we considered in Chapter 3. The other was the growing body of natural resource literature. Here we indicate only briefly the contribution of Charles Darwin, and more extensively that of George Perkins Marsh.

DARWIN

The direct contributions of Darwin to economic doctrine on scarcity and scarcity effect were slight. The indirect contribution, however, was perhaps of major importance. Darwin's own inquiry and results were, he says, influenced by Malthus' *Essay on Population*. Malthus had stated that his principle of a geometric rate of breeding if food supply permits is (with appropriate refinement) applicable to any form of animal or vegetable life. There is thus a tendency within each life form completely to populate the earth. The Malthusian principle thus provides a beginning question for Darwin's analysis of why there is a large number of species. And it provides an abstract theory useful for incorporation in Darwin's answer. Scarcity of food supply induces a struggle for existence, with each species fitting into a niche of the natural environment in which (up to the limits set by the availability of food supplies suited to its particular life technology) it is able to survive. Random mutations, some of which favorably affect biological adaptation to food availabilities, then lead to changes in the types and numbers of surviving species.[12]

[12] Darwin described the influence of Malthus upon his views as follows: "I soon perceived that selection was the keystone of man's success in making useful races of animals and plants. But how selection could be applied to organisms living in a state of nature remained for some time a mystery to me. . . . In October, 1838, that is, fifteen months after I had begun my systematic inquiry, I happened to read for amusement 'Malthus on Population,' and being well prepared to appreciate the struggle for existence which everywhere goes on from long-continued observations of the habits of animals and plants, it at once struck me that under these circumstances favourable variations would tend to be preserved, and unfavourable ones to be destroyed. The result of this would be the formation of new species. Here, then, I had at last got a theory by which to work." From Darwin's *Life,* i. 83, as quoted in G. T. Bettany's Introduction to Malthus' *Essay on Population* (reprint of 6th ed.; London: Ward, Lock, and Company, 1826), p. xxxvi.

In Bettany's opinion, Darwin implicitly elaborated Malthusian doctrine by showing ". . . that the redundant populations are the less fit or the unfit." Bettany writes further: ". . . there is no proved fact which at all touches Malthus's argument for thrift and prudence among the working-classes. Here

The indirect contribution of Darwin to scarcity doctrine by way of influence upon American public opinion and the Conservation Movement was twofold. Darwin, with a social impact perhaps even larger than Malthus' original impact, generalized as a law of nature the concept of the "struggle for food." And, although Malthus, no less than Darwin, claimed to be stating natural law, there was the added force of Darwin's greater prominence, and the facts that his contribution emanated from a practicing scientist and many of the leaders of the Conservation Movement were natural scientists themselves. Second, and more important perhaps, the Darwinian contribution played a central role in the development and propagation of the popularized version of naturalistic philosophy that was so strong in the Conservation philosophy.

MARSH

George Perkins Marsh made his important contribution to the doctrine of scarcity and scarcity effect in a 500-page book, *Man and Nature,* published in 1865.[13] A remarkably talented individual, Marsh was the author of major contributions in English language and literature, a pre-eminent authority on the Icelandic language, as well as an accomplished speaker of most modern European languages. He was an organizer of the Smithsonian Institution; a founder of modern geography; a legislator; and a successful U.S. foreign service officer, spending the last twenty years of his life as U.S. minister to Italy.[14]

Marsh's *Man and Nature* was a pioneering, rather detailed, scien-

---

at least, he stands upon a platform which is really supported by Darwinism, for it is unquestionable that the species can be best maintained and improved by those who become parents producing them at the most mature period of life and under the healthiest conditions as to food, dwelling, etc. Those who do not marry till they can afford it will have the strongest offspring of the best quality, and these will survive in largest numbers; while the weaker, in spite of their reckless early marriages, unthrifty habits, and unwholesome dwellings are inevitably thinned out in the struggle for existence, though they may constantly be getting recruited from the weaker or less provident members of the stronger classes. Whatever may be the value of other remedies for misery and over-population than that of Malthus, Nature is on the side of Malthus, giving evident and great advantages to those who in essential features follow his plan and exercise moral self-restraint." (Pp. xxxii–xxxiii.)

[13] Marsh, *Man and Nature; or Physical Geography as Modified by Human Action* (New York: Charles Scribner, 1865).

[14] *Encyclopedia Britannica,* 11th ed., biography of Marsh.

tific inquiry into physical aspects of the interaction between society and its physical environment. Since he and his important contribution to our subject are little known among contemporary economists and political scientists, Marsh's book is discussed here at some length. The Preface, quoted below in its entirety, epitomizes his views:

The object of the present volume is: to indicate the character and, approximately, the extent of the changes produced by human action in the physical conditions of the globe we inhabit; to point out the dangers of imprudence and the necessity of caution in all operations which, on a large scale, interfere with the spontaneous arrangements of the organic or the inorganic world; to suggest the possibility and the importance of the restoration of disturbed harmonies and the material improvement of waste and exhausted regions; and, incidentally, to illustrate the doctrine, that man is, in both kind and degree, a power of a higher order than any of the other forms of animated life, which, like him, are nourished at the table of bounteous nature.

In the rudest stages of life, man depends upon spontaneous animal and vegetable growth for food and clothing, and his consumption of such products consequently diminishes the numerical abundance of the species which serve his uses. At more advanced periods, he protects and propagates certain esculent vegetables and certain fowls and quadrupeds, and, at the same time, wars upon rival organisms which prey upon these objects of his care or obstruct the increase of their numbers. Hence, the action of man upon the organic world tends to subvert the original balance of its species, and while it reduces the numbers of some of them, or even extirpates them altogether, it multiplies other forms of animal and vegetable life.

The extension of agricultural and pastoral industry involves an enlargement of the sphere of man's domain, by encroachment upon the forests which once covered the greater part of the earth's surface otherwise adapted to his occupation. The felling of the woods has been attended with momentous consequences to the drainage of the soil, to the external configuration of its surface, and probably, also, to local climate; and the importance of human life as a transforming power is, perhaps, more clearly demonstrable in the influence man has thus exerted upon superficial geography than in any other result of his material effort.

Lands won from the woods must be both drained and irrigated; river banks and maritime coasts must be secured by means of artificial bulwarks against inundation by inland and by ocean floods; and the needs of commerce require the improvement of natural, and the construction of artificial channels of navigation. Thus man is compelled to extend over the unstable waters the empire he had already founded upon the solid land.

The upheaval of the bed of seas and the movements of water and of wind expose vast deposits of sand, which occupy space required for the convenience of man, and often, by the drifting of their particles, overwhelm the fields of human industry with invasions as disastrous as the incursions of the ocean. On the other hand, on many coasts, sand hills both protect the shores from erosion by the waves and currents, and shelter valuable grounds from blasting sea winds. Man, therefore, must sometimes resist, sometimes promote, the formation and growth of dunes, and subject the barren and flying sands to the same obedience to his will to which he has reduced other forms of terrestrial surface.

Besides these old and comparatively familiar methods of material improvement, modern ambition aspires to yet grander achievements in the conquest of physical nature, and projects are meditated which quite eclipse the boldest enterprises hitherto undertaken for the modification of geographical surface.

The natural character of the various fields where human industry has effected revolutions so important, and where the multiplying population and the impoverished resources of the globe demand new triumphs of mind over matter, suggests a corresponding division of the general subject, and I have conformed the distribution of the several topics to the chronological succession in which man must be supposed to have extended his sway over the different provinces of his material kingdom. I have, then, in the Introductory chapter, stated, in a comprehensive way, the general effects and the prospective consequences of human action upon the earth's surface and the life which peoples it. This chapter is followed by four others in which I have traced the history of man's industry as exerted upon Animal and Vegetable Life, upon the Woods, upon the Waters, and upon the Sands; and to these I have added a concluding chapter upon Probable and Possible Geographical Revolutions yet to be effected by the art of man.

I have only to add what, indeed, sufficiently appears upon every page of the volume, that I address myself not to professed physicists, but to the general intelligence of educated, observing, and thinking men; and that my purpose is rather to make practical suggestions than to indulge in theoretical speculations properly suited to a different class from that to which those for whom I write belong.

The contributions to the doctrine of scarcity and scarcity effect made by Marsh were several and major. First, Marsh greatly elaborated the conception of the "nature" or "natural resources" variable, relative to the view held by the classical economists. Nature and natural resources were enormously complex and diverse. The properties of natural resources were almost infinite in configuration and variety. Moreover, the natural resources universe was highly dynamic, undergoing change from geological and meteorological forces constantly. In Marsh's view, to consider natural resources as the classical economists did, we infer, was an abominable simplification and abstraction. The essence of natural resources is heterogeneity, complexity, dynamic interaction of components, change. One might as well, we gather from Marsh, describe man as a quantum of weight or a linear dimension and not mention that he is a living organism, or characterize a Rembrandt painting as a mineral-vegetable deposit, or reduce nature to the classical economic quantum "land." In so rich a conception of nature, in the kaleidoscopic panorama of natural resources, the classical economic notion of natural resource scarcity, according to Marsh, is largely devoid of meaning.

A second contribution of Marsh was to enlarge the picture or model of nature, so that it became man and nature. Man changes the natural complex and nature's changes, in turn, exert their major influence on man. The interaction is continuous.

Finally, Marsh implicitly upset the classical economic view of a simple connection between nature's agricultural bounty and man's requirements for subsistence, thereby upsetting the Malthusian and Ricardian doctrines of scarcity. In a sense, Marsh rejected the idea that economic analysis could be isolated from the nature-man continuum. A restricted conception of economic processes was either repugnant or unimportant to him. References to economists or their works are completely absent from his extensive bibliography and from his index. Yet, in many respects, the implications of his work are directed against classical economic doctrine and are damaging to it. As conceived by Marsh, modern man's dependence upon natural resources in a world such as he describes is not that of a simple flow of food from agricultural land, but is much more complex. Man depends upon nature and upon individual components of nature for many products, facilities, and services—material and intangible.

These three contributions by Marsh opened quite new dimensions in a conception of scarcity and scarcity effect.[15] The elements in his dynamic model include man, earth, sea, and sky; man, forests, fertility, river flows, and shore lines; man, climate, and the myriad forms of animal and vegetable life; and so on. Seeding and foreshadowing subsequent Conservation Movement ideas, Marsh states:

> Man has too long forgotten that the earth was given to him for usufruct alone, not for consumption, still less for profligate waste. Nature has provided against the absolute destruction of any of her elementary matter, the raw material of her works; the thunderbolt and the tornado, the most convulsive throes of even the volcano and the earthquake, being only phenomena of decomposition and recomposition. But she has left it within the power of man irreparably to derange the combinations of inorganic matter and of organic life. . . .

> Apart from the hostile influence of man, the organic and the inorganic world are, as I have remarked, bound together by such mutual relations and adaptations as secure, if not the absolute permanence and equilibrium of both, a long continuance of the established conditions of each at any given time and place, or at least, a very slow and gradual succession of changes in those conditions. But man is everywhere a disturbing agent. . . . These intentional changes and substitutions constitute, indeed, great revolutions; but vast as is their magnitude and importance, they are, as we shall see, insignificant in comparison with the contingent and unsought results which have flowed from them.

> The fact that, of all organic beings, man alone is to be regarded as essentially a destructive power, and that he wields energies to

[15] Marsh's description of the physical decay of the Roman Empire and other parts of the old world is especially interesting reading. Although he recognizes the many and complex causes of that early decay, he points out the ways in which, he believes, man was the major destructive influence. (Pp. 3–14.)

resist which, nature—that nature whom all material life and all inorganic substance obey—is wholly impotent, tends to prove that, though living in physical nature, he is not of her, that he is of more exalted parentage, and belongs to a higher order of existences than those born of her womb and submissive to her dictates. (Pp. 35–36.)

There are, in Marsh's view, such extensive possibilities of modification of the balance of man and nature—favorable and unfavorable—that the scarcity doctrines of Malthus and Ricardo presumably could not for him be natural laws. Since scarcity is no longer an ineluctable force, its effects are no longer inescapable. Before Marsh, and in the eyes of the classical economists, there was no question that scarcity was always operative. The conclusion was built into the premises—premises that were equated to natural law. After Marsh, if his lessons are believed, the question became empirical since man and his environment are so susceptible to change.

SYNTHESIS

A comparison of the basic ideas of the Conservation Movement with the major antecedent ideas provides a useful synthesis of Conservation doctrine. On the basis of such a comparison, one is tempted to conclude that the Conservation Movement adopted parts of the classical economic view of scarcity, and grafted onto it the ecological conceptions of Marsh and the revolutionary advances in their contemporary natural sciences. But a sociopolitical movement does not systematically acknowledge its intellectual debts, and we have not undertaken to determine the origins of Conservationist thought. We, therefore, confine ourselves to noting certain suggestive parallels and differences between Conservation doctrine and the antecedent ideas of Malthus, Ricardo, Mill, and Marsh.

The Conservationists reflected America's coming of age and its emergent nationalism after the Civil War and westward expansion. Thus, the relevant natural resource universe for them was not the whole world of the classical economists, but the boundaries of the nation. These were the national equivalents of the Malthusian ultimate limits of the earth; the horizon extended no further. The 1890 census had just announced that America's frontier had disappeared. Given the nationalistic interest, then, the national limits were very important to the Conservationists.

The Malthusian view of population growth did not attract attention. But this is not necessarily because it was found in error. Rather, it was because the Conservationists found, as did Mill and Ricardo, scarcity problems in the resource variables and in a nearer term than when population would press upon ultimate limits. It is also possible that the population dilemma had to be shunted aside as a matter of political expediency. A major emphasis on the Malthusian population growth tendency would have diluted somewhat the effectiveness of the attack on natural resource "waste." As indicated in Chapter 3, acceptance of unending population growth (at the rates prevailing in 1900) would defeat interest in resource management. For if the world or nation will eventually, and not too distantly, run out of standing room—and out of food long before then—it is difficult to become greatly concerned with fuel waste or running out of coal in several hundreds or thousands of years. In strictly logical Conservation theory and analysis, the question of unending population growth would have to be faced; but not in the reality of popular political and social movements. That strand of Conservation doctrine which opposed unrestricted immigration, for example, was far more a reflection of a distaste for diluting native stock with city-oriented foreigners, a reflection of agrarian philosophy, than a concern over Malthusian population pressure upon food supply.

With an advantage over Ricardo of nearly a century of hindsight concerning the effects of revolutionary advances in agriculture and other technology and their focus on physical efficiency, the Conservationists knew far more than he about differential land fertility and its variability. Ricardo's conception of the effects of naturally differential economic qualities of land could not seem wholly realistic to practitioners who wanted (and knew how) to multiply physical yields manyfold and to turn deserts green. Ricardo's analytical scheme, which virtually ignored resource depletion, was an interesting abstraction, but could hardly be a starting point for a Conservation Movement which saw forests disappearing, farms denuded of vegetation and top soil, water polluted, and power sites appropriated by "immoral" monopolies from their rightful owners, "the people." Further, the Ricardian concept of "land" as a factor of production was a far cry from the Conservationists' conception of "nature." The

Ricardian scarcity concept of use of agricultural land in order of differential quality was, in Conservation doctrine, a challenge physically to upgrade the less fertile acres.

On the other hand, there was the Ricardian scarcity *effect*—the tendency toward decline in productivity, and toward ever-increasing costs and prices; and there was the ethical question of unearned increments to private owners of land implicit in the analyses of Ricardo and Mill. These ideas appear in the literature of the Conservation Movement, and were made much of. However, the Conservationists' views of scarcity effect probably derived more directly from the popular writings of the American political reformer Henry George than from the abstract, long-antecedent economic analyses of Ricardo or Mill.

Marsh's ideas of ecological balance, and of scarcity effect from upsetting the balance, reappeared without essential change in Conservationist writings, and were one of the pillars of the Movement's doctrine. His intellectual and historical observations concerning man's predatory raids on the resource environment, and his inquiry into man as a disturber of natural ecological equilibrium, were converted into the Conservation Movement's belief that these were the nation's urgent and pressing dangers—a crucial threat to American social stability.

Interpreting the Economic Doctrine of the Conservation Movement

Our purpose in probing into the Conservation Movement was to improve understanding of this important source of the doctrine of natural resource scarcity, both because the movement was an important development in the nation's history and because much contemporary thinking derives from it. The quest, we think, has been at least partly successful. We have dug out premises, ascertained the structure of the analysis, and detailed the Conservation theses in various ways. We have learned the important fact that quantitative economic analysis of actual economic experience in the nineteenth century did not in any rigorous way enter the Conservationists' analysis of economic resource scarcity and its economic effect.

But a word of warning is appropriate. For a variety of reasons, it is extremely difficult to ascertain and interpret the economic doctrine of scarcity of the Conservation Movement. There is no evidence in the writings of the leading figures of the Movement that they had any substantial training in economic analysis. Thus, there was little or no recourse to precise economic formulation and statement, so that the meanings of terms and the modes of their use are sometimes unclear to economic reviewers of the literature. The difficulty is aggravated by the fact that Conservation writings, being instruments of a political and social reform movement, were several stages removed from scholarly standards, economic or other. At a distance of fifty years, it is not easy to separate the core of these writings from slogans, exhortation, half-truths, and catch phrases. The politically opportunistic character of the Movement increases both the need for sifting and the difficulty of successfully doing so.

Despite the difficulties and uncertainties, we believe that the essential elements in Conservation doctrine which had to do with natural resource scarcity have been accurately characterized here. The Conservation Movement, as it related to natural resources, was enormously successful in its own time. It not only played a major role in several presidential elections, but may have determined the outcome in 1912. Also, its influence reaches down to the present; as in President Taft's time, so today, "A great many people are in favor of conservation, no matter what it means." [16] To the extent that we have been successful, then, the discussion clarifies Conservation beliefs which most of us hold, to some degree, as received doctrine; and it poses some of the fundamental issues to be subjected to analysis in the remainder of this book.

The Conservationists were seriously concerned with ethical revisions of laissez faire and economic atomism—with values involving a holistic conception of man and nature, obligation to future generations, so-called scientific management based on physical values and rejection of the individualistic values of the classicists. They were not concerned with the professional economists' maximizing of the present value of the stream of real income over time, based on consumer sovereignty—which professional economists frequently term "conservation economics." We doubt that economists should so use the

---

[16] *Outlook*, May 14, 1910, p. 57, quoted by John Ise, *The U.S. Forest Policy* (New Haven: Yale University Press, 1920), p. 373.

"conservation" adjective. The term was concocted by a major reform movement for the aggregate of its social objectives and devices. It is misleading, confusing, and inimical to interdisciplinary communication to imply that maximization for present consumers of the present value of the stream of real income over time is significantly related to "Conservation." Both the premises and the interests of the Conservationists were different from those of such current writers on conservation economics as were mentioned in the section on contemporary economic views in Chapter 2.[17]

To an important degree, the leaders of the Conservation Movement—and their followers, too—are themselves responsible for being misinterpreted. This is because the attention they gave to the economic dimensions of such problems as depletion of nonrenewable resources, sustained yield of renewable resources and waste, was without comprehension, or even recognition, of the relevance of economic principles or facts. The Conservationists thus not only laid themselves open to wholly legitimate criticism for dealing fuzzily with concepts requiring rigorous application of an economic benefit-cost calculus, but they made possible the inference that their ultimate objective with respect to the shape of welfare over time was economic efficiency rather than ethical revision based on physical efficiency. By taking it for granted, without careful inquiry, that use of natural resources by a current generation necessarily reduces the productive capabilities of future generations, they were mistakenly led to specify policies of "conservation" and "wise use" which were inappropriate, not only according to principles of economic rationality but also in terms of their own ethical aims, the implications of which they had not adequately examined.

These are important matters. A considerable part of the confusion and misunderstanding is caused, we believe, by a general lack of clarity concerning the meaning and relevance of natural resource scarcity in the modern world. Building on a systematic evaluation of classical doctrine in Part II, we consider its current import in Part III, and the implications of our analysis in Part IV.

[17] Samuel Hays, in *Conservation and the Gospel of Efficiency* (*op. cit.*), writes, "WJ McGee emerged as the prophet of the new world which conscious purpose, science, and human reason could create out of the chaos of a laissez-faire economy where short-run individual interest provided no thought for the morrow." (P. 124.)

PART II

GROWTH AND INCREASING SCARCITY WITHOUT PROGRESS

Chapter 5

BASIC SCARCITY MODELS

THE historical development of the doctrine that natural resource scarcity and economic growth are in fundamental opposition to each other has been briefly traced. Our survey of contemporary and historical beliefs showed that this doctrine embodies three propositions: (1) Natural resources are economically scarce, and become increasingly so with the passage of time. (2) The scarcity of resources opposes economic growth. And (3) ultimately economic growth is prevented by natural resource scarcity. We turn now to a systematic examination of this doctrine, the classical doctrine of diminishing returns to social scale.

Three basic models are set up in this chapter. The first represents the benchmark case, a "Utopian model" where no scarcity exists. In each of the others natural resources are scarce and economic growth is adversely affected, but for different reasons. That is, we affirmatively create rigorous models, each of which simulates, in an abstract way, one of the classic versions of the doctrine of diminishing returns. By so doing, we make explicit the premises necessary for the conclusion that economic growth will be slowed and brought to an eventual halt. This permits us to distinguish the differential effects upon growth of the two basic types of hypothesized resource scarcity. It also facilitates interpretation of the empirical test of the validity of the doctrine, which is undertaken in Part III.

To ground the analysis, we posit the existence of a social production function of the form

$$O = f(R,L,C)$$

where O stands for social output, R stands for indestructible natural resources (hereafter resources), L stands for labor, and C stands for capital. All variables are conceived to be represented by physical quantities.

We introduce initial assumptions customarily employed in so-called static production function analysis. Sociotechnical parameters—primarily social structure and the state of technology—are invariant. In particular, sociotechnical knowledge is constant. Product and each input are either qualitatively homogeneous or constant-proportion vectors. The organization of the production process changes as scale of output increases in such a way as to assure that the most economic method of production is employed for each scale.

Interest focuses on the long-term growth of output per unit of labor, as influenced by a specified natural resource environment. We therefore assume full employment of labor and capital as they increase at exogenously determined rates. Variation of the labor force would introduce irrelevant complications, so labor is assumed to be a constant proportion of population. As we have no interest in cyclical fluctuations, the assumed system adapts instantaneously to increases in labor and capital. It is thus a moving (static) equilibrium system. There is no present need to distinguish labor and capital inputs from each other. We therefore assume that the rates of growth of labor and capital are such as to maintain a constant ratio. This treats labor-capital as a single input, $L + C$.

The basic social production function thus becomes

$$(1) \qquad\qquad O = f_1\ (R, L + C)$$

The function is assumed to be of the frequently posited form in which the marginal and average products of each input increase to a maximum and then decline; it thus obeys the law of variable proportions. The function is also assumed to be homogeneous of the first degree, that is, to yield constant returns to scale. Labor-capital cost per unit of output thus remains constant as both inputs, R and $L + C$, are increased in the same proportion. We call this the *standard constant returns social production function*.

The Utopian Case of No Resource Scarcity

Resource scarcity can be most readily defined, and the effect of resource scarcity on economic growth most easily pinned down, by first setting up the no-scarcity case of abundant resources—the benchmark case in which resources have no effect on economic growth. In the no-scarcity case, society has free and costless access to an indefinitely large stock of currently unused natural resources. Because of costless access, no input of labor-capital is required to bring resources into use: no transportation facilities need be built, no preparatory land-clearing or earth-moving need be undertaken, and so on. Free access also means that there is no charge for the use of resources. The price and the real social cost (labor plus capital cost) of resources, therefore, are zero. Resources are drawn into use without hindrance as needed. There is no natural resource obstruction to economic growth.

Under these conditions, we define the optimal use of resources as that in which idle R has been brought into combination with fully employed $L + C$ up to the point where the marginal product of R is zero. Institutional arrangements are implicitly assumed to be consistent with optimal use as here defined. At this point, the social product will be a maximum for any given amount of $L + C$, and the average and marginal products of $L + C$ will be equal, the average product being maximal. (This implies that the labor-capital supply schedule is perfectly inelastic at each independently defined "full employment" level.) Total and average real cost, meaning labor-capital input per unit of output, will be minimal at the defined social optimum for any given full employment level of labor-capital. The "least-cost combination" for social output at full employment will have been attained.

We call the locus of maximum output (minimum cost) for historically successive amounts of $L + C$ at full employment the *optimal expansion path* for the given conditions. It is represented by OG in Figure 4, where the successive output contours are designated X_1, X_2, . . . Because of the assumption of constant returns to scale, the linear path OG yields constant labor-capital costs per unit as output expands. Resources do not inflict increasing costs on society as the price of growth in the Utopian case. A "law" of historically diminishing returns might exist in the presence of abundant resources, but it would have to be because of the character of the social production process—the consequence of particular institutional or technical conditions, not a consequence of the physical environment. That is, diminishing returns in the no-scarcity case would have to be a sociotechnical, not a "natural," law. Otherwise, under conditions of "abundance," resources do not obstruct economic growth.

Along the expansion path *OG*, the ratio of the marginal product of resources to that of labor-capital is constant as output grows. The

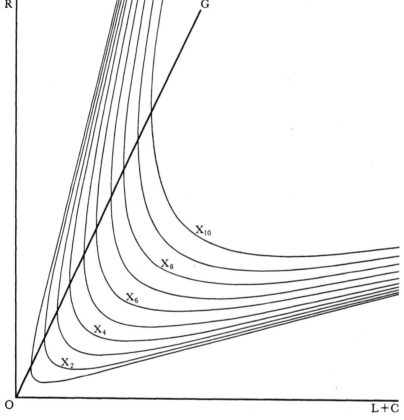

Figure 4. Utopian expansion path: no resource scarcity

assumption that the marginal product of R is institutionally zero at all levels of output is consistent with this condition. But any other assumption of constant marginal product of R would do as well. For example, resources might be available at zero real social cost, but their unchanging supply price—and therefore their equilibrium marginal product—might be greater than zero for institutional reasons. In this case, resource use would be restricted; and full employment of $L + C$ would be reached before its marginal product had reached the maximum that could be attained with greater use of resources. Though its slope would be less, the expansion path would still be linear. Resources would still not obstruct economic growth.

The Utopian no-scarcity case is useful as a frame of reference for the scarcity cases which follow. But it also brings out a point that is sometimes overlooked. *Scarcity of resources is not needed to explain why output is limited.* It is not needed to explain why growth proceeds in a deliberate rather than an explosive manner. With unused resources of constant quality still abundant, output levels and growth rates at any time would be limited by the availability of labor-capital and the given sociotechnical conditions. Great volumes of the world's water, land, and mineral deposits are unused. In the United States, more than 90 per cent of the Alaskan land area is idle. Requirements for resources are never indefinitely large because sociotechnical conditions and the law of variable proportions set a limit to the amount of resources that can usefully be employed with a given amount of labor-capital.[1]

Malthusian Scarcity: Fixed Resource Supply

We now assume a fixed resource availability, so full utilization of available resources becomes a prospect to be reckoned with. The amount of resources available is permanently fixed, as at b in Figure 5. Since fixed resource supply is reminiscent of Malthus, we call this the Malthusian scarcity case.

The optimal Malthusian expansion path is OEH. Resources are not scarce until labor-capital reaches a. The Malthusian path thus coincides with the Utopian path until a units of labor-capital are employed and all of the b units of available natural resources have been brought into use. The path then pursues a less favorable course, toward H. In accordance with the law of variable proportions, the

[1] A constant returns function in which all natural resources would be used, even if almost infinite (i.e., in which there could not be unused resources), no matter how small the $L + C$ input, is mathematically possible. The so-called Cobb-Douglas function is of this type. While such a function might be a reasonable approximation to what happens over a limited range, it is not applicable to the problems dealt with here.

economy runs into diminishing marginal and average productivity of labor-capital (increasing labor-capital cost per unit of output) as $L + C$ expands against fixed R. Output increases at a declining rate to a maximum where $L + C = c$ and then declines. Diminishing

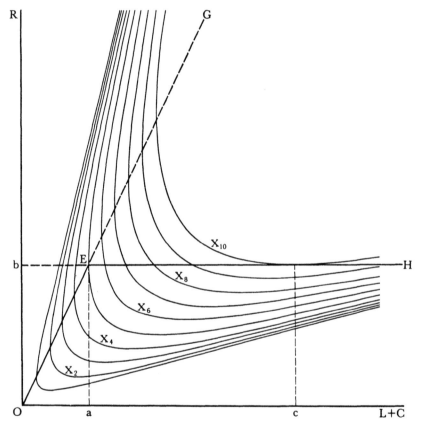

Figure 5. Malthusian expansion path: fixed resource availability

returns retard growth, and ultimately set an absolute limit to it, under the highly restrictive conditions of this type of scarcity.

   This first case of natural resource scarcity and effect, Malthusian scarcity, differs from the no-scarcity case in that total resource availability is fixed and determinate at a relatively small magnitude. Given this condition, and the assumed sociotechnical conditions, we find that:

1) Natural resource scarcity occurs only when—due to growth of labor and capital—a definable economic limit of availability is reached. as at b.

2) Diminishing returns from natural resource scarcity are identifiable as the decline, which occurs from E onward, in the marginal and average productivity of $L + C$, with R availability limited to b.

3) Impairment of economic welfare from natural resource scarcity is identifiable as the decline in output per capita that begins to occur at E.[2]

4) The assumption of the no-scarcity case, that the marginal product of resources is zero, holds only up to the point E. From E onward, the marginal product of resources increases steadily, social output being a maximum for the amounts of resources, labor, and capital available.

Ricardian Scarcity: Declining Economic Quality

The hypothesis that resources are readily available, but only under conditions of declining economic quality, was an essential element in Ricardo's contribution to the theory of economic growth. The model incorporating this hypothesis is therefore called the Ricardian scarcity case.

Incorporation of the Ricardian hypothesis into the analytical framework we have been employing requires a partial relaxation of the assumption that the quality of individual inputs does not change. The Ricardian case recognizes that, owing to the heterogeneous composition of the resource environment, qualitative changes in the physical composition of the resource input will occur more or less continually as the scale of social output expands. New resources, possessing physical and locational properties different from those of resources

---

[2] If we stipulate that economic growth continues so long as total output increases, there is a *cessation of economic growth* from natural resource scarcity after output reaches its maximum level at X_{10}. If $L + C$ continues to expand beyond c, total output will decline absolutely. But there may be a conventional or physical "subsistence" level per unit of $L + C$ equal to k units of output, where k is greater than X_{10} divided by $L + C$. (It seems more reasonable to suppose that subsistence is related to average than to marginal product.) If $L + C$ always increases to the limit of subsistence, the expansion of $L + C$ and the process of economic growth may both cease before maximum output is reached.

in use, are brought into the productive process as the scale of output increases. However, an additional premise is needed for Ricardian scarcity, since the unavoidable changes in the *physical and locational* properties of resources do not necessarily imply adverse trends in changes in *economic quality*—that is, increases in labor-capital cost per unit of output as output expands. Unless society can and does select resources from the untapped reserve in order of their economic quality, the obvious fact that resources differ in their natural properties would establish no presumption of diminishing returns. The presumption is provided by the Ricardian hypothesis that man, in pursuit of economic advantage, will employ economically superior resources before economically inferior ones.

The Ricardian case thus rests on assumptions that society possesses the knowledge required to use resources in order of declining economic quality, and that it is led by the application of a particular economic rationale to use them in this order. This pair of requirements implies: (1) that society possesses appropriate measures of the physical and locational properties of resources; (2) that society accurately translates these into a single index of economic quality related to the product mix and production function; (3) that society arrays resources in order of the index of declining economic quality; and (4) that social behavior patterns are such that resources are used in this order. This is a precise descriptive statement of the informational and behavioral assumptions that are implicit in the original Ricardian model (and in most current analyses) of the relation of resources to growth.

Intuitively we can see that natural resource scarcity, with a consequent inhibition of economic growth, must be present in this Ricardian case. But exposure of the complete characteristics and implications of Ricardian scarcity calls for a rigorously constructed model which explicitly incorporates the assumption that society can and does use resources in order of declining economic quality.

Let R represent resources with homogeneous physical and locational properties, measured in ordinary physical units (for example, acres, tons, barrels); these are "standard resources." Let R_u represent resources measured in the identical physical units, but with unhomogeneous (nonstandard) physical and locational properties. A definition of deterioration in the economic quality of unhomogeneous resources relative to standard resources may then be formulated this way: Resources (R_u) are of lower economic quality than resources (R) if, with no changes in any sociotechnical parameters (and for any criterion of optimality that may be selected), total output and the average and marginal productivities of labor-capital $(L + C)$ are lower for every optimal combination of $L + C$ with R_u in the social production function than for the corresponding optimal combinations of identical amounts of $L + C$ with R.

RESOURCE CONVERSION FUNCTION

We handle declining quality by conceiving of a *resource conversion function*. This shows the amounts of labor-capital and unhomogeneous resources which, taken together, will constitute an input combination that is the equivalent of a given quantity of standard resources, R. Thus, land of inferior fertility or moisture content can be rendered the equivalent of standard land by the use of fertilizer or the provision of irrigation or drainage facilities; from ores of lower mineral content, standard yields of ore concentrate can be obtained by heavier investment in machinery and greater energy input; economically remote resources can be rendered proximate by providing transportation; and so on.

To fix the notion of a resource conversion function, we formalize it as

$$(2) \qquad R = f_2(R_u, L_r + C_r)$$

Here R and R_u are both expressed in conventional physical units (for example, acres); $L_r + C_r$ is the variable amount of labor-capital that must be combined with unhomogeneous resources, R_u, to create an input combination that is the technological equivalent of any given amount of standard resources, R. And because, by hypothesis, unhomogeneous resources are employed in order of declining economic quality, f_2 has the property that $L_r + C_r$ increases faster than R.[3]

---

[3] Although he does not make the distinction we have conceived between conversion and operating costs, S. V. Ciriacy-Wantrup provides many concrete examples of costs entailed by the use of different qualities of resources. See *Resource Conservation–Economics and Policies* (Berkeley and Los Angeles: University of California Press, 1952), especially pp. 70 ff. Also compare Tibor Scitovsky, *Welfare and Competition: The Economics of a Fully Employed Economy* (Homewood, Ill.: Irwin, 1951), pp. 227–28: "As to the initial cost

The resource conversion function thus is a special kind of production function. It shows the combinations of labor-capital and unhomogeneous resources that will, in effect, create a given quantity of standard resources and, therefore, can substitute for that quantity of R in the standard production function.

RESOURCE CONVERSION PATH

A particular solution of the conversion function, which we call the resource conversion path, interests us. It is the solution which shows the minimal labor-capital cost of "creating" each amount of standard

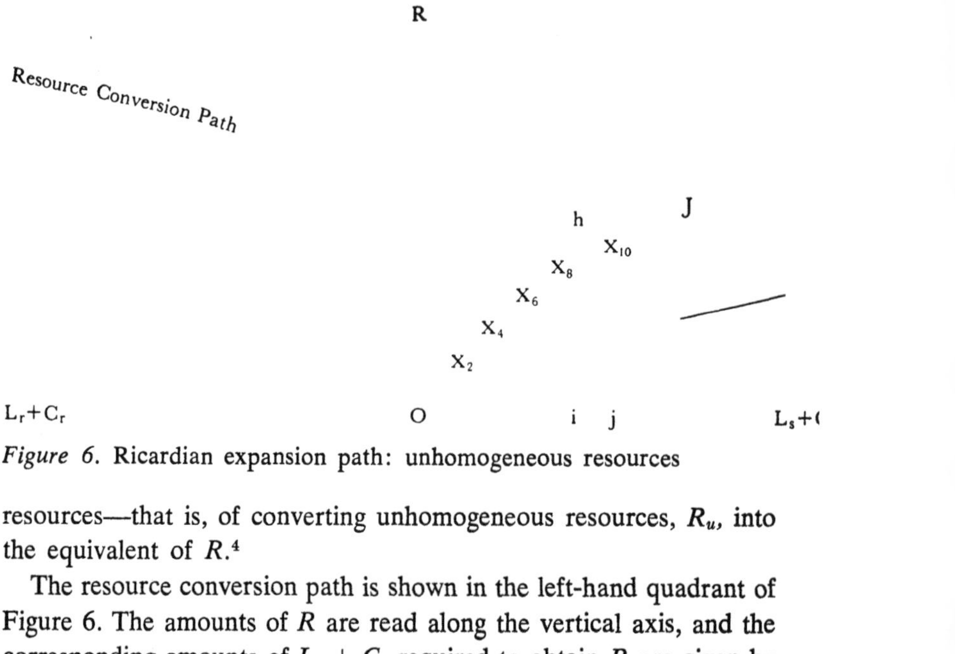

R

Resource Conversion Path

h   J

X_{10}

X_8

X_6

X_4

X_2

L_r+C_r O   i   j $L_s+($

Figure 6. Ricardian expansion path: unhomogeneous resources

resources—that is, of converting unhomogeneous resources, R_u, into the equivalent of R.[4]

The resource conversion path is shown in the left-hand quadrant of Figure 6. The amounts of R are read along the vertical axis, and the corresponding amounts of $L_r + C_r$ required to obtain R are given by the resource conversion path, reading to the left. The amounts of R_u

of production [of land] which we customarily associate with produced factors, we can, if we wish, regard the cost of opening up a mine or clearing a field for cultivation as its initial 'construction' cost, although we must allow, as a limiting case, for the existence of some land whose initial cost of construction was zero."

[4] See Appendix A for a fuller exposition of the resource conversion function and path.

required need not be shown for the reason given below. The fact that $L_r + C_r$ grows at an increasing rate as R (and therefore R_u) increases is both a reflection and a measure of the decline in the quality of successive increments of R_u posited by the Ricardian hypothesis.

Two points may be made concerning the conversion function and path. First, they embody an assumption that resource quality declines continuously. We could also have assumed that resources occur in broad plateaus, each of distinct but internally homogeneous quality— a realistic possibility that we shall consider in later chapters. The conversion surface and path in that case would be composed of segments, one for each quality of R_u, with kinks at the junctures of the segments. The assumption of continuity is a useful first approximation, however. Second, although the conversion path uniquely determines the minimal $L + C$ cost per unit of R as R increases, the Ricardian hypothesis imposes no condition concerning the amount of R_u per unit of R. In general, we would expect this to change in consequence of the change in quality, but there is no reason to suppose that this change must follow a particular, or even a consistent, pattern. For example, it would not necessarily take more than an acre of substandard land, plus a minimal amount of labor-capital, to substitute for an acre of standard land; it could well take less. Thus the relation of R_u to R along the conversion path need not change in a regular way. Actually, the quantity of R_u is unimportant: resource quantity is not a limiting factor in the Ricardian hypothesis, and resources per se are not a social cost. Therefore, it is appropriate to disregard the behavior of R_u as output increases.

One might ask why we resort to the device of a resource conversion path to represent the effects of changes in resource quality instead of employing the method of shifting the production function for each such change. There are three reasons: First, the Ricardian hypothesis postulates that the change in quality is endogenous to the process of growth and has a particular directionality. It therefore requires expression in functional form, rather than merely nonexplicit and nonrigorous reference; if economic quality decline of natural resources is an endogenous feature of the model, it misses the point to treat it as exogenous parametric change. Second, the notion of a resource conversion process and path provides a nontautological definition of decline in resource quality which isolates the phenomenon and (as we show in Part III) clarifies the empirical test of the scarcity hypothesis. Third, incorporation of diminishing returns in a resource conversion path permits Ricardo's resource scarcity hypothesis to be considered independently of, and without prejudice to, the properties of the social production function. This is an important point. Since some assumption concerning the properties of the social production function had to be made, we chose constant returns to scale as the most neutral property. But, as we show later, it is important to be able to consider the possibility of increasing returns to scale, while retaining the assumption of declining resource quality.

RICARDIAN SOCIAL PRODUCTION FUNCTION

We now incorporate the Ricardian resource conversion function in the basic social production function, f_1, previously shown in Figure 4. Substitution of f_2 for R in f_1 gives

(1a) $$O = f_1[f_2(R_u, L_r + C_r), L_s + C_s]$$

where $L_s + C_s$ is the new notation of output with standard resources.[5] Figure 6, which we devised to permit comparison of the standard social production function and the Ricardian one, as well as observation of the resource conversion path, shows the results. Whereas the defined optimal solution of the standard social production function, f_1, yields *constant* marginal and average returns to aggregate labor-capital under conditions of unlimited availability of standard resources, the optimal solution of equation (1a) yields *diminishing* marginal and average returns to aggregate labor-capital under conditions of unlimited availability of unhomogeneous resources. That is, the marginal and average productivities of $L_r + C_r$ and of $L_s + C_s$ both fall along *OJ*.[6] The production contours in the right-hand quadrant of Figure 6 are those of the *standard constant returns func-*

[5] Strictly speaking, it is the particular solution of the production surface that we have called the resource conversion path which is substituted for R in f_1.

[6] Again stipulating that economic growth is increase in total output, that there is a "subsistence" level per unit of $L + C$ equal to k units of output, and that $L + C$ increases to this limit, there will be a stabilization of output and *cessation of economic growth* at some point on *OJ*, where output/$L + C = k$, and not endless increases as in the no-scarcity case. But no matter how small k is, the rate of growth of output will never become negative, as it may in the Malthusian case.

tion, f_1, as shown in Figures 4 and 5. If resources of standard quality were available, the appropriate axis would be the conventional one, labeled R. For the Ricardian case, we employ the resource conversion path as a substitute (curvilinear) vertical axis. By making the Ricardian grids in the right-hand quadrant parallel to this axis, the amount of $L_r + C_r$ needed to obtain each amount of R is automatically added to standard labor-capital, $L_s + C_s$. To interpret Figure 6, follow any curvilinear grid from its point of tangency with any production contour (X_{10}, for example), down to the horizontal axis. If j is the foot of such a grid, the distance Oj marks the aggregate amount of labor-capital that must be combined with converted unhomogeneous resources equivalent to R to obtain the indicated amount of output. The foot of a perpendicular (hi, for example) dropped from a point of tangency of a grid with a contour divides total labor-capital into its two component parts. Thus, Oi marks the amount of $L_s + C_s$ and ij the amount of $L_r + C_r$. The optimal Ricardian expansion path, OJ, is given by the points of tangency between the production contours and the Ricardian grids. The analytical criterion for OJ is that it is the locus of points at which the marginal products of $L_r + C_r$ and $L_s + C_s$ are equal.[7]

Our assumption that there is free and costless access to unhomogeneous resources, and no charge for their use, underlies the specification that the resource conversion path is the solution of the conversion function which minimizes the amount of $L_r + C_r$ per unit of R "created." Unimproved R_u, being costless, is used up to the point where, for each level of R made available, R per unit of $L_r + C_r$ is a maximum ($L_r + C_r$ per unit of R a minimum). If marginal R_u should be presumed to command a price, this would not be the case. Instead, there would be a regular downward shift of the resource conversion path, a progressive rise of resource conversion cost above its minimum level, and further economization of R. Social output would fall below the maximum by a steadily increasing amount.[8]

While it was essential to recognize the independent identities of the resource conversion path and the standard social production function,

---

[7] See Appendix A for more detailed discussion.

[8] The effect is shown in the Ricardian depletion charts in Appendix A. Although these represent conditions of constant output, they also indicate how downshifts of the resource conversion path, whatever their cause, affect the cost and level of output.

the construction that preserves these identities (Figure 6) is not now needed. We, therefore, condense the social production function, equation (1a). To do this, we set $L_a + C_a = (L_r + C_r) + (L_s + C_s)$. Then, since $L_r + C_r$ is uniquely determined for each R_u, we may write

(3) $O = f_s(R_u, L_a + C_a)$

where $L_a + C_a$ includes the amount of $L_r + C_r$ needed to raise a required amount of R_u to the standard of R. This we call the *Ricardian*

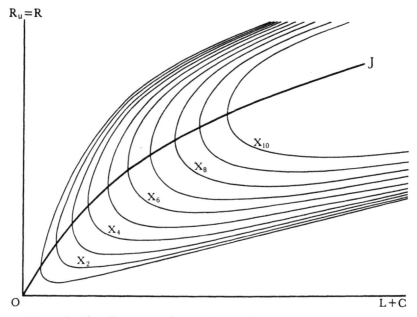

Figure 7. Ricardian expansion path: rectilinear axes

social production function. The production contours for the Ricardian function, f_s, are shown in Figure 7. This figure is derived from Figure 6 by sliding each point on the conversion axis laterally to the right until it coincides with the vertical axis, and shifting the corresponding points on the production contours in the same way.[9] The

---

[9] The path *OJ* in both charts is that which maximizes output for a given amount of aggregate labor-capital. Since the condensed Ricardian production function f_s obliterates the distinction between $L_r + C_r$ and $L_s + C_s$, it is not now possible to speak of equalizing their marginal products. (Indeed, it is not always

Ricardian function, f_3, as derived from the standard constant returns function, f_1, and the resource conversion function, f_2, clearly yields diminishing returns to social scale and to labor-capital along the optimal expansion path. Not only has the function acquired the property of yielding diminishing returns, it has also ceased to be mathematically homogeneous. That is, it is always possible to obtain a larger increase in output, as $L + C$ grows, by reducing the proportion of implicit standard resources, R, to labor-capital than by holding it constant. In Figure 7, for example, the $L + C$ cost of output is minimal for every output along the curvilinear Ricardian path.

SUMMARY OF THE RICARDIAN CASE

We now have a precise formulation of the Ricardian economic growth model in which Ricardian diminishing returns are a rigorously determined result. The characteristics of the model may be summarized as follows: (1) It incorporates the Ricardian premise of an endogenous, scale-induced decline in the economic quality of freely available resources. This premise is the unquestioned physical heterogeneity of the resource base and the assumption that, as new resources are brought into use, society possesses both the knowledge and the will to employ them in order of declining economic quality. (2) The parameters of the model are strictly invariant. The decline in resource quality is wholly endogenous to the model. The product mix is unchanging; and both output and the labor-capital inputs are qualitatively homogeneous. (3) Finally, the standard social production function is specified to provide constant returns to scale, thus assuring that diminishing returns due to declining resource quality will not be over-

possible to segregate these two types of cost in the real world, and where it is possible it may not always be done. Social behavior is determined by the ways in which situations are perceived. If different ways of perceiving the same situation suggest different allocations of costs and benefits, the social behavior pattern will be affected by the mode of perception and, therefore, by the institutional arrangements that determine the relation of the perceiver to the situation perceived. Consequently, allocative decisions made by agencies that undertake both "resource conversion operations" and the corresponding "productive" operations may differ from those made when these operations are undertaken by different agencies. Both situations are encountered in private enterprise societies. And this is one reason why there is often dispute whether capital formation of the kind that has come to be called "social overhead" should be directly undertaken—or subsidized—by public authorities or left to the private sector.)

ridden by the built-in presence of increasing returns to scale in the social production function itself.

These are precise and restrictive conditions. If they are present, a law of historically diminishing returns may be said to follow as a necessary consequence of economic growth.

Conclusions on the Three Models

Suppose we now compare the Utopian, Malthusian, and Ricardian growth paths on the assumption that exogenous growth in $L + C$ is a constant percentage per unit of time. In the Utopian case, growth of output proceeds at the same percentage rate as growth of $L + C$. In the Malthusian case, the percentage rate of growth of output falls relative to that of $L + C$ after a point, eventually becoming negative. In the Ricardian case, output grows at a declining percentage rate from the very beginning, but the fact that availability of unhomogeneous resources is taken to be unlimited means that there is no necessary absolute limit to the growth of output, as there is in the Malthusian case. However, as noted earlier, growth will come to a halt in both cases when output per unit of labor-capital falls to the "subsistence" level.

The Malthusian and Ricardian cases are both genuine scarcity models, but they behave differently. John Stuart Mill, as noted in Chapter 3, emphasized the difference, and argued that Ricardian scarcity was the more important. The scarcity of absolute ultimate limits might be reached in the distant future, he thought, but the scarcity caused by the declining quality of resources was an ever-present obstacle to economic growth.

The Utopian, Malthusian, and Ricardian models represent alternative approximations to reality. Each, as developed in what follows, is a relevant representation of certain situations, but the model of broadest application is the Ricardian one. We therefore devote the remainder of Part II largely to extension and examination of the Ricardian scarcity hypothesis, with only occasional references to the other models.

Resource Extinction

One of the initial assumptions in this chapter was that the processes of production and growth did not affect the resource environment. That is, there was no such thing as resource extinction—no depletion, destruction, deterioration, waste, or ecological damage. Scarcity and its effects in both the Malthusian and Ricardian cases were brought on by growth and nothing else. But, even in the absence of growth, scarcity and its effects can arise, or be aggravated, as a result of the extinction of natural resources.

Mineral resources are depleted when withdrawn from the soil. They are destroyed by use—immediately in the case of fuels, gradually in the cases of other nonmetallic minerals and of metals. Forest resources can be depleted by cutting at rates in excess of growth and destroyed by fire or disease. Agricultural cropland is subject to depletion from erosion, intensive cropping, and appropriation for such nonagricultural purposes as cities, factories, military establishments, mines, and highways. Underground water is depleted by withdrawals at rates faster than natural replenishment; the quality of streams deteriorates with pollution and their quantity with diversion. The atmosphere is tainted by fuel combustion, industrial gases, and radioactivity; its nitrogen content is depleted by manufacture of synthetic nitrates, and its free oxygen lost through combustion and extraction. Fish and game resources can be drawn down, or even eliminated in particular cases, by man's use and by natural forces.

Interesting questions are hidden in the seemingly plain terms, "depletion" and "destruction." Is it economic depletion to take porphyritic ores of less than 1 per cent copper and make them into wire of 90 per cent copper, or to create usable metal from the seas' vast store of magnesium salts? What are the underlying criteria by which we speak of resource depletion when forests are removed to create farm land; or phosphate rock is ground, processed, and employed to enrich soil? Do we or do we not significantly deplete nature's store of usable energy by our activities? If we extend our questions to the notion of ecological "damage," they become even more complex. The ecological concept is merely that at any time, and under any conditions, natural resources constitute a system of interdependent biological and physical variables in static or moving equilibrium. There is an infinite number of possible ecological balances. To speak of certain ones as "damaged," involves a normative judgment, as indicated earlier in Chapter 4. Should the criterion be man's welfare? Sustained biological yields at high levels? A given state of nature? Is there, indeed, an operationally definable criterion of ideal ecological balance?

In this analysis, we pass over these interesting and ultimately relevant questions. As we have simplified the concepts of resource quantity and quality, so we reduce the complex concepts of destruction, deterioration, extinction, waste, and ecological damage to a single idea—depletion. Further, we let the dynamic effects of depletion occur in a manner that will continuously alter a specific parameter of the resource variable in the social production function. This formally preserves the static character of the production process at the cost of permitting variance in a parameter of our constrained models.

DEPLETION EFFECTS IN THE THREE BASIC MODELS

Depletion can have no effect in the Utopian model. Original resources, being boundless and of constant quality, are still boundless after some are extinguished. To handle depletion in the Malthusian and Ricardian models, however, we must take account of the effect of continuing resource utilization on the residual stock and on the marginal quality of available resources.

In the Malthusian case, we may think of b_t, the stock of resources available at any time, as a function of the cumulative amount of resources used since the initial period. Therefore, the current input of resources, R_t, must be less than or equal to b_t—a steadily shrinking magnitude—which we may represent by

$$(4) \qquad b_t = b - \Sigma^t D_t$$

where b is the original stock of resources and D_t is the depletion of resources per unit time. The absolute amount of depletion at any moment is a function of the amount of resources in use at that time, or

$$(5) \qquad D_t = f_\delta(R_t)$$

after the point $R_t = b_t$ is reached, b_t becomes a constraining shift parameter, which falls through time at a rate determined by the depletion function, f_5. Clearly, as long as the amount of resources used is less than the total available stock of resources, b_t, depletion will not affect present production costs in real terms. It is only after the growth of R_t and the shrinkage of b_t has brought these variables into equality that depletion will affect real costs.

Assume an economy in which labor-capital $(L + C)$ is constant through time, $R_t = b_t$, and there is continuing depletion. In this case, both b_t and R_t will fall continually, and the constant flow of $L + C$ will yield an ever-decreasing flow of output. In this case (and also in the case where labor-capital continues to grow), the optimal expansion path will shift downward as b_t declines (see Appendix A). This may be expressed by rewriting the standard production function with the shift parameter, b_t, explicitly represented as

(6) $$O_t = f_6 [R_t, (L + C)_t; b_t]$$

where the value of the parameter b_t is determined by equations 4 and 5. Although equation 6 is static, the two preceding equations introduce a dynamic element into the Malthusian depletion model (after the point $R_t = b_t$ is reached) via their determination of b_t.

The situation is different in the Ricardian depletion case. Here depletion changes the whole spectrum of resource quality, though the precise manner of the change is open to speculation. The Ricardian resource conversion function will yield changing conversion costs due to depletion from the outset. The Ricardian depletion effect will vary according to both the rate of growth of output and the qualities of resources being depleted. Once the latter are specified (as they implicitly are in our model), the time path of depletion and its effect on the quality of the resource input variable, R_u, at each point of time are both functions of the time path of the system.

Consider this further. Under static Ricardian scarcity, the marginal economic quality of resources declines as a function of the quantity used. Still, for any given value of the independent variable, labor-capital, there is a single stable equilibrium level of output. In the depletion case, this is no longer true, for the quality of resources now declines not only as a function of the equilibrium quantity of R for each level of $L + C$ but also as a function of cumulative resource utilization since the initial period, t_o. Therefore, a resource conversion function, defined for a situation in which there is no extinction of resources, cannot provide a unique determination of the "least-cost combination" of R_u and $L_r + C_r$ required to obtain a given amount of R for a situation in which extinction does occur.

If we introduce cumulative depletion into the conversion function as a continually changing parameter, the function may be written as

$$(7) \qquad R_t = f_7 \left[R_{u_t}, (L_r + C_r)_t; \Sigma^t D_{u_t} \right]$$

where the depletion term is defined in a manner corresponding to that employed in the Malthusian case. The conversion function retains its static character, but a dynamic element has been introduced by the way in which the depletion parameter is determined. However, since depletion simply adds a feedback relation to the determination of the otherwise exogenous time paths, the departure from strictly static analysis is not a departure from sociotechnical parametric invariance in the production functions.

Any realistic accounting for resource extinction phenomena would have to be exceedingly complex. Even at the highly abstract level of our parametrically invariant model it would have to say something concerning the sociotechnical parameters that characterize institutional arrangements and social philosophy with respect to resource management. Private ownership of depletable resources, for example, might translate anticipations of depletion and consequent future scarcity into higher supply prices—and hence lower rates of use and depletion—than indicated in our models. Changes in relative prices would modify the economics of scrap recovery and, therefore, the degree of physical waste. Forest ranger stations would decrease depletion by increasing the chances of discovering and extinguishing fires, but the concomitant access roads, if permitted to facilitate recreational use, would enhance fire risk. We have simplified greatly.

RICARDIAN DEPLETION EXAMPLES

Ricardian depletion has interesting implications which are readily illustrated in simple arithmetical examples. For purposes of illustration, we assume that 20 per cent of the resources in use at the beginning of a time period have been depleted by the period's end. We also assume, as a first possibility, that the resources of better quality are depleted first; and we describe the quality of resources by hypothetical "quality indexes." The lower the value of the index attached to un-homogeneous resources, R_u, the more units of $L + C$ are necessary to convert R_u into units of R. An index number of 100 represents a unit of standard resources, and the difference (100 minus quality index) measures the amount of $L_r + C_r$ applied to unhomogeneous resources to provide a unit of R. The resource environment involved in the Ricardian model is thus described by a set of unhomogeneous resources, the quality indexes of which decrease as shown in Table 1.

Assume that the first five units, as shown in the upper part of Table 1, are in use. According to our assumption, 20 per cent of these R_u units deplete—the best unit vanishes. Thus the unit with the quality index of 99 is used up. The resource conversion situation then changes to that in the lower part of Table 1. Before depletion, the total cost of providing five R units equaled 35 units of $L_r + C_r$; after depletion it equals 55 units of $L_r + C_r$. Now assuming R equal to five units in the second period, depletion would again extinguish the best unit in part B of Table 1. This view of depletion removes the resources of best quality continually from the resource spectrum, but does not change the qualities or quality-order of the remaining un-homogeneous resources. Graphically, this means that the original curvature of the resource conversion path remains unchanged, since depletion simply cuts off a certain part of the path, and shifts the remainder to the origin.[10]

Extinction of the best unit is only one among a large number of possibilities. If several units of exhaustible R_u are in use at the same time, each may be depleted somewhat. Assume that each of five units in use is depleted by the same amount per period. All five units will be reduced to miniscule residuals after a time, and be virtually replaced by the next five. Individually, the units that have been longest in use will drop out successively, to be replaced by others, lower in the quality array.

The foregoing cases involve the implicit assumption that the original economic quality of a unit of resources is unaffected by depletion—

[10] The successively downward-shifting paths of Appendix Figure A-6 are constructed and drawn according to this pattern of depletion. For each new conversion path there is a new set of grids and a new expansion path.

that it continues to provide the same flow of resource services at the same conversion cost throughout its useful life, and then disappears. Examples of this sort of depletion might be underground fossil water which provides a continuous pumped supply until exhausted; and forests, or open-cut mines, if there were no appreciable increase in

TABLE 1. Quality Ordering of Unhomogeneous Resources: (A) Before Depletion and (B) After Extinction of Best 20 Per Cent

Initial Quality Rank of R_u Unit [a]	Quality Index	Cumulative $(L_r + C_r)$
A. BEFORE DEPLETION		
Resources in use:		
1	99	1
2	97	4
3	94	10
4	90	20
5	85	35
Resources not in use:		
6	79	56
7	72	84
•	•	•
•	•	•
•	•	•
B. AFTER EXTINCTION OF FIRST UNIT		
Resources in use:		
2	97	3
3	94	9
4	90	19
5	85	34
6	79	55
Resources not in use:		
7	72	83
8	64	119
•	•	•
•	•	•
•	•	•

[a] By a unit of unhomogeneous resources we mean here whatever quantity (of the indicated quality) is required, in combination with the indicated amount of $L_r + C_r$, to replace a unit of standard resources.

transport costs as the reserves were drawn down. In many, perhaps most, cases, however, depletion causes the original economic quality of the resource in use to deteriorate: petroleum ceases to flow under pressure of natural gas and must be pumped; mine shafts become deeper and underground tunnels longer; soils are gradually exhausted or eroded; ecological balances are disturbed; and so on.

To consider this possibility, assume that (1) all five units in use are simultaneously depleted, and (2) that depletion reduces not only the quantity, but also the original economic quality, of each unit of resources. The effect will be achieved if we assume that depletion has the effect of decreasing the quality index of each R_u unit in use by the same percentage. In the illustrative case shown in Table 2, the quality index of every unit used during each period is assumed to decrease by 25 per cent; and during each period five units of R_u are used. These five units, together with the indicated amounts of $L_r + C_r$, are always equivalent to five units of standard resources.

Comparing the quality indexes of R_u units over the four periods of Table 2, two phenomena appear: First, partial depletion of the R_u units which are used causes a reordering of the units. Second, the quality differences between the R_u units become smaller as a result of partial depletion and consequent reordering. The curvature of the conversion path changes continually, and tends to become more linear as the quality indexes of the better existing R_u units decline. This is shown by the ordering in Period 4 of Table 2. Depletion thus reduces the original quality differences of the Ricardian model.

This increasing trend toward a more homogeneous resource spectrum would also result under the assumption that the quality of the R_u units in use declines by equal absolute amounts. In fact, the shift toward homogeneity occurs whenever depletion affects quality adversely, requiring a reordering of the resource spectrum. The phenomenon of reordering is readily observable in the real world. Several million acres of New York farm land, formerly of high quality and now partially exhausted or eroded, have fallen so low in the quality spectrum that they have been removed from agricultural use.

The quality indexes of the units in use become closer to each other as better resources are degraded and become similar to poorer ones. At complete homogeneity—that is, when the resource conversion path has become a straight line—conversion costs are high, but constant; the resource scarcity effect changes neither as a result of growth

TABLE 2. Successive Quality Orderings of Units of Unhomogeneous Resources When Depletion Causes Quality to Decline ᵃ

1st ordering (period 1)		Quality index after depletion	2nd ordering (period 2)		Quality index after depletion	3rd ordering (period 3)	Quality index after depletion	4th ordering (period 4)
Quality index	Cumulative $(L_r + C_r)$		New order of quality index	Cumulative $(L_r + C_r)$		New order of quality index		New order of quality index
			RESOURCES IN USE					
99	1	74	79	21	59	68	44	55
97	4	73	74	47	56	64	42	55
94	10	71	73	74	55	64	41	54
90	20	68	72	102	54	59	40	53
85	35	64	71	131	53	56	40	45
			RESOURCES NOT IN USE					
79	56	79	68	163	68	55	55	44
72	84	72	64	199	64	55	55	42
64	120	64	64	235	64	54	54	41
55	165	55	55	280	55	53	53	40
45	220	45	45	335	45	45	45	40
34	286	34	34	401	34	34	34	34
22	364	22	22	479	22	22	22	22
.	.	.	.	.	.	.	.	.
.	.	.	.	.	.	.	.	.
.	.	.	.	.	.	.	.	.

ᵃ During each period it is assumed that only the best five R_u units available at the beginning of the period are used.

nor as a result of depletion. The situation has become what we termed Utopian at a low level of resource quality.

To summarize, resource extinction adds a new dimension to the analysis of scarcity. Scarcity is not simply a scale-induced phenomenon, it is also time-induced. In the absence of sociotechnical progress, therefore, societies cannot avoid scarcity and its effects simply by standing still.

Chapter 6

MITIGATIONS OF SCARCITY
IN COMPLEX ECONOMIES

THE scarcity models have yielded a slow-down in the growth of output; decline in output her capita; and increase in the labor-capital cost of output. These results were built into the models, not only by explicitly defining and introducing increasing natural resource scarcity, but also by subjecting them to a set of highly restrictive constraints. The most rigorous of these constraints was the exclusion of sociotechnical change. In addition, we assumed a standard social production function that yielded constant returns to scale and diminishing marginal productivity to any factor of production as it increased relative to other inputs. We assumed a homogeneous product mix in the strict sense of unchanging proportions of the component products, so that product substitutions were ruled out. Except for the precisely defined endogenous variation of natural resources in the Ricardian model, we assumed homogeneous inputs; resources and labor and capital were each fixed packages, which could be combined with each other in varying proportions, but were each invariant in internal composition. Substitutions within the resource sector and the labor-capital sector were thus also ruled out.

Now we relax the initial constraints to observe mitigation of resource scarcity or its effects. The frame of reference continues to be consistent, so far as possible, with both classical growth theory and neoclassical stationary equilibrium theory. In particular, we continue to exclude the possibility of sociotechnical change, and defer until Parts III and IV the admission of this possibility. We do this because we designed the basic scarcity models to capture and present the essence of certain significant historical and contemporary ideas concerning natural resource scarcity; and because, as shown in Part I,

126

widely held views of scarcity are based implicitly on a conception of natural resource availability, economic activity, and growth occurring with a minimum of parametric change. Major segments of public belief and opinion rest on assumptions and reasoning essentially like those embodied in these models.

In this chapter, we first assume the presence of Ricardian scarcity and ask how the scarcity force might be mitigated by price-induced substitutions or by favorable, though constant, structural characteristics of conceivable kinds. And then we examine the validity of the Ricardian scarcity premises.

Substitutions in the Ricardian Scarcity Model

Our original social production function involved a single product, a single production process, and two homogeneous inputs—one consisting of labor and capital in fixed proportions. Now let us assume that the economy can be sensibly conceived as having four sectors. These are a resource conversion (or R) sector and three producing sectors: extractive goods (E), intermediate goods (N), and final goods (G).

The resource conversion sector is that in which nonstandard, unhomogeneous resources are conceived to be converted into standard, homogeneous resources. It is the locus of the resource conversion process, the distinguishing feature of the Ricardian model. However, we cannot readily distinguish the resource conversion process from the other extractive processes with which it is closely integrated. Therefore, we collapse the R sector and the resource conversion process into the empirically identifiable extractive sector. In this schematization, the extractive sector utilizes resources and produces basic extractive products, such as grain or ore concentrate. In addition to resources, the extractive sector uses direct labor and capital, some of its own output, and intermediate materials produced by the N sector. The intermediate goods sector produces materials for the three other sectors, and a variety of other intermediate goods for its own use. And the final goods sector produces finished consumption and capital goods, employing labor, capital, extractive goods, and intermediate goods. Except for timing, the value of the output of this

G sector is equal to the social product designated as O in the preceding chapter. Each of the inputs to each of the E, N, and G sectors is of constant quality. The sector production functions are subfunctions of the standard social production function, f_1.

The simple, two-input, one-output production function of Chapter 5 excluded from the production process nearly all of the flexibility that is characteristic of productive activity as we know it. The increase in the number of input and output variables in the three-sector model just outlined is a first step toward development of a conception that captures the essential complexity and flexibility of a modern economic system, and permits important cost-saving substitutions. Let us briefly consider how substitution operates in a three-sector model in which the items comprising the product mix for each of the output aggregates do not change, and in which every input, similarly, is qualitatively homogeneous.

Since the real unit cost of R is presumed to rise—that is, the economic quality of R_u is presumed to decline—there is an inducement in the extractive sector to substitute the now relatively less costly intermediate goods inputs for R.

As a result of the substitutions in the E sector, the cost and price of extractive goods rise proportionally less than the cost and price of R. Yet, despite this mitigation, extractive goods do become more expensive. Similar substitutions of intermediate goods inputs for extractive goods inputs, therefore, take place in the N and G sectors so that cost and price of intermediate and final goods rise relatively still less than they do for extractive goods. Thus, the effects of resource adversity are mitigated in each of the three producing sectors by substitutions that reduce the use of those inputs whose costs increase relatively as a consequence of increasing scarcity. This, in the last analysis, economizes R. Requirements for R and R_u will increase more slowly than total output, and the rate of decline in the quality of R_u will be retarded. That is, less R will be employed than if substitution were not possible. Therefore, the cost and price increases of E, N, and G are, relatively, each successively less. Given our restrictive assumptions, however, the scarcity effect can only be mitigated, not fully overcome, by such substitutions. A model with three sectors and substitutable inputs in each provides many opportunities for avoiding the effects of increasing resource scarcity, but the force of scarcity is present and is felt in some degree.

Conceive, now, without relaxing the parametric constraints of the model, that products and processes are many and diverse, and that inputs are similarly multiplied in number. Each of the several input and final output aggregates represented in the three-sector social production model would then be composed of an exceedingly large number (millions) of qualitatively distinct component items. And, while we shall continue to exclude the possibility of innovations, we shall permit price-induced changes in the relative proportions of the components of the several aggregates. We relax, that is, the strict homogeneity requirement hitherto enforced with respect to the product mix and input factors. Thus, R_u is no longer an invariant package of resources that decline homogeneously in economic quality, but a vector symbol for a great variety of resources, which decline in quality at different rates. Similarly, R, E, N, and G are vector symbols for a great many standard resources, extractive products, intermediate goods, and final goods. Inputs of L and C are no longer required to be used in constant proportions. Moreover, each of them represents a large number of distinct labor and capital items, the proportions of which may change within each of the aggregates, although in the economy as a whole the ratio of capital to labor is constant.

With the model elaborated as just specified, three points need to be stressed. The first is that we have vastly multiplied the substitution possibilities and, therefore, the avenues through which the scarcity effect may be ameliorated. As before, but now in much greater degree, substitutions in response to scarcity-induced price change reduce the rate at which new resources of lower quality are brought into use. In this, and other ways, the impact of scarcity on the cost and price of final goods is mitigated.

The second point is that, in general, no matter how numerous the potential substitutions may be, they cannot wholly eliminate the effects of scarcity. So long as we remain faithful to our assumptions—permitting only price-induced substitutions within an otherwise restricted framework, and accepting the hypothesis that resources decline continuously in over-all quality—it is certain that there will be a degree of scarcity effect on growth, even though the effect is much reduced by taking advantage of substitution possibilities. It is possible that the effect will be insignificant. But whatever its magnitude, we can only contemplate mitigation, a reduced significance, not complete escape from the scarcity force. Any reaction that more than overcomes the scarcity force is out of the question, given our assumptions so far.

The third point is that near-perfect substitutes are better scarcity mitigators than imperfect ones. If consumers are virtually indifferent to whether they obtain Btu for heating, cooling, and lighting from gas, coal, or electricity, a change in the proportions in which these commodities are used will not, in itself, affect welfare. The same is true of rayon or silk, cinder-block or wood-frame construction, margarine or butter, and so on. The point is relevant to the present discussion because, by and large, scarcity-induced substitutions often involve commodities that can be employed or consumed in widely varying proportions without making much difference in welfare terms. Preferences for different forms of heating fuel, construction, clothing, or even foods are largely matters of socially conditioned taste, and are therefore quite flexible over time. Long-run elasticities of substitution are thus greater than short-run elasticities.

In the fuel area, for example, consumers have choices among bituminous coal, anthracite coal, manufactured gas, natural gas, fuel oil, and electricity. Any onset of relative scarcity in one fuel would swing consumers to the less scarce substitutes. Fuel substitution may also be brought about through increased use of such commodities as storm windows, insulation, sweaters, and thermostats. Trivial increases in fuel prices would produce little if any substitution, but large price increases would produce important substitutions over the long term in a parametrically invariant economy. The fact that residential use of electricity in areas of the United States where electricity costs are low is five to ten times that in high-cost areas suggests the force of significant price differentials.

The extent to which substitution will mitigate the scarcity effect depends, of course, not only on the increase in the cost that would occur in the absence of substitution but also on the array of substitution possibilities. Magnesium and aluminum are substitutes for lumber and steel. Plastics are substitutes for agricultural fibers, leather, rubber, and metallic minerals. Substitutions during World War II are reminders of the possibilities. This array should not be viewed too narrowly—things that are not alike in a physical sense may be economic substitutes. For example, broadcasting may be substituted for newsprint; sedentary vacations for peripatetic ones; public transportation for operation of private cars; wintering in Florida, or emigration to southern California, for fuel.

And food is a significant example. An average caloric in-take of, say, 3,000 calories per day has variable acreage implications, depending upon the type of food consumed. Animal proteins and dairy products require several times as much acreage per calorie as root foods and cereals. The scarcity effect on food prices would, if substantial, set in motion a major adjustment in the composition of the diet. Such adjustment could not fully overcome the resource scarcity (cost) effect, given our assumptions, but it could substantially mitigate this effect.[1]

For convenience in the earlier chapters, capital was assimilated to the labor factor, and these two inputs were assumed to be applied in constant proportions—were in effect a single input. We now consider how relaxation of this assumption might affect the impact of resource scarcity in our models. What are the opportunities over the long term for reallocating a given quantity of capital in response to scarcity-induced changes in relative costs? Such reallocations would, necessarily, require changes in various capital-labor ratios—increases in some, decreases in others—but, for the present, we are assuming that the ratio of total capital to total labor is unchanged.

The cases in which reallocation of capital may mitigate scarcity are rather interesting. One such case arises when the effect of greater scarcity is to raise marginal productivity of capital relative to that of labor. If both marginal products fall in consequence of increased scarcity, the marginal productivity of capital may fall less. As access roads are pushed farther into timberlands and logs have to be hauled farther to mill, for example, more capital-intensive methods of lumbering are introduced. The same is true of mining operations, as shafts become deeper and longer or as ores of lower yield must be processed. Increased resource scarcity frequently requires either longer haulage, more intensive processing, or both. Since these operations tend to be relatively capital-intensive when carried out on a large scale with

---

[1] This is a clear case of very imperfect substitution with respect to welfare.

optimal organizational efficiency, their extension is typically accompanied by an increase in the capital-labor ratio in the resource sector. The economies that result from raising the capital-labor ratio instead of holding it constant may significantly forestall the scarcity effect.

Another major type of capital substitution is represented by what may be called resource-saving uses of capital. An example appears in thermal electric generation. As fuel rises in price, it pays to introduce more capital-intensive methods in order to achieve higher initial and lower terminal temperatures, and to use mercury in place of water as the boiler fluid. Such a case is found in the thermal efficiencies and capital intensities of power stations in the United States; on the average, these have been higher (until recently, at least) in the areas of high fuel costs than in the cheap natural gas area of the Southwest. As water becomes more costly, it pays to employ condensers to economize it, and so on. At a more homely level—and without venturing into the vast field of improvements in resource-saving technology (which is blocked off by our present restrictive assumptions)—we may note that many uses of capital on farms, such as feed and water-storage facilities, belong in the resource-saving category of price-induced capital substitutions, becoming increasingly economic as the costs of feed, water, and so on, increase.

Changes in the durability of capital also enter into the question of substitutability. Capital in existence possesses different temporal characteristics—different longevity, participation in productive processes of different duration, and construction periods of different length. To maintain the stock of capital over time, society has to allocate a certain amount of inputs to replace what has worn out. But to say only that a fixed amount of inputs is used for replacement leaves the temporal characteristics of the new capital unspecified. Given society's time preference and its production function, particularly the additional construction cost as longevity of a piece of equipment is increased, a certain structure of capital is optimal.

In the case of Ricardian depletion, the downward shifting resource conversion path brings resources of successively lower qualities into use. Although the structure of capital was optimal at one time, it is unlikely that the same structure will be optimal later, after depletion has changed the character and quality of resources. More specifically, the aggregate labor-capital cost, including $L_r + C_r$ pro rata, of producing a unit of capital equipment—or of final consumption goods—increases as resource quality declines. Increased labor-capital cost changes the optimal longevity of capital equipment since new machines, for example, now contain more of the input $L + C$. Output per unit of $L + C$ will fall, but it falls less in any period if society changes the structure of its capital when making replacements. Under these circumstances, whether longevity should be increased or decreased, whether the duration of productive processes or construction periods should be lengthened or shortened, depends critically upon the way in which declining resource quality alters conditions of production for capital goods relative to consumer goods.

There is no need to enter into a detailed discussion of possibilities. We wish only to note that society, by changing the structure of its stock of capital by replacement, can ameliorate the effects of increasing resource scarcity. This can occur under a given technology; the model is still parametrically invariant.

Attention has been focused on a single country or region, isolated from trade with the rest of the world. We must now take note of the great increase in substitution possibilities available to a member of a world trading system as compared to an isolated economy. To eliminate the effect of changes in international relations and institutional arrangements, we assume free trade throughout the world economy. Under this assumption, the potential gains from trade that are inherent in the structure of comparative advantages existing at any time are already fully realized, and there is instantaneous adjustment to changes reflecting declining resource quality—the only changes in the structure permitted in the presently constrained framework.

A world economy, as here conceived, differs from a national economy in two major respects. First, the mobility of labor and capital is more restricted among national economies than within them. Second, the varieties of resources are much more numerous and the quantities of each variety are far greater in the world as a whole than for a national economy. This broadens the substitution potential for national economies that belong to the world trading system as compared to those that do not. Yet international substitutions, like their national counterparts, can only mitigate the effect of increasing resource scarcity; they cannot fully, or more than fully, offset it. This follows from our assumption that all gains from trade are realized at all times —that the assumptions of the Ricardian model hold for the world trading system as a whole. Otherwise the realization of a hitherto unrealized opportunity for gain might more than offset the impact of a given increase in resource scarcity.

Given our assumptions, international trade creates no opportunities not already covered in the preceding discussion, but it vastly enlarges the scope of possible substitutions. In short, the significance of trade is that it dilutes the impact of scarcity by distributing it over a wider area than the national economy under observation. Just as trade among sectors within a national economy partly reduces the over-all scarcity effect and partly distributes the residual cost increase among the several sectors, so international trade reduces and redistributes the scarcity effect for the world economy.

Procurement from foreign producers of extractive goods for which domestic costs would otherwise rise sharply is the most obvious and impressive of the substitution possibilities available under international trade. In exchange, the domestic economy exports goods or services which it can produce on relatively more favorable terms. The opportunity for mitigation of the resource scarcity effect, however, is rather greater than this simple statement suggests. Extractive commodities are diverse in type and in their natural origins. Thus, for example, the United States has a zero net balance in foreign trade of agricultural products and an import balance in minerals. In the agricultural category, grains are exported and coffee and beef imported; in the minerals category, coal is exported and oil is imported. Holland and Denmark import minerals and grain and export dairy and meat products. India exports manganese ore and jute and imports grain and petroleum. All of these represent possibilities for price substitution of a kind made feasible by international differences in natural resources and cost structures.

Beyond extractive commodities, the resource content per unit value of semiprocessed and finished goods ranges from miniscule proportions in, for example, electronics gear, to major proportions in heavy machinery, newsprint, and motor fuel. The whole vast range of commodities produced throughout the world provides latent opportunities for mitigating effects of resource scarcities by international trade.[2]

[2] But there are also possibilities, perhaps, for eventually exacerbating scarcity.

International trade opportunities to escape increasing domestic resource scarcities do not require that other countries be free of scarcity effects. They require only that nations differ somewhat in resources, in other endowments, or in sociotechnical parameters.

Substitutions That Ameliorate Resource Extinction

Substitutions, to some extent, directly reduce the rate of resource extinction itself, and thus retard the development of increased resource scarcity at its source. The recovery and use of various kinds of scrap and waste—steel and other rarer metals, paper, glass, sewage, and so on—amount to a substitution phenomenon, made economical by the rise in the cost of extractive materials relative to recovery, and by the accumulations of a growing economy. Scrap is a special kind of intermediate good recovered from the productive processes of the several sectors. The scrap recycling phenomenon by-passes R_u and R, and sometimes E, as productive inputs. To the extent that this occurs —and it occurs increasingly as the costs of R and E rise—resource extinction does not take place. Nor should it be thought that the possibilities of by-passing resource extinction are narrowly limited. Once the relative cost inducement is strong enough, organic and mineral compounds extracted from the soil can be returned to it far more systematically and completely than is done in most industrial societies at present. Even the seemingly evanescent escape into the atmosphere of organic and inorganic compounds contained in the hot gases of combustion and reduction processes can be, and is, forestalled when the price is right. At one time, and perhaps still, the operating

---

The bite of scarcity is felt sooner, possibly, by the countries that export extractive materials than it would be in the absence of export. We say "possibly" because trade is a two-way street, and it is by no means certain that countries that export resource-intensive products of some kinds and import others, or export resource-intensive products and import those that are not, are hurt thereby. More specifically, it would be hard to establish that, in the absence of such trade, the countries in question would grow more rapidly, or achieve a higher per capita income at any time, than with trade. It must be recognized, however, that trade between pre-modern and modern societies may not be to the advantage of the former under some circumstances. From a substantial body of literature on this point, we call attention to the papers by John H. Adler and C. P. Kindleberger in Joseph J. Spengler, ed., *Natural Resources and Economic Growth* (Baltimore: The Johns Hopkins Press for Resources for the Future, 1961). Both provide extensive references to other discussions.

costs of the assay office of the Federal Mint in New York were met by the recovery of gold, platinum, and other rare metals in the gases of the melt and the wash water of employees.

Indeed, and this seems worth stressing, the earth's waters form the "waste trap" of the terrestrial globe. Eventually, most of what is eroded from the soils, discharged into the atmosphere, or simply added to the world's accumulated rubbish, is carried by rain, stream, and wind into the earth's open and landlocked waters—there to be held in solution or suspension, to be transformed into organic life, or to accumulate as silt in streams and lakes and on the ocean floor as coagulated nodules of nearly pure mineral. The earth's waters, in short, are not simply a stock of resources; they are a stock that is being steadily augmented. The rate of augmentation is, in a relative sense, small, but the absolute additions of usable substance per unit of time are far from trivial. Technicians know many of the secrets of extracting materials from the sea; and the economics of resource scarcity has already brought some of the known methods into application. Further increases in the relative cost of exploiting other resources would lead to expansion of ocean-based extractive industries, even if there were no further advance in scientific knowledge.[3]

We have gone far enough to show that, even in our simple, parametrically invariant models, price substitutions are induced by initial resource scarcity effects, and the effects are thereby significantly ameliorated. Without further technological change, the opportunities are as numerous as the products and processes employed in the economy. Chemical fertilizer and water are substitutes for agricultural land, and so are insecticides, fungicides, and power. Chemicals used in mineral flotation are substitutes for some mineral ores. In coal mining, pit-props are substitutes for coal pillars. In oil production, water injection substitutes for new wells. The list is virtually endless in a scientifically and technologically advanced society. Thus, to the extent that existing technology has already provided a long list of opportunities—as it has in the world of the mid-twentieth century—the impact of scarcity is much weakened. This leads to consideration of

[3] See, for example, John L. Mero, "Minerals on the Ocean Floor," *Scientific American*, Vol. 203 (December 1960), and "Economics of Deep Sea Mining," *Mining Congress Journal*, Vol. 47 (September 1961).

the existing structural characteristics of technologically and institutionally modernized societies, which may produce a similar result; or even, in conceivable circumstances, might more than offset the effect of scarcity.

Structural Characteristics of the Economy

A basic structural characteristic of our initial models was that labor and capital grew at the same rates and maintained constant proportions. Earlier in this chapter, we removed this restriction for specific production processes, but did not permit total capital to grow faster than total labor. However, capital may grow faster than labor, as it has in the United States. At least in part, an increase in the ratio of capital to labor will offset the declining output per capita caused by resource scarcity in our Ricardian model of Chapter 5.

Rising income per capita is possible, even under parametrically invariant conditions of increasing resource scarcity, provided the ratio of capital to labor increases fast enough, or if there are economies of social scale. If, with rising per capita incomes, expenditures were allocated among all consumer goods and services in fixed proportions, no modification in the scarcity effect could be inferred. But if the built-in structural response to rising per capita incomes were such as to alter the proportions of the items in the consumer basket in a regular way, the scarcity effect would be systematically modified.

Available evidence indicates that consumer expenditure obeys Engel's law: as income per capita rises, expenditure on basic food, clothing, and other essentially biological necessities increases less than proportionally. These necessities are more R-intensive—at least in the sense of agricultural land—than the service and luxury items that are consumed in relatively increasing amounts as living standards improve. That is, the latter items call for more "value added" and require different types of extractive products from the former. They tend to make different and less demands on agricultural land. To the extent that this is the case, then, the requirements for agricultural land increase more slowly than income. Pressure on the land base, as defined at any point in time, thus increases less as growth occurs than it would in the absence of Engel's law, and the scarcity and scarcity effect are ameliorated in this relative sense. But the shift toward protein foods as income per capita rises exerts an offsetting influence.

Economies of social scale may also counteract scarcity. When, for purposes of the models constructed in Chapter 5, we assumed that the standard social production function yielded constant returns to scale, this was more than an analytic simplification. The assumption played a crucial role in determining the consequences of resource scarcity, especially of the Ricardian type. The scale-induced decline in resource quality hypothesized in the Ricardian model is, in effect, a diseconomy of social scale. Thus it will inevitably produce diminishing returns in the Ricardian production function if, and only if, offsetting economies of social scale are not built into the standard function. The assumption of constant returns to scale met this requirement.

But what is the possibility that the standard social production function yields increasing, rather than constant, returns? If increasing, the effects of scarcity will be mitigated and, if the economies of scale in the standard production function are strong enough, the Ricardian form of the function may yield constant or increasing returns, at least over part of its range.

The fact that the Ricardian hypothesis of declining resource quality might be valid, and yet conceivably not yield diminishing returns because of overriding economies of social scale, could be important. A strong tradition in economic theory holds (largely on the basis of a priori reasoning) that production functions, when defined so that all parameters are rigidly invariant, must yield constant returns to scale. This is a rather precarious premise, especially when related to society as a whole, and we are now concerned simply with calling attention to the fundamental importance of the shape of the social production function, without committing ourselves to any particular shape. We incline to the view that increasing returns to scale characterize production as a whole in modern societies. But in the absence of evidence concerning the shape of the social production function, any conclusion based on the assumption that the function has a particular shape should be regarded as an untested hypothesis. It is important to stress that the occurrence of Ricardian diminishing returns can only be postulated with certainty if the possibility of offsetting increasing returns to scale is denied or assumed away.

Premises Concerning Natural Resource Availability

We now turn to a consideration of the hypothesis of increasing resource scarcity itself—in its Malthusian formulation of an absolute limit to the availability of resources, and in the Ricardian form of continual decline through time in the economic quality of resources. We treat the Malthusian case very briefly, and the Ricardian one at some length.

The Malthusian hypothesis posits an absolute fixity in the stock of natural resources—a perfectly inelastic ultimate supply of this productive input. It has been applied by many analysts to the world as a whole, because the earth is finite. But it is clearly wrong to identify the entire terrestrial globe, only a fraction of which has been disturbed by the hand of man, with the resource-input factor in the social production function. Malthusian scarcity thus is not the situation presently confronting man on a global scale. It is probable that some societies, those too primitive to engage in extensive interregional trade and employed almost wholly in agriculture, experience Malthusian scarcity. This does not mean that all the physical resources of their entire natural endowment are being put to full use, but only the resources—primarily agricultural land—which they have the knowledge to use. Their low state of economic welfare results from an interaction of two factors: one representing their fertile land relative to population numbers, and the other one representing the spectrum of their available institutional opportunities and technologies. Such a resource environment with few acres per capita is more limiting than one with many, because a larger stock of technical knowledge and institutional relations is required to conquer its intractabilities.

This way of stating the case emphasizes that a society would have to be both primitive and largely isolated if it is to be persistently subject to Malthusian scarcity. While such a society can validly be characterized as being held down by Malthusian scarcity, we wonder whether this is a highly significant description. No society can escape the general limits of its resources, but no innovative society need accept Malthusian diminishing returns. Through interregional trade and the interchange of knowledge, the effective resources of each nation are greatly extended by the increased diversity of the natural and the sociotechnical environments at the effective command of all.

Thus, the analytical problem in applying the Malthusian hypothesis to contemporary societies is one of defining the limit of resource availability in realistic terms, of determining whether or not the limit has been reached, and of identifying the relevant sociotechnical parameters. The more complex the society, and the greater its contact with the world, the more impossible it is to define a Malthusian limit which has any operational meaning or significance for policy. The Malthusian scarcity hypothesis, therefore, has rather specialized and limited relevance, and so is not generally useful, even under conditions of parametric invariance.

The Ricardian hypothesis asserts that resources decline in economic quality as the quantity of output increases under strict parametric constraints, or as resources are extinguished through use or fortuitous circumstance. The reasoning underlying this hypothesis, which we now propose to examine, warrants restatement: Rational man possesses a given fund of knowledge concerning the extent and qualities of resources, productive techniques, modes of technical and social organization, and the goods and services to be produced. Possessing also a given set of canons of taste and an economic calculus, man endeavors to minimize the labor-capital cost of output. Since, in general, equal areas of the earth's surface and equal volumes of its crust contain different assortments of the kinds of physical resource properties useful to man, and since they are also differentially accessible to the established centers of population, any enlargement of the scale of social output makes it necessary to choose which of the then unutilized resources shall be brought into use. Assuming that the requisite information is available, and that the choice is made in accordance with a rational economic calculus, those resources will be employed first that entail the smallest labor-capital cost per unit of output. These are the implicit assumptions of the Ricardian hypothesis. Our problem is to consider more closely the conditions under which, in a parametrically constrained world of the kind here assumed, this would be the case.

For the Ricardian hypothesis to be valid in the rigorous form developed in Chapter 5, the following specific conditions must be satisfied:

1) The physical quantities and properties of all resources should be fixed and known, insofar as they are relevant to the known techniques of production, for otherwise fortuitous discovery might upset the quality ordering. Then, given the known properties, the cost effects on extractive output of all possible input combinations must also be known, and must guide behavior.

2) For the economic ordering of resources to be fixed, the accessibility element should be invariant under change of social scale. Hence, given the irregularity of resource distribution, population increases must not alter the initial geographical distribution of population: all increases must occur at the initial inhabited sites. Further, scale economies in transportation incident to growth must not be of a magnitude to affect the ordering of resource use.

3) There must be no institutional obstacles to using resources in accordance with the quality ordering rendered possible by the preceding conditions.

4) Resource "plateaus"—that is, large blocks of resources having constant quality—must be of negligible significance.

5) Changes in the ecological balance must not cause costs to decrease.

These conditions are clearly very strict; we now examine them individually.

KNOWLEDGE OF RESOURCES: SCALE-INDUCED DISCOVERY

For knowledge of economic quality, it is necessary not only to know the physical properties and quantities of resources, but also to translate this knowledge into an economic—that is, a cost—spectrum.

With respect to knowledge of physical properties and quantities, the Ricardian assumption is a difficult one, even for a society with unchanging science and technology. Such understanding will vary, depending upon the particular society, its particular stage of socio-economic development, and its particular resource endowment. Very little was known about the physical properties of most resources in the United States of 1850. Today, information on the properties and quantities of agricultural lands, forests, and surface waters is quite good; on underground water and ultimate coal deposits is less good;

on ultimate oil and gas pools, fair to poor; and on ultimate metallic and nonmetallic mineral deposits, poor or very poor. Thus, significant ignorance concerning subsurface resources still exists with respect to individual quantities, locations, depths, and physical characteristics.

Yet it is not sufficient to know simply the physical properties and quantities of all resources. Suppose for a moment that this information is available; and that each resource of a given kind can be rated relative to others of that kind in terms of every relevant physical property. Each acre of agricultural land, for example, can be rated in terms of its chemical content, moisture availability, friability, hours of daylight and sunshine, average and range of temperature, length of growing season, and so on. Similarly, every ore deposit can be ordered according to each of many dimensions—such as the degree of concentration of minerals, the mechanical and chemical forms of their occurrence, the number and kinds of impurities to be removed, hardness, depth of location, type of overburden, and so on. But ordering each unit of a given type of resource in terms of each of these dimensions separately would not order one unit in relation to another in economic—that is, relative cost—terms. Physical properties alone provide insufficient information for the Ricardian premise, which requires knowledge of the relative cost of output from each acre of land as compared with all others, each ore body compared with all others, and so on. It is necessary to know the effect on costs of using each available type of resource. And it is necessary to know this for each of the alternative extractive products or product combinations that might be produced from each resource; otherwise, substitutions might alter the quality ordering of the resources. To the extent that economic knowledge adequate for marginal decisions is imperfect, inferior resources will often be used before superior ones.

How closely is the condition concerning knowledge of resources approximated? Clearly, it does not hold in high degree for any existing societies, and cannot even be imagined to hold for the world as a whole. Cost characteristics of known, but untried, natural resources cannot be specified with precision, if at all. And the time is still far distant when, if ever, we can say that there is nothing further to be learned concerning our resource endowment, even though we disregard for purposes of the present analysis the effect of advances in science and technology. As man pushes farther along the surface of the earth and penetrates more deeply into its crust, he learns—by mere virtue of these more extended activities—more about the natural environment at his disposal. Society is pleasantly surprised more often in the case of subsurface resources than those on the surface; more often in lightly settled areas than in dense ones; more often, perhaps, in advanced than in primitive societies; and, no doubt, further generalizations are possible. To the extent, therefore, that increasing knowledge is a scale-induced phenomenon, we may regard it as an offset to the decline of quality that does not materially violate—as technological advance would—our basic assumption of strict parametric invariance.

The condition of perfect and unchanging knowledge of the cost profile of the resource base, which is necessary for the *economic* hypothesis of declining resource quality to be valid, thus is only a rough approximation. If societies were completely without such knowledge, each resource to be used would be selected at random, and quality would not change in a systematic way. Viewed with hindsight, the ordering is neither perfectly systematic nor perfectly random. Man can only order resources in terms of economic quality subject to his ignorance. There have probably been few societies that did not discover—purely as an aspect of their expansion—new resources superior in economic quality to some of those already in use. The fact is that man is neither all-knowing nor all-ignorant concerning the resource potential; he occupies an intermediate position. There is certainly a tendency to use known resources in order of declining quality in a parametrically constrained situation. But it is hardly the simple and clear-cut law which Ricardo assumed for agricultural land in the England of the early nineteenth century.

SCALE-INDUCED CHANGE IN RESOURCE ACCESSIBILITY

The accessibility dimension adds a further complication. By accessibility we mean the distance of the resource from the centers of use of the final output to which it contributes, together with all the obstacles—such as bringing minerals to the surface—that add to the cost of traversing this distance. Overcoming the obstacle of distance entails "transport cost." In our rational, cost-minimizing world, therefore, it will be necessary to array known but unused resources according to the properly weighted transport costs entailed in their use. This means that we should use nearby resources with unfavorable physical properties if they permit sufficient transport savings to overcome the intrinsic quality advantages of more distant resources.

But the size of transport costs depends in part on the distribution of population. If population grows at its existing sites, population growth will have no effect on the ordering of resources in terms of transport costs (except as differential economies of scale in transport occur). But it is more realistic, and does little violence to the assumption of strictly limited parametric change, to suppose that population, as it increases, disperses itself and thus alters costs of transport.

Given the geographical spread of a growing population, a rational society could at times find itself in a situation where resource quality would increase with growth. Remote resources of superior intrinsic physical properties, which had not been previously employed because their transport costs were too high, as the result of population spread, would be brought progressively into use. Under conditions of perfect rationality, each such superior resource would be employed as soon as the transport cost entailed by its use had fallen to the point where it just matched the disadvantage of processing physically inferior, but more accessible, resources. Thereafter, as population density in the vicinity of the new resources increased and transport cost fell further, average costs would decline. Thus, it is possible for growth of population and output to occur, under otherwise constant sociotechnical conditions, without encountering the Ricardian condition of declining resource quality.

Nor should it be argued that this result is impossible because population would be initially located as close as possible to the best resources. To assume that population centers, or the directions of population movement, are solely determined by the natural resource productivity criterion would far exceed the reasonable and usual assumptions of such a model and violate the criteria of social behavior. Rather, it is clear that many factors, among them resource quality, account for the concentration of population in particular centers, as well as for absolute and relative population movements. Resource quality, in the sense used here, is not usually conceived to be the sole, or major, force determining population locations. The settlement of the United States in the seventeenth century and its subsequent expansion westward provide illustrations.

INSTITUTIONAL EFFECTS ON THE ORDER OF RESOURCE USE

Institutional features of modern societies sometimes prevent resources of higher quality from being used before those of lower quality. Three of these features are of particular interest here.

One institutional feature relates to the manner in which investment decisions are reached in a private enterprise society. Incremental capital is not perfectly mobile (that is, indifferent as between applications), because its availability entails charges for real or presumed risks. Risk decisions involving new ventures are often taken, or influenced, by financial institutions—insurance companies, investment trusts, pension funds, and so on—which are noted for their caution, as well as by the less inhibited nonfinancial enterprises. None of these investing groups is omniscient concerning risk. In general, capital is more readily available for exploiting familiar resources in familiar and developed locations than for new ones. Within the United States, and even more in the world at large, capital flows more readily to places where it is already employed than elsewhere. But if capital is available only on relatively disadvantageous terms for newer resources and locations, then resources of higher intrinsic quality may lie unused, while those of lower quality are employed.

International boundaries and impediments to international trade and factor movements are also serious obstacles to the uniform use of resources of higher quality before those of lower quality. The labor-capital cost of Middle Eastern and South American oils, for example, is much lower than the cost for U.S. resources. The same is true, to a degree, for lead, zinc, and copper. Yet U.S. imports of these items are restricted by tariffs and quota limitations; therefore, U.S. resources for which labor-capital costs are higher (thus, resources of lower quality in this discussion) are still employed. The obstacles to use of world resources in order of decreasing quality include not only commercial but also foreign exchange restrictions, national security policies, and the relative immobility of labor and capital as between national entities.

Even within a single country, where there are subordinate governmental units with significant sovereignty, governmental boundaries may interfere with the use of natural resources in order of declining quality. For example, restrictions on oil and gas output in Texas and Louisiana, but not in California, result in utilization of reserves of inferior quality in the latter state while superior quality reserves in the former states are shut back. Also, prorationing techniques within states which employ quotas discriminate against the earlier utilization of lower cost resources. Prohibitions of the export of hydroelectric power from Maine to neighboring states is another example. Reservation of high-quality resources—forest lands, so-called naval oil reserves—or the imposition of restrictions on their use by the federal government, are other examples of institutional blocks to employment of resources in descending order of quality.

In short, we observe another source of interference with utilization of the best grades of resources first. Even if the world's resources could conceivably be arranged in order of declining economic quality, there would be no assurance that this array would be the order of use. Biased appraisals of risk often intervene. And governmental restrictions involve unintended or deliberate reservation of resources of higher quality.

RESOURCE PLATEAUS OF CONSTANT QUALITY

The entire analysis up to this point has rested on the assumption that resource quality declines continuously as the quantity used increases; that is, that the resource conversion function is continuous. This was a methodologically convenient, but unrealistic, assumption that we may now discard. If we assume that, under appropriate conditions, quality ordering is possible, it does not follow that the curve of quality will decline monotonically. It may flatten out over indefinitely long stretches as a result of the occurrence of large resource "plateaus" of constant quality. This being a somewhat abstract discussion, it is perhaps not necessary to establish that these plateaus are empirically important, but the examples we have mentioned elsewhere are potentially significant. We are not referring to developments that depend on technological change, but only observing that (1) an assumption of resource use in order of decreasing economic quality in a static model does not necessarily imply that quality declines continuously; and (2) plateaus of constant quality may be very extensive. The manner in which resource plateaus affect the conversion path is shown in Figure 10 in the next chapter.

The existence of plateaus does not affect the Ricardian hypothesis in the same way as the points made earlier about other conditions. The plateau argument suggests only that resources may decline in quality discontinuously rather than continuously. The consequent change in the shape of the resource conversion path would provide no grounds for denying the reality of the path's existence unless the "plateau" were indefinitely large. But some of the ineluctable character of scarcity and scarcity effect is lost.

BENEFICIAL ECOLOGICAL DISTURBANCE

Disturbances of ecological equilibrium have usually been accused of creating difficulties for man, of imposing added costs on his efforts to wring a satisfactory life from a reluctant nature. But there seems to be no inherent reason why this should always be the case. What are usually observed and noted are the adverse effects: increased erosion and flooding caused by deforestation, dust bowls caused by overgrazing, and so on. But there are favorable effects of ecological disturbance, such as the spread of deltas and cultivable flatlands and creation of farms, lakes, and parks. This may, or may not, be an important qualification of the Ricardian hypothesis, but it is a possibility which provides further reason why resource quality may not always decline.

This concludes our discussion of constrained scarcity models. The conditions which must exist if there is to be a clear presumption of diminishing returns in a parametrically invariant world are far more restrictive than is commonly realized. This is what we have tried to demonstrate in the two chapters of Part II.

The plain fact, however, is that the acceleration of sociotechnical change has now become the dominant influence on economic growth. Parametrically constrained models thus do not, and cannot be made to, represent twentieth-century reality. We therefore turn to analysis of the hypothesis of increasing resource scarcity under conditions of change in the modern world.

PART III

RESOURCES IN A PROGRESSIVE WORLD

Chapter 7

A PARAMETRICALLY VARIANT, STATIC, AND HISTORICAL GROWTH MODEL

PERHAPS the premises and conclusions of classical economics concerning natural resources and economic growth have gone largely unquestioned because they are difficult to test. Subjection of these premises and conclusions to analytical and empirical investigation involves three steps. The first, undertaken in Part II, was to examine the two basic classical models—the Malthusian and Ricardian—within the framework of their own restrictive premises. The second step, undertaken in this chapter, is to remove these restrictions and provide an analytical framework that takes account of historical changes in the parameters. The third step, which we undertake in further chapters, is empirical investigation and evaluation of the role of natural resources in the growth process.

Shift from Parametric Invariance to Parametric Change

The models of Part II were characterized as parametrically invariant. They were also static, and only to a limited degree historical.[1] We now wish to modify these models so that they can take account of any relevant type of historical change.

Our initial basic social production function in Part II was in this static and nonhistorical, or stationary, form: [2]

---

[1] For an explanation of our usage of these terms see Chandler Morse, "A Note on Static, Dynamic, and Historical Analysis," *Southern Economic Journal*, Vol. 27 (January 1961), pp. 237–39. The static and parametrically invariant status of the models in Part II was mildly prejudiced by modifications introduced in Chapter 5, but they retained essentially their initial characteristics.

[2] Again, *O* equals social product, or output; *R* equals natural resources; *L* equals labor; and *C* equals capital.

$$O = f(R,L,C)$$

This was an abridgment of a more complete statement

$$O = f(R,L,C;A,B \ . \ . \ .)$$

in which $A, B \ . \ . \ .$ are variables that reflect sociotechnical conditions. In the models developed in Part II, the variables A and B were assumed to be constant—that is, they became sociotechnical parameters. Being constant, they were omitted from the stated functional relationships of the model. The above forms of the social production function were also stationary, since they made no provision for growth of $R, L,$ or C. But we required a historical growth model. We, therefore, specified that the labor and capital variables, which we combined into a single variable, $L + C$, were to be viewed as growing through time at an exogenously determined rate. Employed resources, R, also grew through time, but at a rate determined by the optimal equilibrium requirements for R (up to the point, in the Malthusian case, where R was fully employed). The basic social production function then implicitly became

$$O_t = f(R_t, L_t + C_t; A,B \ . \ . \ .)$$

where the absence of time subscripts for the sociotechnical parameters indicates their continuing status as constants. Again, it was convenient to employ an abridged form of the function, omitting the constants. And, for convenience, the t-subscripts were not shown, although they were understood to be present:

$$O = f_1(R, L + C)$$

Alternative definitions of equilibrium yield alternative equilibrium solutions of this function. As $L + C$ grows, equilibrium solutions trace out "moving equilibrium" paths through time, among them the optimal expansion paths of Part II. Introduction of exogenous time into the models, via influence on $L + C$, thus converted them from static and stationary to static and historical. But they remained parametrically invariant. The historical element was limited, being confined to the autonomous growth of $L + C$, with historical change of the sociotechnical parameters, $A, B \ . \ . \ .$ explicitly excluded.

Malthusian resource scarcity was then defined as an absolute limit to the availability of R. Malthusian scarcity necessarily yielded increasing average $L + C$ cost of a growing output after the limit of R was reached. Ricardian scarcity was defined as an increasing cost of converting substandard, unhomogeneous resources into standard resources as the required quantity of the latter increased. Constant returns to scale having been built into the standard social production function, Ricardian scarcity also necessarily yielded increasing average labor-capital cost of output.

To take account of depletion, the major type of resource extinction, we had to recognize that it was a function of both time and the quantity of resources in use. This introduced a dynamic element into the models, and, to a limited extent, they became dynamic and historical. But depletion, though a function of both time and scale, merely aggravates the influence of growth on scarcity. It was, therefore, practical and convenient to regard depletion (and, more generally, all forms of resource extinction) as a special type of parametric change related to the resource variable.

Analysis could therefore be conducted flexibly within a static, historical, and still invariant sociotechnical framework. Consideration of various hitherto unanalyzed characteristics of the models then led us to observe that:

1) The occurrence and increase over time of natural resource scarcity and scarcity effect must be regarded as a hypothesis, not a self-evident fact, even in parametrically constrained models subject to depletion.

2) The character of the social production function, and therefore of the determining social, technical, and cultural environment of the production process, might play a crucial role in determining whether the resource scarcity hypothesis is or is not valid.

We now remove the constraints to which we adhered in Part II. From this point on, we take explicit account of historical changes in the sociotechnical parameters, A, B . . . , that result from such phenomena as resource depletion and discovery, the accumulation of knowledge, technological innovation, the progress of training and education, improvements of social organization, and so on.

To the extent that changes in the sociotechnical parameters may be regarded as purely historical events, exogenous to the model, no analytical problem arises. By releasing the parameters, and giving them time subscripts to signify that they are no longer assumed to be constant through time, they become free to change, continuously or discontinuously, with the passage of time. Further, if labor and capital are viewed as growing at different rates, the standard social production function needs to be written:

$$O_t = f(R_t, L_t, C_t; A_t, B_t \ldots)$$

Of course, at any point in time, the model is static and stationary. But between two points in time, it is no longer parametrically constrained; its parameters have been freed from all restrictions, and the model has become historical in the fullest possible sense.

The above function (plus analogous reformulations of the other functions of Part II) provides an analytical framework that permits us to handle complex phenomena by the essentially simple method of "continuing comparative statics." In this method, changes in parameters—whether continuous through time or occurring at discontinuous intervals—shift the functions to which the parameters relate. In the absence of parametric change, the growth of labor and capital causes the system to trace out optimal equilibrium expansion paths, as in Part II. In the presence of parametric change, the economic variables are assumed to adjust instantaneously from their former (moving) equilibrium values to their new ones. The method of continuing comparative statics suffers from the disadvantage that the time paths of adjustment processes following the occurrence of parametric changes are ignored, and that the influences of all such changes are merged. But these are matters that can be disregarded in long-term trend analysis such as that employed here.

In this method, parametric changes may be viewed either as exogenous historical phenomena or as (endogenous) feedback effects. If exogenous, the parametric changes reflect accidents, or political forces, or any other cause, but not operation of the economy. If endogenous, they are induced by the growth and performance of the system under analysis. For example, reductions in the stock or quality of resources induce exploration and research leading to resource discovery and to resource-saving changes in products and processes. Cost increases induce labor-saving and capital-saving technological innovations which may increase the resource intensity of social output, and so on. Our method of continuing comparative statics permits us to regard parametric changes as *caused within the system* that is being analyzed, but not to specify the set of functional relationships through which the processes of causation operated. Since this method conforms to the spirit—though not, perhaps, to the strict definition—of dynamic analysis, it is now permissible to refer to our analysis as "dynamic," in contrast with the static analysis of Part II.

Parametric Change and the Trend of Cost

Every change in knowledge about the resource spectrum, in the qualities of labor and capital inputs, in the quality or composition of output, in institutional arrangements and, generally, in any socio-technical characteristic that affects the parameters of the social production process as a whole—all of these changes are now to be regarded as involving a shift to a new function, a change in or from the existing function. Resource extinction, discovery, and development are treated as causing parametric shifts, along with technological advance, new products, changes in preferences, new legislation, and so on. Consequently, the mathematical forms of the relevant static functions cease to be the sole, or possibly even major, determinants of changes in the real social cost of output as scale increases. Parametric shifts of the functions or changes in their form now acquire major, often dominant, importance.

The following discussion of the effects of parametric change will be built around the Ricardian model, with Malthusian aspects treated incidentally. We shall distinguish two groups of historical influences, one affecting what we shall call the "trend of real social cost," the other operating upon the "trend of resource conversion cost."

TREND OF REAL SOCIAL COST

The trend of real social cost is defined by a time series of observed points. The relation of each point to that preceding necessarily represents either (1) a movement along a static function, (2) a functional shift, or (3) some combination of both. Figure 8 illustrates these alternatives. The trend line *ah* in each of the panels represents a hypothetical series of average labor-capital cost points. The general

trend of the dynamic cost curve *ah,* which is identical in each of the
panels, is downward despite the differences in static cost conditions.

The dynamic *ah* curve corresponds to experience in the United
States since 1890 at least, as shown in Figure 9. In fact, the curve *ah*

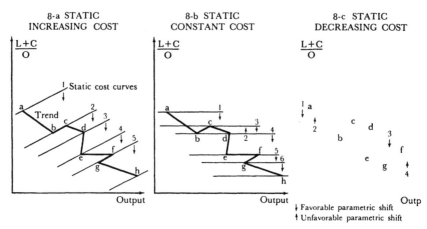

Figure 8. Schematic trend of real social cost

consists of segments like those that make up the connected point
curve in Figure 9.

Panels 8-a, 8-b, and 8-c explain the dynamic trend of *ah*
primarily in terms of assumed parametric shifts of increasing, constant, and decreasing static cost curves. Each of the static cost curves
implies a different static social production situation. The increasing
cost curves in panel 8-a, for example, fit the Malthusian and Ricardian cases; the constant cost curves in panel 8-b fit the Utopian case.
The decreasing cost curves in panel 8-c can be taken to imply increasing returns to scale. The dynamic trend of average real cost is
clearly seen to be the result of (1) the character of the static social
cost function, and (2) parametric changes—that is, the number,
speed, size, and direction of the shifts of the function itself. The
greater the increasing cost tendency of the function, the larger must
be the postulated down-shifts in order to produce the observed downward trend of average real cost. But increasing static cost functions
do not, in that case, generate an increasing trend of social cost. If,
on the other hand, the static social cost function is constant or de-

clining, the observed downward trend of cost relies less heavily on downward shifts of the function itself.

In the following discussion, we suppose that the observed down-trend of social cost in the United States is the consequence of favorable parametric change superimposed on one of the basic resource

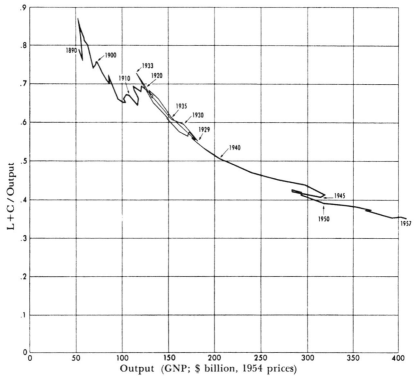

Figure 9. Trend of average real cost of output in the United States, 1890–1957

situations implied by the slope of the postulated cost curves in panels 8-a and 8-b. The possibility that the downtrend of the observed dynamic *ah* curve might be due to a decreasing-cost, static social production function is not considered here. It is an explanation that does not necessarily depend on parametric change, and has already been dealt with in the discussion of parametrically invariant models in Part II. In the following paragraphs, we consider three basic types of parametric change.

Institutionally Generated Changes in Social Costs.   In Part II, we defined the optimal expansion path as that associated with a zero price for resources. If, for institutional reasons, there is a positive reservation price for resources, they will be used less liberally. Output will be less at every level of labor-capital availability, and labor-capital cost per unit of output will be higher. In the models of Part II this would mean that the expansion paths would all lie closer to the $L + C$ axis than the optimal paths as we defined them. Under these conditions, a favorable institutional change, resulting in a reduction in the reservation price for resources, would reduce average social cost. Conversely, an increase in the reservation price would raise average cost.

With multiple products and inputs (as in Chapter 6), there is a different maximum output (welfare optimum) and a different cost minimum (least-cost combination) for every set of prices. For institutional reasons, actual observable expansion paths are not maximal, or cost functions minimal. The criteria actually employed in the economy for choosing the scale, composition, and method of production are at best only approximations of those embodied in traditional economic theory, being based on rules of thumb and incomplete knowledge. In addition, markets are variously imperfect, and prices are subject to manipulation in varying degree. It seems probable that, in the United States since the Civil War, changes in the reservation prices of resources have been such as to increase, rather than reduce, the labor-capital cost of output. The reason is that virtually free land, abundant at the beginning of the period, is now almost nonexistent. This is not because all land is now "in use," but because all land is in private or public hands, from which, even if idle, it can be dislodged only at a price. The price may sometimes consist heavily of taxes, but nonetheless is relevant in influencing social cost by influencing the input structure in extractive industries. To determine how much reservation price has increased would require a special study on the economically effective terms by which access to natural resource services can be obtained.

Sociotechnical Changes that Shift the Social Production Function. Since the social production function is defined only for a given set of sociotechnical conditions, change in any of these conditions will shift the function. In general, the influence of these other socio-technical changes is that the production function of a modern, technologically advanced society will consistently shift downward. The effects of cumulatively increasing knowledge usually will result in cost-reducing shifts by improving the quality of labor and capital, by stimulating labor-saving, capital-saving, and resource-saving innovations, and by inducing social and administrative innovations that improve the economic efficiency of sociotechnical organization. These influences operate regardless of the resource situation, and we know that historically they have been of major and increasing importance.

Autonomous changes in the product mix also may shift the production function. As new products are introduced, the number of resource-saving or cost-saving substitutions is increased, and new gains (similar to those discussed in Part II) become available. Even without introduction of new products, there may be changes in tastes toward, or away from, relatively resource-saving, capital-saving, or labor-intensive commodities, with consequent shifts in the social cost functions and effects on the trend of average real cost.

Changes in the resource intensity of final demand may reflect changes in the whim of fashion, in which case they have no assignable directionality; or they may be partly induced, like those discussed in Chapter 6, which reflect operation of Engel's law. But increased income per capita also induces a desire for high protein and other protective, or prestige, foods, which often are relatively resource intensive. Similarly, modern industrial techniques require large amounts of mineral resources, metallic and nonmetallic, including fuels. On the other hand, the increased use of resource-intensive products induces the adoption of resource-saving technologies and substitutions and, more important, an intensive scientific search for such possibilities.

CHANGE AND THE TREND OF RESOURCE CONVERSION COST

First recall the initial shape of the resource conversion path. The continuous and smooth conversion path employed in Part II was a convenient first approximation, but the discontinuous and kinked path, *Oab* . . . , shown in Figure 10 is more realistic. The latter explicitly recognizes that resources occur in relatively large plateaus,

some of which, represented by linear segments, are of essentially
constant quality. Horizontal segments in the discontinuous path represent situations in which a lumpy outlay is required to reach a new
resource plateau of variable or constant quality. Examples are
bridges across rivers or canyons; oil wells and mine shafts; forest
roads; irrigation and reforestation projects. Vertical linear segments
represent plateaus of resources that, once reached, are of standard

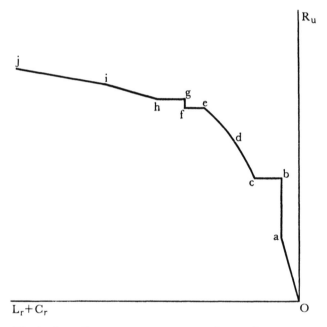

Figure 10. A discontinuous resource conversion path

quality; there being no variable resource conversion cost, total labor-
capital cost does not increase as more resources are used. The left-
ward-sloping linear segments represent plateaus of resources of constant but substandard quality: since conversion cost per unit is
constant, total labor-capital cost increases, but by a constant amount
per unit of R_u employed. Curvilinear segments represent blocks of
resources of continuously declining marginal quality.

We have assumed that the conversion path, like the social cost
function, is a least-cost solution that minimizes labor-capital cost
per unit of standard resource equivalent. Assumption of a different

benefit-cost calculus, or the existence of institutional arrangements that prevented effective application of this criterion, would yield a different result. Consequently, changes in business rationale, in the reservation price of resources, or in other relevant institutional influences will alter the parameters of the resource conversion path and cause it to shift, with resulting effects on the trend of cost.

Certain parametric changes may be classified according to whether they alter the processes of resource extinction or contribute to expansion of the resource base. The factors affecting resource extinction are changes in the resource intensity of the product mix; technological changes affecting rates of depletion and destruction; technological and other changes affecting the degree of waste or failure to use resources; and modifications of processes that tend to produce ecological unbalance. Factors contributing to resource expansion are the discovery of new supplies of familiar resources and new types of resources; development of new conversion techniques and new uses for available, known types of resources; and changes that increase the quantity or quality of resources.

Extinction shortens and eventually eliminates segments of the discontinuous resource conversion path, and thus alters the shape, as well as the position, of the conversion path. Similarly, discovery of new supplies of old resources, or of entirely new resources, alters old segments or creates new ones which must be introduced at their proper position in the quality scale, thus also altering the shape and position of the conversion function. Development of new uses for plentiful elements of the environment will improve resource quality and shift the corresponding segments to new, improved positions on the conversion path.

Resource extinction is a continuous function of the aggregate of production over time. Resource expansion may also be if, as we believe, resource searching, finding, and innovation are built-in responses of a growing economy in the modern age. When the costs of nuclear power are reduced, atomic fuels may come to occupy positions in the quality spectrum superior to fossil fuels. Thus extinction and expansion are two among the many relevant historical developments determining the trend of social cost.

Technological advance and change in the quality of labor and capital affect the resource function in more complex ways. Technological improvements that reduce the conversion cost of a particular type of resource are a clear case of an increase in resource quality that favorably shifts the affected segment in the quality spectrum. One may also imagine that new methods of resource conversion might change substandard resources into "superstandard" resources—that is, resources that reduced aggregate social cost below that attainable with former "standard" resources. This could be represented by a new segment of appropriate slope (necessarily at the base of the resource conversion path), lying wholly to the right of the initial origin. Some changes, such as deterioration in the physical vigor or training of labor or management, or in social organization, may shift the function in the contrary direction, and vice versa.

Summarizing, the effects of sociotechnical change on the resource conversion function and path produce through time a trend of resource conversion cost analogous to the trend of social cost. As growth proceeds, society may be presumed to follow a given resource conversion function and path so long as no parametric change occurs. With change, it will shift to a new function and follow that. The new function will reflect influences that may have shifted it vertically downward or upward; reduced or increased the degree of curvature, and, in the limiting case, made it linear; or altered the angle to the horizontal. These influences, which may affect the path over all or part of its range, are brought about by resource extinction and expansion and by technological, ecological, institutional, and other changes that alter the labor-capital cost of resource conversion. The historical record—the resultant of all these conditions and of growth —could clearly trace out a path quite different in shape from that of the postulated static resource conversion path. This new dynamic path, which would be analogous to *ah* on Figure 8, and could easily be supposed to have a similar downward inclination, would be the trend of resource conversion cost.

The trend of social cost and the trend of resource conversion cost have been identified. The former, it must be emphasized, includes the latter. In other words, all parametric influences that affect the resource conversion function are transmitted to the social production function. But the social cost function, the social production function, and the expansion path are each subject to parametric changes of their own. For this reason, the record for the United States presented in Figure 9, which shows increasing returns in the social production process as a whole, is entirely consistent with a hypothesis that the trend of resource conversion cost was increasing.

In our empirical tests in the next two chapters, we would like to examine resource conversion costs to ascertain whether the trend for these has been upward. But resource conversion cost cannot be observed and measured directly because, in fact, the economy does not upgrade resources to standard, and then engage in extractive activity. Rather, the resource conversion process and the extractive production process are combined activities in most resource industries. The method we are forced to adopt is to measure changes in the real cost of producing extractive output, E, this being the earliest resource activity for which time series data on output and costs can be obtained. As in Chapter 6, we collapse the resource conversion process into the extractive sector, hoping that evidence of increasing resource scarcity, if it exists, will not be lost among the other influences that affect the cost of extractive output.

Chapter 8

THE UNIT COST OF EXTRACTIVE PRODUCTS

A QUANTITATIVE test of the observable presence or absence of "increasing economic scarcity of natural resources" in the United States, from approximately 1870 to the latter part of the 1950's, is attempted in this chapter. The hypothesis to be tested grows out of the model of historical growth, which showed that increasing natural resource scarcity would reveal itself in an increasing trend of unit cost of resource conversion as reflected in extractive products. For the test, we have chosen the United States—not only because the requisite data are more readily available than for other countries, but also because the economy is dynamic and the ratio of population to resources has experienced great change.

Setting for the Quantitative Test

Our decision to cover a long period was deliberate. One rather obvious reason is that the scarcity doctrine is usually applied to the long term. Business cycles, wars, and other transitory influences, in the short term, could obscure the hypothesized long-term tendency. The other reason for having chosen a period of almost a hundred years is less obvious, but quite important. According to received doctrine, scarcity and its effects increase as population and incomes grow and as depletion cumulates. A long period permits observation and comparison of data for the beginning and ending subperiods.

The latter reason is particularly important with the United States as subject of the case study. At the beginning of the period, the nation was an "underdeveloped" country. Its population was less than 40 million. Prior to World War I, the United States was only thinly settled in its western areas. The nation was anxious to bring resources into use for political as well as economic reasons. Final land entries under the Homestead Act rose persistently. The population density west of the Mississippi River did not reach 15 persons per square mile until 1920. The extent of western lands without population was so great early in the period that it was urgent public policy to foster settlement. Great volumes of land were given to the railroads to subsidize transcontinental construction. On one basis or another, land was made available at nominal fees to settlers. Until approximately World War I, the government policy was to attract population to the United States.

The important point is that the early part of our long period might be considered quite close to the Utopian case of no resource scarcity. And the latter part might be viewed as beyond the time when unused resources of standard quality were available. In a comparison of the early and later years, important contrasts in the record of economic growth may be detected. Population has multiplied more than four-fold. The annual output of goods and services today is roughly twenty times as great as in 1870, and consumption of the products of agriculture, mining, forests, and fisheries is some six times as great. Only in gross area is the economy virtually unchanged. The increase has been only 11,000 square miles—the bulk of it in Hawaii and Puerto Rico. This increase is less than one-third of 1 per cent of the 3.6 million square miles of 1870.

The nation had thus passed from underdevelopment to an advanced economic status. The process was continuous, and it is not possible precisely to date the transition. If it is useful to visualize a date, there may be merit in one in the neighborhood of 1920. The Conservation Movement, concerned with agitating for revised natural resource policies, had its terminus about then. Final homestead entries reached a peak decade in 1910–20, and thereafter declined very sharply. By the close of World War I, the United States had become the world's greatest financial creditor, rather than a debtor. Relative to its former open immigration policy, the United States virtually closed its doors to foreign settlers in the 1920's. And it was about that time when the United States ceased to be a net exporter of extractive products.

Thus, in the period that is covered by our quantitative test, one

could expect to find evidence of increasing economic scarcity of natural
resources. The United States has been a rather free economy in which
the forces of demand and supply have had ample opportunity for
mutual adjustment. Sociotechnical changes have been many and
major. Production and consumption have increased many times. Yet
the nation's geographic boundaries, and thus the physical resource
limits, have increased little. On the one hand, there has been ample
opportunity for depletion of exhaustible resources and intensive pressures on renewable ones; on the other, there have been discoveries,
technical advances, and substitutions. Finally, although rapid growth
has characterized our whole history, it is possible to break the almost
century-long period into two roughly equal parts: the first, a time of
underdevelopment relative to physical resources; the second, a growth
period of an advanced and mature industrial economy.

The case is thus the actual historical situation of a society undergoing change in its natural resource availability and in other technical
and social conditions. The hypothesis to be tested is that there was an
increase in natural resource economic scarcity and effect and, as
already indicated, that it will be revealed by an increasing trend in
the unit cost of extractive products.

Test of the Hypothesis

We now turn to our test for increasing natural resource scarcity by
examining the trend of unit cost of extractive products in the agricultural, mineral, forestry, and fishing industries. We are concerned
only with trend—with long-term movements, largely shorn of business
cycles and the influences of weather, war, and other transient aberrations. The following definitions are used:

L = Labor input, or the number of workers employed in the respective extractive industries or the nation as a whole.

C = Capital input, or the volume of capital employed in the respective extractive industries or the nation as a whole, measured in constant prices.

Gross O = Gross output of the respective industries, in physical units. When unlike units are aggregated, the units are weighted by their relative values or prices per unit in a base period.

Net O = Net output of the respective industries, or gross output adjusted downward to exclude the value of purchased materials used in producing the output.

Thus, $L + C/Net\ O$ is the labor plus capital required to produce a unit of net extractive output. And $L/Net\ O$ is the labor required to produce a unit of such output. Our preferred measure is $L + C/Net\ O;$ we use this to the extent available. For reference (and in the case of capital input because its measurement is more precarious than the measures of labor and output), we also show *Gross O, L,* and $L/Net\ O$ in the figures accompanying the text.

Since index numbers are used throughout, the absolute levels of the measures are irrelevant. The *relative changes* are what concern us. We therefore use ratio charts, in which slopes of the lines show relative changes.[1]

AGRICULTURE

In Figure 11, we present salient information for the test of the agricultural scarcity models. Measured at decade intervals, both the gross and net output curves have increased persistently, although irregularly, over the whole period since 1870. By 1957, gross output of agriculture had increased to more than four times the original level. Net output was more than three times the original level. There is thus no question that there has been opportunity for diminishing returns caused by growth-induced resource scarcity to manifest itself. Data on labor and labor plus capital inputs in agriculture are also shown on Figure 11-a for reference.

Figure 11-b indicates that the increasing scarcity hypothesis was invalid for agriculture for the period 1870 to the present. According to the hypothesis, scarcity and its increase would force the unit cost of agricultural output to rise. But not only did unit cost of net output fail to rise during this period, it actually experienced a downward trend—whether cost is measured in labor plus capital or in labor alone. From the beginning to end of the period, unit cost of agri-

[1] See Appendix B for a brief discussion of statistical sources and techniques.

cultural products declined by more than half, if cost is measured in labor plus capital. The decline is about two-thirds if unit cost is measured in labor alone.

Analysis of the time sequence is particularly damaging to the hypothesis that scarcity increases with economic growth and time. Instead of the expected less favorable unit cost record during the later period than during the earlier one, Figure 11-b shows that the reverse

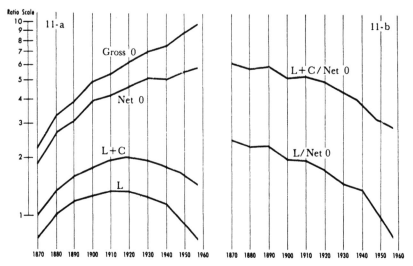

Figure 11. U.S. agriculture: output, labor and capital inputs, and cost per unit of product, 1870–1957

actually occurred in agriculture. The period 1870–1919 was characterized by a mildly declining unit cost of agricultural products. During the period 1919–57, when the scarcity mechanism of the model was supposed to be much stronger, agriculture actually experienced a more sharply declining unit cost. During 1870–1919, unit cost in terms of $L + C$ declined by a compound rate of 0.4 per cent per year. But comparable unit cost during 1919–57 declined by 1.4 per cent per year.

An accounting for these phenomena appears in Figure 11-a. The increase of agricultural output in the early period was accompanied by an increase in labor and labor plus capital. The somewhat less rapid increase of output after 1919, on the other hand, was achieved

while labor and labor plus capital inputs to agriculture were substantially declining. Results in agriculture, therefore, offer adverse
testimony, rather than support of the scarcity hypothesis.

MINERALS

Because minerals have been subject to depletion to a far greater
degree than most other natural resources, there is particular interest
in applying the scarcity hypothesis to this industry. Also on the score
of growth impact, the case is particularly interesting. Demand for
minerals has increased enormously since 1870—perhaps forty times
—and thus more than national demand for all goods and services
as a whole.

Figure 12-a presents the data for minerals output and for labor and

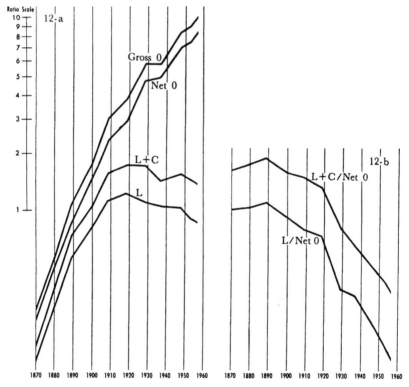

Figure 12. U.S. minerals: output, labor and capital inputs, and cost per
unit of product, 1870–1957

capital input. Except for interruption by the depression of the 1930's, output has increased rather steadily, although with retardation in the rate of increase. Unlike agriculture, the rate of increase in net output was as rapid as in gross output. As in agriculture, employment of labor and labor plus capital increased during the early portion of the period, and then declined in the latter.

The quantitative test for scarcity-induced increasing cost is presented in Figure 12-b. The factual result is, again, exactly the opposite of hypothetical predictions, except during 1870–89 (when, coincidentally, the data are rather weak). From 1890 onward, costs per unit of net mineral output, measured in either labor or labor and capital, have declined rapidly and persistently. By the end of the period, the cost of labor and capital per unit of product was only one-fifth as large as in 1889. The decline is even greater for labor cost alone. Again, the increases in productivity were more rapid in the latter half of the period than in the early half. From 1889 to 1919, it is estimated that the $L + C$ unit cost of minerals declined at the rate of 1.2 per cent per year; from 1919 to 1957, the rate of decline was 3.2 per cent per year.

In summary: Instead of increasing unit costs in the minerals industry, as called for by the scarcity hypothesis, a declining trend of cost was experienced. And the more sharply increasing returns occurred later, contrary to the hypothesis. This is so with respect to both labor plus capital and labor alone.

FORESTRY

Salient data for forestry, so far as we have them, are presented in Figure 13. The forestry output curve increased steadily to about 1910 (in annual data, the peak occurred in 1907). Since then, it has had no persistent upward or downward trend; in annual data, the output has shown considerable short-term fluctuation.

The second curve from the top shows the output of lumber alone. The next curve shows labor input in logging (that is, the cutting and hauling of lumberable logs). The use of lumber only is necessary since there are no adequate data on employment in the gathering of pulpwood or fuelwood. The labor input in logging increased to the 1920's, and has had a level trend since, although fluctuating considerably.

Data on capital input are not available. Finally, the lowest curve shows the unit cost of sawlogs—labor cost per unit of output of lumberable logs. On balance, this increased to 1920, and since has remained roughly constant or trended downward.

The forestry evidence for the period as a whole (but not since 1920) thus supports the increasing scarcity hypothesis. Unit cost experienced an increase over the 87-year period, averaging 0.9 per cent a year. Further, it is very likely that, if capital input data were avail-

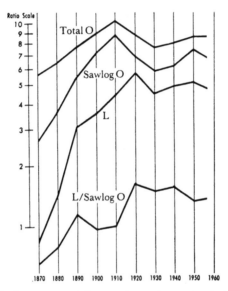

Figure 13. U.S. forestry: total output, sawlog output, labor input for sawlogs and cost per unit of sawlog output, 1870–1957

able for forestry, we would find that the rate of increase in unit cost in terms of labor plus capital was somewhat greater than in labor cost alone. This suspicion is based on a surmise that the ratio of capital to labor has increased in forestry, as it has in agriculture. Thus, we believe that, if capital data were available for forestry, the scarcity hypothesis for the 1870–1957 period would be more strongly supported than it is by the statistical evidence represented in Figure 13.

Again, however, as in the case of agriculture and minerals, the time sequence of cost movements is adverse to the hypothesis. The unit cost record is more favorable in the late period than earlier. But this opposition to the hypothesis is less serious in forestry than in agriculture and minerals. In forestry, output did not increase in the latter subperiod. There have been major substitutions away from lumber, forestry's major component, as the result of absolutely increasing unit costs up to World War I, and relatively increasing unit costs as compared with other structural material since that time. This undoubtedly retarded the pressure upon forest resources in the latter period.

COMMERCIAL FISHING

The relevant data for the commercial fishing industry are shown in Figure 14. Both the gross output and employment statistics are of poor quality, particularly for the early years, and neither net output nor capital input data are available. To the extent the data are valid for our problem, they contradict the scarcity hypothesis. The trend of output has been upward, while labor has trended horizontally, with the result that labor cost per unit of output has declined since the end of the nineteenth century.

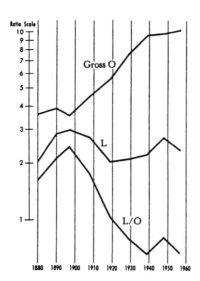

Figure 14. U.S. commercial fishing: output, labor input, and cost per unit of product, 1870–1957

EXTRACTIVE OUTPUT AS AN AGGREGATE

While extractive activity in our analysis includes agriculture, minerals, forestry, and fishing, the first two industries dominate it. This is shown by the bars of Figure 15. Together agriculture and minerals have accounted for about 90 per cent of the value of extrac-

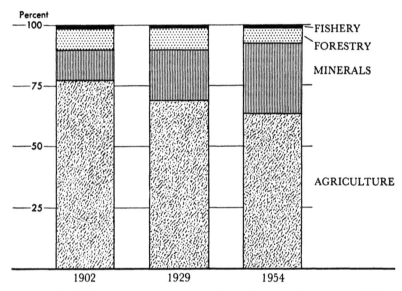

Figure 15. U.S. extractive output: value of output in current dollars, percentage composition, 1902, 1929, and 1954

tive output (quantities multiplied by prices in the respective years) since at least the beginning of the century.[2]

The figure also shows that: (1) agriculture has been, and is, the major extractive industry, even though it has been relatively declining; (2) mining has been steadily becoming a more important extractive industry; (3) the third industry in economic importance is

[2] If Figure 15 had been compiled in terms of value added, rather than value of output, the rise in importance of minerals relative to agriculture would be greater, as shown by the following comparative figures:

Minerals relative to agriculture	1902	1929	1954
Value of output	18%	28%	36%
Value added	18	29	46

forestry, but its economic importance has been relatively declining; and (4) relative to the other extractive industries, fisheries are of minor economic importance.

We now examine the statistical record of these major extractive industries as a whole for signs of increasing unit costs. When the preceding data for agriculture, minerals, forest products, and fishing are combined, with appropriate weights based on economic values, they yield the curves which appear in Figure 16.

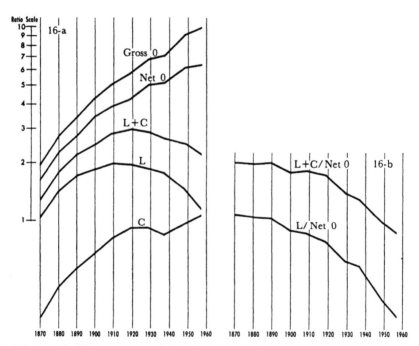

Figure 16. U.S. extractive industries: output, labor and capital inputs, and cost per unit of output, 1870–1957

Extractive output has increased steadily since 1870, gross output somewhat more rapidly than net. Labor and labor plus capital inputs to the extractive industries increased less rapidly than output during the first half of the period; they then began a persistent decline, which has now continued for forty years or so.

As shown in Figure 16-b, unit costs of extractive goods have declined during the period under review. Not only does this contradict the scarcity hypothesis, but there is further contradiction in the fact that declines in unit costs have been significantly more rapid in the period since World War I than before.

We thus find by empirical observation that the natural resource scarcity hypothesis, as formulated earlier in this chapter, has been invalid in the United States during 1870–1957. Contrary to the hypothesis which called for increase in the labor-capital cost of extractive output, the unit cost of extractive output has declined. How do we account for this outcome?

The implications of the foregoing factual evidence are our concern in the remainder of this chapter. We consider the quantitative importance of each of several influences by which, conceivably, the economy escaped the prediction of increasing natural resource scarcity—and thereby increasing unit costs of extractive goods—under conditions of economic growth. In this empirical accounting, cessation of population growth is ruled out as a contributory cause, since U.S. population grew at the substantial rate of 1.7 per cent a year.

We treat, in order, the following influences:

1) The weighting system used in the output indexes.
2) Substitution of extractive commodities with relatively lower or declining costs.
3) Recourse to foreign supplies of extractive goods as a means of averting economic pressure on indigenous natural resources.
4) Changes in natural resource availabilities.
5) Technological advance in the resource conversion function (where, conceptually, low-quality resources are upgraded to standard) and in the production of extractive goods.

A sixth influence is government intervention, which undoubtedly has played a role in facilitating the decline in unit costs of extractive goods. The government has provided large volumes of services to the extractive sector. These have been, in whole or in part, paid by general governmental revenues and not assessed as a charge upon the extractive sectors. We suspect that the extractive industries have differentially benefited from this phenomenon, as compared with similar assistance to manufacturing and services. But we have not made an attempt to investigate this hypothesis.

The Weighting System

Different weighting systems could affect the aggregate unit cost indexes. Figure 17 shows the index of labor-capital cost per unit of output in extraction based on three different sets of weights for output. In each case, every commodity's output in the extractive cost index is weighted by the price of that commodity relative to other prices in the extractive sector, the prices being those of the widely separated years, 1902, 1929, and 1954.

The comparisons in Figure 17 show that the weighting system for the output indexes has not been primarily responsible for the contra-

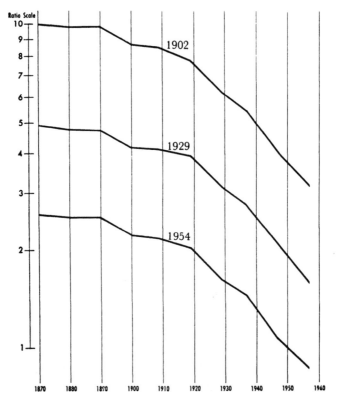

Figure 17. Labor and capital cost per unit of U.S. extractive output, 1902, 1929, and 1954 weights

diction of the scarcity hypothesis in our test. The extractive cost index declines at similar rates irrespective of the weighting system. In the 1902 price-weighted index (of gross output), the unit cost of the extractive goods index has an average decline of 1.32 per cent per annum; this compares with 1.25 per cent for the 1954 index, and an intermediate figure for the 1929 index.

We obtained similar results in both agriculture and minerals by varying the weight of output of individual commodities according to their prices in 1902, 1929, or 1954. Figures 18 and 19 show these comparisons. The 1954 weighting system which we have used does not primarily account for the fact of declining unit cost in total agriculture. The situation is similar in minerals as an aggregate. All three weighting systems show substantial and similar declining unit costs.

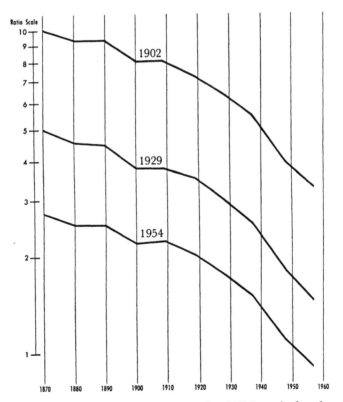

Figure 18. Labor and capital cost per unit of U.S. agricultural output, 1902, 1929, and 1954 weights

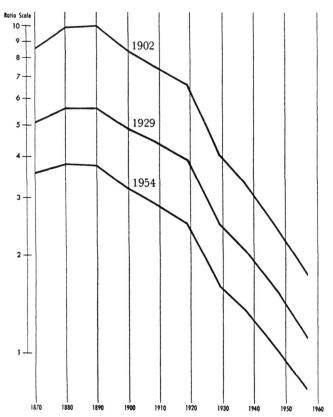

Figure 19. Labor and capital cost per unit of U.S. mining output, 1902,
1929, and 1954 weights

Substitutions of Less Costly Commodities

A major type of accounting leads us to examine individual commodities within agriculture, minerals, and the other extractive industries. That this may be extremely important for understanding the
declining unit costs can be easily shown. Assume, as one possibility,
that natural resource scarcity had been operative in half of the major
agricultural and mineral commodities, and that the opposite had
occurred with equal force in the other agricultural and mineral commodities. Then the observed significant declines in unit costs for all
of both agriculture and minerals would have been the result of shifting
from commodities with increasing costs to those with decreasing costs.
The latter would be progressively accounting for larger and larger

shares of total agricultural and mineral output, and thereby of total extraction.[3] If, on the other hand, the great majority of the individual major commodities in each of these industries experienced declining unit cost, then evidence of denial of the scarcity hypothesis is more pervasive, and there must be further reasons for the phenomenon. In the first case conjectured, the test of the scarcity hypothesis produces negative results because substitutions away from rising-cost extractive commodities favorably change the composition of our aggregate measures; this is less so, or not so, in the second case.

UNIT LABOR COSTS IN THE AGRICULTURAL AND MINERAL SECTORS

There is a simple way to demonstrate that demand-induced and cost-induced substitutions away from extractive commodities with increasing costs do not primarily account for the fact of declining unit cost in extraction as a whole, or in either agriculture or minerals. This is simply to examine individually the unit cost records of the major commodities and groups in each of the extractive sectors. In this procedure, only labor costs and gross outputs can be used, since neither capital input data nor net output figures are available for the individual commodities. For reference, we show the analogous labor per unit of gross output in the aggregates.

For agriculture, this is done in Figures 20 and 21. In Figure 20, the trend of labor cost per unit of output is shown for all agricultural crops and for nine major commodities. In Figure 21, the labor cost per unit of total agricultural output is shown, along with that for livestock and products, including poultry, milk cows, and meat animals. Both figures show that the rates of decline in unit labor cost have been quite varied. Cost has declined less rapidly in livestock and products (particularly meat animals) than in crops. Among crops, vegetables and tobacco have experienced smaller cost declines than grains, oil crops, sugar, and cotton. But, without exception, the indexes show declining unit labor cost, most of significant rates.

All minerals, as well as the three major mineral groups—fuels, metals, and nonmetals—are shown in Figure 22. Clearly, substitutions among the three groups do not primarily account for the fact of de-

---

[3] This, of course, would show up to some degree if weights were changed as in the preceding discussion.

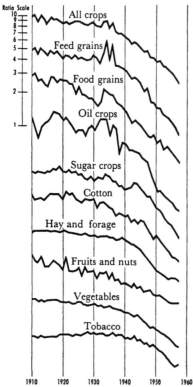

Figure 20. U.S. agriculture: labor cost per unit of output in all crops and nine major commodities, 1910–57

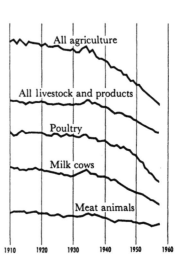

Figure 21. U.S. agriculture: labor cost per unit of total output and of output of livestock and products, 1910–57

cline in the all-minerals unit labor cost, since each group has itself experienced rapid decline in unit labor costs.

Pursuing experience with minerals farther, we show in Figure 23 the unit labor cost record for the mineral fuels aggregate and its components—petroleum and natural gas, bituminous coal, and anthracite coal. Here we observe two significant developments. First, each of the mineral fuels has experienced major decline in unit labor cost; and, therefore, shifts among these fuels do not primarily account for the fact of significantly declining fuel cost in the aggregate. Also, there has been a substantial shift in the composition of fuel output, from coal to petroleum and natural gas. Since labor cost per unit of

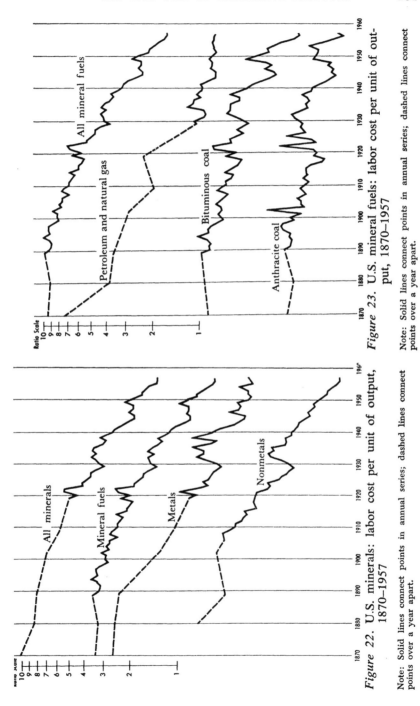

Figure 23. U.S. mineral fuels: labor cost per unit of output, 1870–1957

Note: Solid lines connect points in annual series; dashed lines connect points over a year apart.

Figure 22. U.S. minerals: labor cost per unit of output, 1870–1957

Note: Solid lines connect points in annual series; dashed lines connect points over a year apart.

output is, and has been, lower in these latter fuels than in coal, some of the rapidity in the decline in labor cost per unit of mineral fuels as a whole results from the substitution of oil and gas for coal.

A further breakdown is shown in Figure 24, which presents the indexes of unit labor cost of all metals, iron ore, copper, and lead and zinc. The rapid decline in the all-metals series is roughly matched in iron ore and copper; but the decline in lead and zinc is quite small. We know that domestic lead and zinc outputs have fallen since World War I and the late 1920's because the economy has made substitutions for lead. Here, then, is a case in which a part of the decline of unit costs of aggregate metals can be accounted for by substitution away from the commodity with a relatively unfavorable cost per-

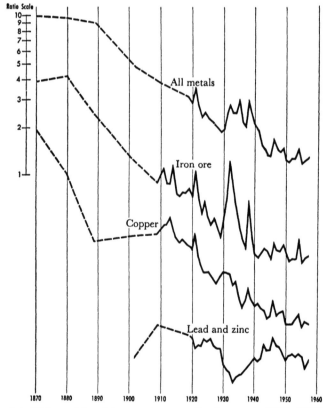

Figure 24. U.S. metals: labor cost per unit of output, 1870–1957

Note: Solid lines connect points in annual series; dashed lines connect points over a year apart.

formance—presumably because of natural resource scarcity. The marked decline in unit cost of metals in the aggregate is accounted for primarily by decline in the most important of the individual metals, rather than by substitutions among the metals.

A similar operation for all nonmetals and for five components— sand and gravel, stone, phosphate rock, sulfur, and fluorspar—is performed in Figure 25. All have declined in unit labor cost; and substitu-

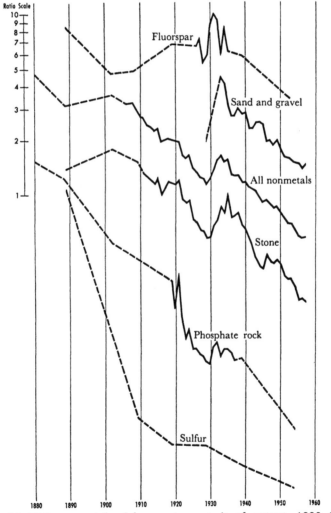

Figure 25. U.S. nonmetals: labor cost per unit of output, 1880–1957

Note: Solid lines connect points in annual series; dashed lines connect points over a year apart.

tions do not account for the decline in the aggregate index of non-metals.

By value, forestry was about 9 per cent of the extractive industry in 1902, and about 7 per cent in 1954. The influence of forest products in aggregate extractive unit costs, therefore, is not large. For forest products, the statistical quality of the data is somewhat more uncertain than in agriculture and minerals. But, subject to this drawback, we have concluded the following: (1) There have been significant cost-induced substitutions away from forest products and toward mineral-based ones. Alone among extractive groups, unit labor costs of forest products have increased since 1870; relative prices have increased correspondingly; and the volume of output is no higher than half a century ago. (2) It is our judgment, based on indirect evidence (primarily relative price performance), that labor cost per unit of lumber has increased significantly relative to labor cost per unit of pulpwood, veneer, and naval stores. And we think it is only lumber among the forestry products for which the economy has made significant substitutions on cost grounds. (3) The greatly increased use of cost-induced and preferred substitutes—such other structural materials as metals, masonry, and plastics—has significantly eased the pressures on timber resources. This seems to be an important reason why unit cost of forest products has held constant, rather than increased, since about 1920.

SUBSTITUTIONS FOR AGRICULTURAL AND FOREST LAND

The substitution of minerals for fertile land is even more pervasive and significant than the substitution of structural materials for lumber. For our interest in the whole spectrum of natural resources, it is useful to elaborate on this phenomenon which has greatly eased the pressure on agricultural land because of the reduced need for increased agricultural and forest output.

The substitution of mechanical and electrical power equipment for work animals through the entire economy, no less than on farms, involved substitution of mineral fuel calories for agricultural feed. A rough calculation based on Btu's of mineral fuel indicates that if the United States today had to rely upon work animals for its "horse-power," the feed would require 15 to 30 times as many acres of cropland as are in use in the country. The substitution of mineral fuels for fuel wood was similarly important. The innovation of chemical fertilizers in farming has meant, ultimately, a substitution of fuels and the other minerals from which they are made for agricultural land. The substitution of synthetic fibers and plastics for natural fibers involves use of mineral fuels instead of agricultural and forest lands. At present yields, the land which would be required to furnish natural fibers equal to the present production of synthetic fiber is about 5 to 10 million acres. In effect, insecticides and fungicides, which primarily derive from mineral materials, also represent a mineral substitution for land.

It is clear that the internal dynamics of the extractive industries and of the industries which consume raw materials have, under conditions of technological change, worked very strongly to substitute natural resources which are economically more "plentiful" for those which are less so.

The Influence of Foreign Trade

Our effort to account for the observed statistical contradiction of the scarcity hypothesis continues with an examination of foreign trade in the extractive industries—but, in the case of minerals, gold and silver are excluded, since foreign trade in these is governed by monetary policy. The United States has not, by hypothesis, experienced increasing economic scarcity of natural resources, except in timber in the period preceding World War I—this, we have already determined. The question now is: "To what extent have increases in the quantity of imported extractive goods (net imports valued in constant prices) been responsible for the avoidance of increases in unit costs of extractive products?"

EXTRACTIVE GOODS AS AN AGGREGATE

First, we observe the statistical record. The United States was a net exporter of extractive goods at the beginning of our period, in 1870. Annual net exports increased at an irregular pace to reach a peak about the turn of the century. They then declined to a zero figure in the 1920's. Annual net imports were about $1 billion (in 1954 prices) in the late 1930's, and reached about $2 billion after 1950. In summary, the United States became a net importer of extractive goods in the interwar period, after having been a net exporter previously.

How large are the net foreign trade magnitudes relative to U.S. consumption of extractive goods? Figure 26 shows net U.S. exports

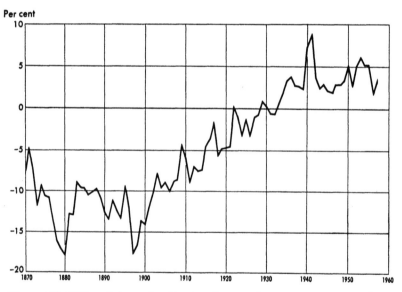

Figure 26. U.S. net imports of extractive goods as a percentage of consumption, 1870–1957

or imports of extractive commodities as a percentage of consumption —both in 1954 prices. Net imports, consistent since the early 1930's, have been small in relative size. They were 2.5 per cent of consumption in 1937–39, and increased to 4.1 per cent in 1951–57. Viewing extractive goods as an aggregate, net imports have thus moderated domestic demand for indigenous natural resources by a small figure in the period since the United States ceased to be a net exporter.

FOREIGN TRADE IN AGRICULTURAL GOODS

In agricultural commodities, also, the United States shifted from a
position of annual net exports to annual net imports in the 1920's or
1930's. Here, too, the magnitudes of net imports have since been
quite small. In absolute terms, expressed in 1954 dollars, there has
been no trend; most of the magnitudes fall below $1 billion. Relative
to U.S. production and consumption of agricultural goods, net imports have trended downward since the 1930's, as shown in Figure 27.

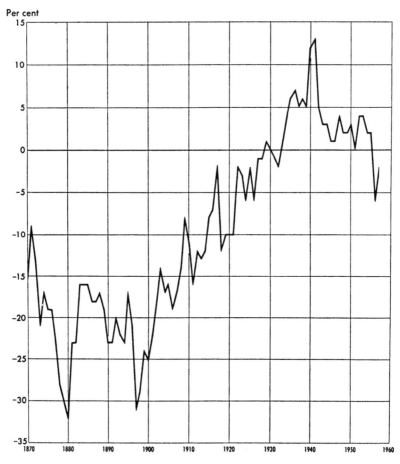

Figure 27. U.S. net imports of agricultural commodities as a percentage
of consumption, 1870–1957

Net imports of agricultural goods from 1950 through 1957 were less than 1 per cent of consumption of such goods. Net imports have been becoming absolutely smaller; in 1956 and 1957, for example, the United States again was a net exporter. If agriculture is viewed as an aggregate, net imports have not played a significant role in facilitating the decline in unit cost of U.S. production of agricultural goods.

This is true for agriculture as a whole, but it is proper to ask which agricultural commodities we are now importing. Since agricultural products are so varied, it is possible that tendencies toward increasing cost of certain domestic products have been avoided by the substitution of imports. The answer, as indicated by Table 3, turns out to be

TABLE 3. U.S. Agricultural Foreign Trade, 1870–1957

(In billions of 1954 dollars)

Year	Exports (1)	Supplementary imports (2)	Exports less supplementary imports (1) less (2) (3)	Complementary imports (4)	Net exports or imports [a] (3) less (4) (5)
1870	1.07	0.10	0.97	0.21	0.75
1880	2.57	0.16	2.41	0.34	2.07
1890	2.63	0.27	2.36	0.44	1.92
1900	3.58	0.40	3.18	0.60	2.58
1910	2.76	0.57	2.19	0.75	1.44
1919	4.07	1.25	2.82	1.31	1.51
1929	2.92	1.29	1.63	1.86	−0.23
1939	2.16	1.14	1.02	2.02	−1.00
1949	3.23	1.27	1.96	2.41	−0.45
1954	2.67	1.24	1.43	2.04	−0.61
1957	4.04	1.30	2.74	2.31	0.43

[a] Net imports are identified by minus signs.

quite interesting. In the table, imports are classified in two groups: supplementary imports of commodities produced in the United States, the two largest being sugar and apparel wool; and complementary imports of commodities not produced in this country, chiefly coffee, cocoa, tea, carpet wool, bananas, rubber, and silk.

The United States is still a net exporter of the types of farm goods permitted by its climate. Thus, for these commodities, foreign trade has not moderated pressure upon indigenous agricultural land and is not responsible for the declining unit costs of U.S. agricultural goods.

The factor which has swung the United States into the net import column for agricultural goods is complementary imports—the gradual increase in imports of the "exotic" commodities which have always come from foreign sources. Of these, coffee imports alone have been running annually at about $1.4 billion (in 1954 prices) since World War II, after having risen during the interwar period from about $700 million to about $1 billion a year.

FOREIGN TRADE IN MINERALS

The foreign trade situation in minerals (still excluding gold and silver) is quite different from that described for all extractive goods and for agriculture. Summarized, it looks as follows: (1) The United States ceased to be a persistent net exporter of minerals about the time of World War I. During the 1920's and 1930's, it was roughly in a balanced position. It was a net exporter for 12 years and a net importer for 8 years. Since World War II, the United States has become a large net importer of minerals—in absolute terms, about $1.5 billion (as large as coffee); and in relative terms, about 8 per cent of minerals consumption. (2) In certain mineral commodities, partial substitution of imports for domestic production facilitated the decline in unit costs of such domestic production, by moderating demand pressures upon limited domestic resources. Except for the substitution of imports, the record of very rapidly declining unit costs of domestic mineral products in the aggregate, and of some major commodities, might have shown a more moderate decline. And in the case of lead, zinc, and fluorspar, the relative substitution of imports may have averted a unit cost increase in domestic production.

Figure 28 presents mineral imports as a percentage of domestic consumption—both valued in 1954 prices. Before World War I, production exceeded consumption, and the excess went into exports. Following the irregular, but close balance in the 1920's and 1930's, net imports became the rule and the trend in the absolute and relative volume of net imports is upward.

Domestic consumption increased by about a third in the decade following World War II. About three-quarters of the incremental U.S. demand was provided by U.S. output, and about one-quarter by net imports. In the increase of net imports, mineral fuels played the

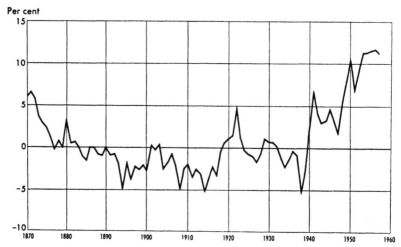

Per cent

Figure 28. U.S. net imports of minerals as a percentage of consumption, 1870–1957

largest role, metals a significant one, and nonmetallic minerals a very minor one.

Mineral Fuels. Until World War II, the United States had generally been a net exporter of oil and coal. In the postwar period, as shown in Table 4, coal exports continued, but net imports of oil began and increased rapidly.

TABLE 4. U.S. Foreign Trade in Petroleum and Coal, 1947–57 [a]

(In millions of 1954 dollars)

Year	Petroleum	Coal Bituminous	Anthracite	Total
1947	15	309	73	397
1948	−148	206	57	115
1949	−322	124	42	−156
1950	−552	113	33	−406
1951	−427	255	50	−122
1952	−527	214	39	−274
1953	−641	151	23	−467
1954	−705	139	24	−542
1955	−891	231	27	−633
1956	−1,021	308	44	−669
1957	−1,021	343	37	−641

[a] Net imports are identified by minus signs.

The change in the position of petroleum requires that we focus on oil for our question of whether substitution of imports, by moderating pressure on domestic resources, significantly accounts for the declining labor-capital cost record per unit of mineral output. The relative substitution of petroleum imports for domestic production in meeting incremental consumption needs has been substantial. As Figure 29

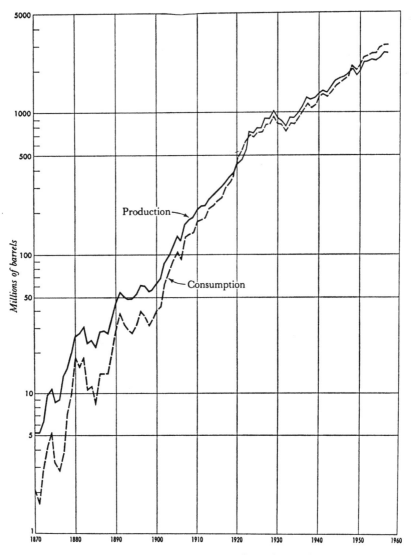

Figure 29. U.S. production and consumption of petroleum, 1870–1957

shows, petroleum imports in 1957 had reached a level amounting to about 12 per cent of U.S. consumption.

Did the advent of imports following World War II significantly facilitate the decline of labor-capital unit costs of petroleum and natural gas which we observed earlier in Figure 23? It could be so. But it is quite uncertain. In fact, it is possible that the labor-capital cost per unit of domestically produced petroleum and gas during the decade of the 1950's might have declined a bit faster if the increase in imports during that period had been smaller. Since the early 1950's, the domestic industry has been operating at far less than efficient scale for its capacity. Texas, which is the source of more than half of domestic supply, for example, has been operating on quotas of less than 15 days per month, usually less than 10 days. Costs of capital input per barrel of output and, to a degree, labor cost per barrel of output are higher under these operating conditions than they would be if national production were, say, 10 to 15 per cent higher (approximately the amount of net imports). Up to the present, net imports of petroleum would not appear to have been primarily responsible for the declining unit cost of domestic output. Of course, the answer could be different in the future, as present reserves are more fully utilized and new—possibly more costly—sources are discovered and brought into production.

With respect to mineral fuels as an aggregate, it would be difficult to believe that, in the absence of the relative substitution of oil imports for indigenous fuel output, the unit cost declines would have been very different, at least to the present.

Metallic Minerals and Metals.   The United States has always been a net importer of metallic minerals, except for a few scattered years. (As elsewhere in this discussion, gold and silver are not considered.) But following both World War I and World War II, the volume of net imports has bounced to higher levels, and more metals have gradually joined the list of net imports, as shown in Table 5.

Our general question is whether, in the absence of the increased net imports, additional U.S. output would have been forthcoming only at higher unit costs than actually prevailed. One particular form of this question is whether the relative substitution of imports for domestic production of metallics is significantly responsible, through moderating demand pressures on domestic resources, for the declining unit cost records of domestic production which appeared in Figure 24. No rigorously provable answers are possible, but it is our judgment that the answers are: (1) "Yes," for copper, lead, zinc, bauxite, and metallic minerals as an aggregate; (2) "No," for iron.

TABLE 5. U.S. Consumption and Net Imports of Metallic Minerals and Metals, 1880–1957

(Dollar amounts in millions at 1954 prices)

Year	Significant net imports relative to consumption	Net imports	Consumption	Net imports as per cent of consumption
1880 . . .	Tin	$31	$121	26%
1890 . . .		32	246	13
1900 . . .	Add ferroalloys	2	421	—
1909 . . .		9	759	1
1919 . . .		111	883	13
1929 . . .	Add bauxite	256	1,447	18
1937 . . .		254	1,213	21
1948 . . .	Add lead, zinc, copper	571	1,856	31
1954 . . .	Add iron	821	1,920	43
1957 . . .		910	2,212	41

Another form of the question, even more difficult to answer, is whether in the absence of relative import substitutions for domestic output, the decline in unit costs would have occurred. Our view (more a guess than an estimate) is that the slight decline in unit costs of lead and zinc would have been reversed, and that declines in unit costs of iron ore, copper, and metallic minerals as an aggregate would have occurred, although at less rapid rates.

Nonmetallic, Nonfuel Minerals. The chief commodities among the nonmetals, an indication of their net position in the foreign trade of the United States, and the value of 1957 U.S. consumption (in 1954 prices) are shown in the following listing:

Trade unim- portant:	Consumption	Substantial net exports:	Consumption
Stone	$687 million	Sulfur	$143 million
Sand and gravel	480 million	Phosophate	71 million
Salt	123 million		
Cement rock	108 million	Substantial net imports:	
Clays	86 million		
Potash	78 million	Diamonds	177 million
Gypsum	35 million	Asbestos	60 million
		Fluorspar	31 million

The first two categories in the list are not relevant to the question of whether net imports primarily, or significantly, account for the rapidly declining cost record of U.S. output. Only the third category, in which the United States is, relative to consumption, a substantial net importer concerns us. With respect to diamonds and asbestos, U.S. outputs are, and always have been, trivial; reliance has always been placed on imports. The United States has always been a net importer of fluorspar, but imports began to increase sharply about the time of World War II, and by 1957 the great majority of the U.S. supplies were coming from foreign sources. In the absence of the import increase, it is quite likely that unit costs would have increased rather than declined.

For nonmetallic minerals as a whole, and for its chief commodities, the record of declining unit cost is not attributable to relative import substitutions for domestic output.

FOREIGN TRADE IN FOREST PRODUCTS

The labor cost per unit of forest products as a whole rose from 1870 to 1920, and then became approximately stable in the 1920's and 1930's. Substitution of imports for indigenous output probably contributed significantly to the stabilization, by moderating pressure upon domestic forest resources, since the United States shifted from net exporter to net importer of forest products as an aggregate during these two decades. If, in fact, net imports played this role, they did so primarily by supplying a considerably increased volume of pulpwood, while the United States continued to export lumber and other forest products.

The level of unit labor costs continued stable from the 1930's to the present. In this period, pulpwood imports continued to increase, and the United States imported substantial volumes of lumber and veneer logs. The evidence is clearer in this later period that imports of forest products significantly contributed to the stability of unit cost of domestic output and that, except for imports, unit costs might have turned upward.

Natural Resource Availability

The scarcity hypothesis has been contradicted by statistical evidence; unit costs of extractive products declined instead of increasing. But why was the hypothesis in error during the 1870–1957 period? So far, we have found that the declining unit costs of extractive goods were very pervasive among individual commodities and groups and that declining unit costs in several commodities were facilitated by substitution of imports for domestic output. We now ask: "Did the availability of natural resources increase? If so, did the increases significantly account for the statistical record of declining unit cost?"

AVAILABILITY OF AGRICULTURAL AND TIMBER ACREAGE

The land area of the United States has changed little during our 1870–1957 period. The *Statistical Abstract*[4] shows that in 1870 the land area amounted to 2,970,000 square miles; in 1958, it was 2,971,000 square miles.

The farm area during the period has been subject to increase as a result of new settlement, forest removal, and land reclamation. But lands also have been withdrawn from agriculture for cities, roads, dams, parks, defense purposes, and so on.[5] Land once used for farming has also become idle for economic reasons. The more than doubling of farm land during the early half of the period, an increase of almost 500 million acres, could have facilitated the decline of 0.4 per cent per year in the unit cost of agricultural products in the 1870–1910 period, previously shown in Figure 11. But during the

[4] *Statistical Abstract of the United States, 1961* (Washington: GPO), p. 5.
[5] For a discussion of changing farm acreage, see Marion Clawson, R. Burnell Held, and Charles H. Stoddard, *Land for the Future* (Baltimore: The Johns Hopkins Press for Resources for the Future, 1960), p. 200.

period since 1910, when the average annual decline in unit cost accelerated to 1.4 per cent, farm land increased less than 300 million acres, and cropland did not increase at all. Only a minor part of the decline in unit cost, therefore, can be attributed to increase in the amount of agricultural acreage. Most, by far, of the reason for the decline in unit cost of agricultural products must be found in other causes.

According to the U.S. Department of Agriculture, timber acreage declined substantially between 1870 and 1954.[6] All of the decline in timber acreage occurred in the period up to World War I, and it is easy to believe that the record of increasing unit cost from 1870 to World War I was associated with this reduction in available resources. Since World War I, timber acreage has increased a little, coinciding with a period of constant unit cost of timber products. The inference is that the maintenance of timber acreage in this latter period may have been partly responsible for preventing further rises in unit costs of timber products.

AVAILABILITY OF MINERALS

New domestic reserves of minerals have been found, or have become economically accessible, more rapidly than old ones have been used up. This generalization has a few exceptions—lead, zinc, and bauxite—among the major commodities within the United States. But for oil and gas, coal, iron, copper, sulfur, and other major commodities known and usable U.S. reserves have increased, and this has facilitated the rapid decline in unit cost of the extractive products.

There are two reasons for the augmentation of economically useful reserves, both contradictory to the premises of the usual depletion models. Whereas the models assume complete initial knowledge of all mineral resources, in actuality the improvement of knowledge generally, and of the earth's crust in the United States in particular, has led to discovery of new reserves. The Ricardian-type assumption of invariant technology in the resource conversion function (the provision of standard resources R from R_u) meant, for example, that immense deposits of taconite, even though known, were not viewed

[6] Clawson *et al., op. cit.,* p. 39.

as usable iron reserves; or that known offshore oils were not accessible; or that porphyries of low percentage copper were not economical resources. What happened, however, is that technological change made these resources into incremental R_u reserves (which ultimately have yielded standard or superstandard resources at declining unit costs).

The facts that mineral resources have been found, because of advances in geological knowledge and search techniques, and added to reserves, because of similar advances elsewhere in the economy (particularly in the resource conversion and extractive sectors), thus have been significantly responsible for negating the scarcity hypothesis.

Technological Advances in the Resource Conversion Function and in Extractive Production

Far-reaching technological advances in the resource conversion and extractive sectors have accounted to a considerable extent for the declining unit costs of both extractive products as an aggregate and the separate component commodities.

TECHNOLOGICAL CHANGE IN AGRICULTURAL AND TIMBER PRODUCTS

Among the pervasive influences in reducing the labor-capital cost per unit of agricultural goods—along with economizing on farm land —have been the introduction of mechanical power and the use of artificial fertilizer and irrigation water to offset declines or deficiencies in resource quality. Of these, the effects of substituting mechanical power for animal and human effort have been especially interesting. This substitution not only has reduced cost per unit by decreasing the pressure upon the land required to provide calories for work animals. It also has saved more in labor per unit than it has cost in capital. Another of these major influences has been the discovery and introduction of improved breeds, weedkillers, controlled feeding, and improved fungicides and insecticides. Hybrid seeds and crossbred livestock have increased the yield from a given volume of labor-capital, since they frequently are more resistant to disease and drought. These innovations not only have been factor-saving in land, but also in labor and capital.

Technological change has been primarily responsible for preventing the moderate increases in timber production per unit cost experienced since 1870 from turning into a sharply increasing trend. The most important technical advance has been development of the substitutes discussed earlier—mineral fuels for fuel wood; and metals, masonry, plastics, and sheet metals (rock and sand materials, asphalt, and pressed woods) for saw lumber. Timber production itself has benefited from other technological advances—chief among them the self-powered chain saw and tractors for bringing logs out of the forest.

TECHNOLOGICAL CHANGE IN THE MINERAL GOODS SECTOR

Earlier we discussed technological advances in finding minerals and augmenting reserves. Here we are concerned more directly with technological advances in the resource conversion function and in the extractive goods production sector.

Technological advances in minerals conversion and extractive goods production have been of major importance in accounting for the decline in labor-capital cost per unit of minerals output. In coal, the advent of, and increasing reliance upon, strip mining has greatly reduced unit cost. As a rough indicator, in 1959, average output per worker in bituminous strip mining was 22.6 tons per day compared with 10.1 tons per day in deep mines. Labor cost per ton of coal from shaft mines has also fallen substantially due to longwall mining techniques, power transportation in mines, power drilling equipment, and improved explosives.

In natural gas and liquefied petroleum gases, the technological advance has taken a different form with the advent of long-distance gas pipelines. Once pipelines were built, producing gas wells, which formerly had no markets and whose gas was shut in or flared, became large suppliers of extractive products after World War II. In turn, this successful and profitable experience encouraged development and exploration for further gas resources. The larger outputs at the fields then justified construction of natural gasoline plants in the fields to scrub the dissolved liquids from wet gas. As a result, by 1957, natural gas provided 28.5 per cent of total U.S. production of all mineral energy, and natural gas liquids were 8 per cent as large as crude oil output.

In other minerals, too, there have been major advances. Taconites, concentrated to 60 per cent and pelletized, provide an input available for charge to blast furnace with a unit labor-capital cost per ton of pig iron which is reported to be less than that formerly obtained by high-grade ore. Some offshore oil deposits yield crude oil at a labor-capital unit cost smaller than that formerly obtained from continental deposits, because of improved drilling techniques. Porphyries of less than 1 per cent copper content yield copper concentrate at a lower unit cost per ton of copper content than former high-grade ores, because of advances in open-pit, earthmoving, and digging techniques and the discovery of selective flotation techniques to concentrate the copper content of pulverized ore. Sulfur costs have been driven down primarily by development of the Frash process, and secondarily by extraction of sulfur from stack gases. More recent innovations of considerable promise include production of minerals from sea water; newly devised furnaces for refining titanium; and the introduction of gaseous oxygen into blast furnaces, which cuts by about three-quarters the time necessary to reduce the ore to pig iron, and thereby reduces labor and capital costs per unit of product.

Conclusions of Our Quantitative Test

Our empirical test has not supported the hypothesis—let us call it the "strong hypothesis"—that economic scarcity of natural resources, as measured by the trend of real cost of extractive output, will increase over time in a growing economy. Observing the extractive sector in the United States from 1870 to 1957, we have found that the trend in the unit cost of extractive goods as a whole has been down—not up.

In the cases of agriculture and minerals, which account for the bulk of the value of extractive output, costs not only declined, but declined more in the latter part of the period—when according to the hypothesis they should have increased sharply. In both forestry and fishing data are inadequate. But it appears that forestry as a whole more nearly supported the scarcity hypothesis while commercial fishing contradicted the hypothesis.

The next step was to look at influences which might have brought about this invalidation of the resource scarcity hypothesis in a growing economy. First we found that different weighting systems did not account for the declining unit costs of all extractive goods or for total agriculture and mining.

Then we examined the possibility that substitutions away from individual agricultural and mineral commodities whose unit labor costs actually rose, or failed to fall, might have been primarily responsible. This, however, was not the answer since actual declines in unit costs were extremely pervasive throughout the extractive industries. Conversely, when we asked whether substitutions among extractive commodities and groups played a major role in averting cost rises and in fostering cost declines, we had a different answer. By shifting demand pressures from agricultural and forest lands to mineral resources, and from less plentiful to more plentiful mineral resources, substitutions favorably influenced declining unit costs.

Another question was whether imports of extractive products, by moderating pressure upon domestic resources, were significantly responsible for the favorable record of unit costs of domestic output. In general, we found that they were not; but in the case of nonferrous metallic minerals and forest products, they probably were.

Our question on the effect of resource availability resulted in a mixed finding. The answer to the question, "Does the finding and creation of additional unhomogeneous natural resources—that is, augmentation in the availability of R_u—significantly account for the record of declining unit cost?" for agriculture and timber was a definite "no." For minerals, the answer was just as definitely "yes." Augmentation of mineral R_u was a major reason for the declining unit cost of most minerals, and for minerals in the aggregate, in view of rapid depletion of originally known R_u reserves in most major minerals— oil, iron, copper, and others. And for extraction as a whole, the answer was a combination of these two unlike situations—minerals accounting for one-fourth to one-third of the aggregate and agriculture and timber for two-thirds to three-quarters.

Finally, as we have just seen, technological advances in the resource conversion and the extractive sectors were important in total agriculture, timber production, and mineral products, as well as in separate commodity components, in reducing the unit costs of output.

With evidence of an increasing trend of cost of extractive output adverse to the scarcity hypothesis, we are forced to retreat to the weaker proposition that the cost of extractive output would have increased had it not been for sociotechnical progress in the economy as a whole. In Chapter 9, therefore, we examine a "weak hypothesis." This is the proposition that natural resource scarcity is an obstacle to economic growth which, since it operates more strongly in the extractive sector than in the nonextractive sector, will show its effects in a rise in the unit cost of extractive output *relative* to that of nonextractive output.

A WEAK SCARCITY HYPOTHESIS
AND ITS TEST

ACCORDING to the weak scarcity hypothesis just suggested, a downward trend of costs of extractive goods can occur. This is possible because favorable sociotechnical change and economies of scale operative throughout the economy can be strong enough to overwhelm the hypothesized tendency for resource conversion costs to increase. The weak hypothesis asserts, nevertheless, that increasing resource scarcity is a fact in the changing real world which it is important to understand and measure, even though its effects may be offset and obscured.

Our aim in this chapter is to determine, within the limits of available data and techniques, whether there is evidence which supports or fails to support this weak hypothesis. We are very doubtful that it is possible directly to remove the effect of economy-wide sociotechnical change from the extractive production process, while still leaving the sociotechnical changes which, like depletion and improved techniques for drilling oil wells, are somehow defined to be particular to the extractive sector. Nor do we believe that, if it were possible, it would be proper to do so in a test of a dynamic scarcity hypothesis in a dynamic economy.

We have decided to employ two devices and sets of evidence to test the weak hypothesis. These are tests of the relative costs and the relative prices of extractive goods.

The Relative Cost Test

The relative cost test is simply a measure of the trend in the cost of a unit of extractive output relative to that of a unit of nonextractive output. That is, it is a measure of the trend of the ratio

$$\frac{L_e + C_e}{E} \bigg/ \frac{L_n + C_n}{N}$$

where E and N represent the net output of the extractive and the nonextractive sectors of the economy, and the subscripts indicate labor and capital inputs to these sectors. We call this ratio of unit costs the "relative cost of extractive output."

Interpretation of the relative cost test will be facilitated by noting its implications. Let us write the production functions, net of purchased materials from the E sector and N sector, for each sector as follows:

$$E = f_e(R_u, L_e, C_e; T_e)$$
$$N = f_n(L_n, C_n; T_n)$$

In each case, T is a collective shift parameter that represents sociotechnical conditions in that sector. The weak hypothesis postulates that, because of declining quality of R_u, f_e through time will yield increasing costs relative to f_n. This is because f_e utilizes resources, while f_n does not.

Our relative cost test of the weak scarcity hypothesis may be viewed as proceeding on either of two assumptions:

On one assumption, the trend of T_n/T_e is assumed to be approximately level. In this case, the hypothesis for a dynamic economy is that there is operative in the E sector a retardation influence, natural resource scarcity, which is not present in the N sector, as both sectors experience the same improvement in sociotechnical conditions. Our measurement through time of

$$\frac{L_e + C_e}{E} \bigg/ \frac{L_n + C_n}{N}$$

will test this hypothesis.

On the other assumption, the trend of T_n/T_e is declining. This is because there is operative in the E sector a retardation influence, natural resource scarcity, which is not present in the N sector, which induces more rapid progress in T_e than occurs in T_n. The hypothesis is that this built-in antidote to natural resource scarcity will nevertheless be insufficient to overcome all of the differentially adverse effect upon $L_e + C_e/E$. Our measurement through time of the above ratio will also test this hypothesis.

In slightly different terms: We are concerned about possible dynamic natural resource scarcity because of its relatively adverse cost consequences through time and its retardation of economic growth. Either: (1) It manifests this relatively adverse cost consequence while the natural resource sector is enjoying the same sociotechnical progress as the remainder of the economy. Or (2) it manifests this relatively adverse cost consequence despite the automatic antidote or self-correction it generates in the form of an induced, more rapid rate of sociotechnical progress than in the remainder of the economy. Or (3) it does not manifest a relatively adverse cost consequence, which means that both hypotheses fail. The failure in the first case would be because natural resource scarcity did not occur in a progressive economy. The failure in the second case would be because natural resource scarcity in a progressive economy generates differential progressive forces which completely nullify its incipient influence.

One final word before presenting the test data. For the measure of N, we have used figures for deflated gross national product less that portion of GNP which originates in the extractive sector. For the measure of E, we use, as in the preceding chapter, *net* output (that is, value added) in constant prices. The data are briefly described in Appendix B.

AGRICULTURAL COSTS

The relative cost series of net agricultural output is defined as cost of agricultural products in terms of labor plus capital relative to unit cost of deflated nonextractive GNP (as just described). If the weak scarcity hypothesis were valid, the trend of relative cost would rise. But we find that the data do not support the hypothesis, as shown in Table 6. The trend of relative $L + C$ cost per unit of agricultural output is approximately level throughout the period. There are short-term movements, due to differences in cyclical behavior and, partly, to other phenomena, which do not concern us. Over the long term, however, relative agricultural costs per unit of product have not risen.

The measurement of capital for use in the production function, and its addition to the labor input to provide combined labor-capital cost, constitute hazardous statistical operations. Not only are nineteenth-century statistics of poor quality, but also dividing one relative cost series by another may compound the probable errors in each. We, therefore, are curious about the findings when unit cost is defined as labor alone. A measurement of the labor cost per unit of agricultural product relative to the labor cost per unit of national product is included in the lower portion of Table 6. The adverse finding continues to hold when relative unit cost is defined in labor alone. (Further, the recent data show significant declines in relative cost, also contrary

TABLE 6. Relative Unit Costs of Net Agricultural Output, 1870–1957

(Unit cost index numbers, 1929 = 100)

Item	1870–1900 Av.	1900	1910	1919	1929	1937	1948	1957
Labor-capital cost per unit of output:								
Agriculture	132	118	121	114	100	93	73	66
GNP less extractive goods	136	126	115[a]	118	100	102	80	68
Relative, agriculture to GNP	*97*	*94*	*105*	*97*	*100*	*91*	*91*	*97*
Labor cost per unit of output:								
Agriculture	151	130	130	115	100	92	66	53
GNP less extractive goods	162	137	121	126	100	103	83	69
Relative, agriculture to GNP	*93*	*95*	*107*	*91*	*100*	*89*	*80*	*77*

[a] 1909 data.

to the hypothesis.) Our incorporation of capital estimates, therefore, is not responsible for the statistical results. Labor is the more influential factor in these ratios, both in its statistical weight and its movements.

MINERAL COSTS

The comparison of the labor-capital cost per unit of mineral products with the $L + C$ cost per unit of all nonextractive goods in the economy is presented in Table 7. As shown, until 1909 or 1919, the trend of relative unit cost of minerals is approximately horizontal. Declines in unit cost of mineral goods kept pace with declines in the rest of the economy. This evidence fails to support the weak scarcity hypothesis.

The evidence in the latter half of the period, from 1919 to 1957, is more strongly adverse to the hypothesis in two ways. First, the decline in unit cost of minerals relative to other goods is so substantial that it is unlikely to be due to cyclical aberrations, measurement errors, and unusual short-term phenomena. The rate of decline fol-

TABLE 7. Relative Unit Costs of Net Minerals Output, 1870–1957

(Unit cost index numbers, 1929 = 100)

Item	1870–1900 Av.	1900	1910	1919	1929	1937	1948	1957
Labor-capital cost per unit of output:								
Minerals	211	195	185	164	100	80	61	47
GNP less extractive goods ..	136	126	115	118	100	102	80	68
Relative, minerals to GNP ..	*155*	*155*	*161*	*139*	*100*	*78*	*76*	*69*
Labor cost per unit of output:								
Minerals	285	234	195	168	100	96	65	45
GNP less extractive goods ..	162	137	121	126	100	103	83	69
Relative, minerals to GNP ..	*176*	*171*	*161*	*133*	*100*	*93*	*78*	*65*

lowing 1919 is 1.8 per cent per year. And, second, the sequence which appears in the data—decline of relative cost in the latter part of the period, after depletion and large-scale industrial demands have had opportunity to exert influence—is just what we do not expect in a scarcity conception.

Again, as in the case of agriculture, in order to see to what extent the capital factor was responsible for the results, we have constructed a relative cost series in terms of labor cost alone. The series, shown in the lower portion of Table 7, is similar to the relative labor-capital cost results. It shows an approximately level trend to about 1920. And then it shows a pronounced down-trend to the present, as did the relative $L + C$ cost per unit of minerals output. Neither of these results, of course, is anticipated from the weak scarcity hypothesis.

COSTS OF FOREST PRODUCTS

Forestry presents a significant example in support of the weak scarcity hypothesis. Table 8 presents evidence on the labor cost of

TABLE 8. Relative Unit Costs of Output of Sawlogs, 1870–1957
(Unit cost index numbers, 1930 = 100)

Labor cost per unit of output	1870– 1900 Av.	1900	1910	1920	1930	1940	1950	1957
Sawlogs	59	65	67	108	100	104	88	90
GNP less extractive goods ..	162	137	121	126	100	103	83	69
Relative, sawlogs to GNP ..	*36*	*47*	*55*	*86*	*100*	*101*	*106*	*130*

sawlogs—those cut into lumber. There is one period of relative cost stability in these data—the 1930's and 1940's. But except for this, the record is one of almost uninterrupted relative increase in unit costs. Further, the increase is at a sufficiently substantial rate to leave no doubt that this is increase and not stability (this is particularly helpful, since the quality of forestry data is not very good).

Two further points: First, the fact that the rate of increase has slowed since the 1920's, though contrary to the hypothesis, does not crucially detract from it, since increase has persistently occurred. Second, the need to use relative labor cost data (in the absence of capital information) should not be disturbing. As was seen in agriculture and minerals, inclusion of capital changed the results but little. We would guess that inclusion of capital cost in forestry, if we had the data, and correspondingly using $L + C$ input data for the non-extractive GNP, would also show a rising relative cost trend, at a rate slightly more rapid than for relative labor cost alone.

COSTS OF TOTAL EXTRACTION

Six curves for total extraction are shown in Figure 30. One shows labor plus capital cost per unit of net output for all of agriculture, minerals, forestry, and fishing. A second shows only the labor cost per unit of net output for this aggregate of the extractive sector. The next two curves show the same information for GNP less the extractive sector. And the final two curves show these unit costs of extractive goods relative to comparable unit costs of GNP less extraction. The aggregation process reduces the variability found in the individual industry series. Certainly this aggregate series does not support the weak hypothesis that relative unit costs in extraction will increase due to scarcity.

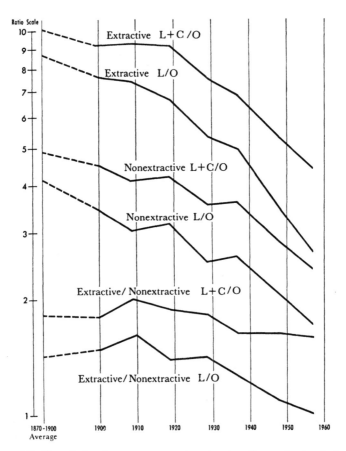

Figure 30. Trends in the cost per unit of extractive output relative to nonextractive output in the United States, 1870–1957

The Relative Price Test

The effort to find evidence of increasing scarcity in a rising trend of relative extractive costs has opened the way for application of a similar, but more comprehensive test—that of relative price. All the tests so far have employed data expressed in "real" terms—that is, values in constant prices, or actual physical quantities of goods and numbers of workers, and indexes based on these.

It is also possible to test the hypothesis of increasing relative costs by comparing the unit prices of extractive and nonextractive output. This is simply the ratio of price per unit of extractive goods divided by price per unit of nonextractive goods. (See Appendix B for a brief discussion of sources and data.)

One of the assumptions in such a test is that the trends of prices of inputs other than natural resources (of wage, interest, and profit rates and prices of purchased materials) into the extractive sector will not, for reasons unrelated to natural resource scarcity, be significantly different from those in the nonextractive sector. Unless this assumption is approximately true, then differential changes in the degree of unionization of labor in the two sectors, for example, could affect the trend of relative wage rates and, therefore, the trend of relative prices. Or differential changes in the degree of monopoly in various sectors of the economy might systematically alter the relative prices of purchased inputs and outputs as well as profit rates. Similarly, trends of taxes, subsidies, and transport cost may have been different in the extractive relative to the nonextractive sector; if so, some of these differentials need not have been indicators of change in resource scarcity. To illustrate, we write the equation for the price of any product as

$$P = \frac{\Sigma(P_L L + P_M M + P_F F)}{Q}$$

where P_L, P_M, and P_F represent the prices; L represents the quantities of labor; M, the purchased materials inputs; and F, all other inputs (capital, entrepreneurship, government services, and so on) plus profits. In other words, changes in the prices of inputs—P_L, P_M, and

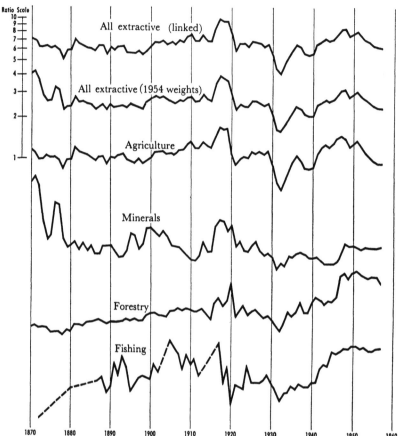

Figure 31. Trends in unit prices of extractive products relative to non-extractive products in the United States, 1870–1957

Note: Solid lines connect points in annual series; dashed lines connect points over a year apart.

P_F—may occur for what we may broadly call institutional reasons. Such changes, to the extent that they have significantly *differential* trends in the two sectors, will cause relative prices of extractive versus all other goods to change for reasons unrelated to change in resource quality.[1]

[1] We do not include changes in demand among the "institutional" factors. As we observed in the previous chapter, and shall observe in the following one, changes in demand affect natural resource requirements, both absolutely and per unit of GNP. They, therefore, help to ameliorate or aggravate, as the case may be, any tendency for resource scarcity to increase; and if these effects show up in relative price, this is precisely what we want to detect.

The measurement of change in absolute money costs per unit, because of inflation and deflation, would be statistically meaningless as a test. But the measurement of unit prices of extractive products relative to nonextractive products, which is the method we follow here, overcomes this defect.

Comparison of prices of extractive and nonextractive goods has important advantages over the relative cost measure. It is comprehensive as regards cost coverage in its inclusion of all purchased inputs. Also, price quotations are more plentiful, and are frequently of superior objectivity and statistical quality to measures of labor input and capital input over the long term. Further, the relative price measure is statistically independent of the relative cost measurement, and thereby provides a check on its results.

Figure 31 presents the essential data for this second test of the weak scarcity hypothesis. It shows the annual data of the unit prices of extractive goods as an aggregate and of the two major and two minor commodity groups. In its essentials, the story is simple. Where the trend of relative price is upward—certainly in forestry and possibly in fishing—there is support for the weak form of the natural resource scarcity hypothesis. Where the trend is approximately horizontal—in agriculture, minerals, and total extraction—the scarcity hypothesis fails, even in its weak form.

AGRICULTURAL PRICES

There is certainly significant material for analysis of cyclical, intermediate-term, and war-induced influences in the long-term series of agricultural prices relative to nonextractive prices. The punishing effects on farmers in the deep depressions following 1873 and 1929 appear in the form of declining farm prices relative to other prices. The more rapid recovery following the earlier of the two depressions is visible. The effects of the two World Wars show themselves as roller-coaster ascents and falls in farm prices as compared with other prices. Government protection of farm prices slowed the decline after World War II but did not prevent it.

There is also a slow but rather steady upward movement of relative farm prices in the two or three decades preceding World

War I. Although the increase is not large as compared with effects of cycles and other short-term forces, conceivably this represents the operation of a natural resource scarcity force, relevant to the weak scarcity hypothesis. If it is this, however, the scarcity hypothesis, even in this weak form, is embarrassed by the later evidence. The increase of about one-fourth in the two and a half decades preceding World War II has since been reversed. The decline is contradictory to the scarcity hypothesis, both as simple decline and also in that the hypothesis contemplates increase in resource scarcity as the economy grows.

We conclude that agricultural scarcity according to the weak hypothesis probably has not occurred. Or, if it has, it has been a transient or minor force as compared with other influences operative upon farm prices which are not related to resource scarcity.

MINERAL PRICES

The price data for minerals relative to nonextractive products are quite "jumpy." The key to understanding the "saw-teeth" is the short-term relative inflexibility of minerals output to changes in demand from movements in the economy as a whole. The minerals supply tends to be inelastic in the short term and intermediate term for reasons related to organizational structure of the minerals industry, lead times to develop new sources, and several types of uncertainty and risk.

Mineral prices fluctuate with other prices, but with more amplitude. For example: (1) Prices in general declined from the 1870's to the 1890's, but prices of minerals declined more. (Price data for this period are better than data on labor and capital inputs and real output, but they are still thin, and should not be "over-interpreted.") (2) Prices in general rose from a trough in the 1890's to a peak in World War I. But mineral prices rose more. (3) From the peak of World War I, prices in general declined to a trough in 1932–33. Mineral prices declined more. (4) Since the trough of the 1930's, prices in general have risen, with mineral prices rising more. (5) The relative movements have tended to be similar in the shorter cyclical swings.

Short-term movements aside, the trend of relative mineral prices has been level since the last quarter of the nineteenth century. This does not support the weak scarcity hypothesis.

PRICES OF FOREST PRODUCTS

The next extractive category, forest products, was about 11 per cent of extractive output value in 1870, 9 per cent in 1902, and 7 per cent in 1954. The price record of forest products is interesting enough to discuss its two major components, lumber and pulpwood, as well as the aggregate.

By the 1950's, relative prices of "all forest products" had increased to two and a half times the level of the 1870's. Moreover, they increased with some persistence, although very unsteadily. There was an increase in most decades. This is very promising evidence in support of the weak scarcity hypothesis. There is further support when the price history is related to production. Present output levels are no greater than at the turn of the century—peak output was reached a bit later, in 1907—while present prices relative to non-extractive products are nearly twice as high. It is interesting that the case of forests, which was of major influence in inciting the original Conservation Movement, yields the only striking evidence of economic scarcity. Gifford Pinchot was certainly correct in his forecast of price increases, although not in his appraisal of the economic consequences of scarcity.

> For example, it is certain that the rate of consumption of timber will increase enormously in the future, as it has in the past, so long as supplies remain to draw upon. Exact knowledge of many other factors is needed before closely accurate results can be obtained. The figures cited are, however, sufficiently reliable to make it certain that the United States has already crossed the verge of a timber famine so severe that its blighting effects will be felt in every household in the land. The rise in the price of lumber which marked the opening of the present century is the beginning of a vastly greater and more rapid rise which is to come. We must necessarily begin to suffer from the scarcity of timber long before our supplies are completely exhausted.

> It is well to remember that there is no foreign source from which we can draw cheap and abundant supplies of timber to meet a

demand per capita so large as to be without parallel in the world, and that the suffering which will result from the progressive failure of our timber has been but faintly foreshadowed by temporary scarcities of coal.

What will happen when the forests fail? In the first place, the business of lumbering will disappear. It is now the fourth greatest industry in the United States. All forms of building industries will suffer with it, and the occupants of houses, offices, and stores must pay the added cost. Mining will become vastly more expensive; and with the rise in the cost of mining there must follow a corresponding rise in the price of coal, iron, and other minerals. The railways, which have as yet failed entirely to develop a satisfactory substitute for the wooden tie (and must, in the opinion of their best engineers, continue to fail), will be profoundly affected, and the cost of transportation will suffer a corresponding increase. Water power for lighting, manufacturing, and transportation, and the movement of freight and passengers by inland waterways, will be affected still more directly than the steam railways. The cultivation of the soil, with or without irrigation, will

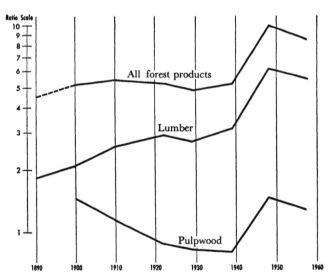

Figure 32. Trends in unit prices of forest products relative to nonextractive products in the United States, 1890–1957

Note: Because there were no pulpwood figures for the period, the dashed line shows extrapolation.

be hampered by the increased cost of agricultural tools, fencing and the wood needed for other purposes about the farm.[2]

Before 1900, our forest products price series is composed of lumber alone. The relative price history of the forest products aggregate and of its two major components, lumber and pulpwood, since then is shown in Figure 32. It provides interesting insight. The slight upward trend of the aggregate series between 1900–02 and 1939 is an offset result of contrary movements of the components —a rising lumber price index and a declining pulpwood index. The steep rise in the aggregate from 1939 to 1948 results from steep increases in both components; both components also contribute to the moderate decline from 1948 to 1957. The lumber record tends to confirm the weak scarcity hypothesis; the pulpwood record does not.

Comparison of Relative Cost and Price Tests

A comparison of the results of the relative cost and relative price tests in terms of support of the weak hypothesis is given in the listing below. The single words used to summarize the test results with respect to support of the weak hypothesis are, of course, oversimplifications.

Support of weak hypothesis	Relative cost test	Relative price test
Late 1800's to 1920's:		
Extractive	No	No
Agriculture	No	No
Minerals	No	No
Forestry	Yes	Yes
1920's to 1957:		
Extractive	No	No
Agriculture	No	No
Minerals	No	No
Forestry	Yes	Yes

[2] Pinchot, *The Fight for Conservation* (New York: Doubleday, Page and Company, 1910), pp. 15–17.

For confidence in the data and the results of these tests of the weak scarcity hypothesis, it is significant that both produce the same conclusion. In large degree, the relative cost series for the extractive sector was founded on counts of the physical output of individual products and counts of physical numbers of workers involved in their production. The relative price measure had, as its basic component in both sectors, market price quotations of individual products. Thus, elements of the basic data were sufficiently different so that, in view of data imperfections, it was not inevitable that the two series should give the same final results. And they do not for short periods. But the results are the same for the long-term analysis of the weak hypothesis. And this reinforces confidence in the findings.

Chapter 10

AMBIGUOUS INDICATORS OF
RESOURCE SCARCITY

A NUMBER of other indicators of scarcity have been implicitly or explicitly employed by other writers concerned with natural resources. We here examine some of these indicators. We present the requisite data, when they are available, and explain why, in general, we regard these indicators as inferior to those we have used in Chapters 8 and 9. The indicators have one feature in common: each is a *partial indicator* of increasing resource scarcity and, under certain conditions, will reflect changes in scarcity. Because they are incomplete, they include built-in ways for evidence of increasing scarcity to be hidden by other influences; or for such influences to make the indicators behave as if scarcity were increasing when it is not. The alternative tests are thus considerably more ambiguous than our own.

The partial scarcity indicators fall into four groups. One reflects the view that increasing resource scarcity will force the nation's labor or capital to be diverted from nonextractive to extractive activities. A second group involves the premise that scarcity will increase the value of extractive output relative to total output in current prices. A third group of indicators reflects the proposition that resources will be economized as they become scarcer and more costly. Finally, a fourth group would involve direct observation of change in the quality of resources.

Increasing scarcity, according to one view, will reveal itself by a steady increase in the proportion of the total labor force engaged in the resource-exploiting (that is, the extractive) sector of the economy. Whether this tests our scarcity hypothesis or not, these are important data. The data on labor used in extractive industries as a percentage of total U.S. labor were among the first we examined. What we found, as Figure 33 shows, was that the percentage of the labor force engaged in extraction has been declining rapidly in the United States for a long time. But these data are quite inconclusive for a valid test of the scarcity hypothesis as we conceive it.

The percentage of the labor force in extraction is affected not by one set of influences, but by at least three. These are: (1) socio-technical advance and economies of scale, which primarily determine whether output per capita will grow; (2) cost and preference trends,

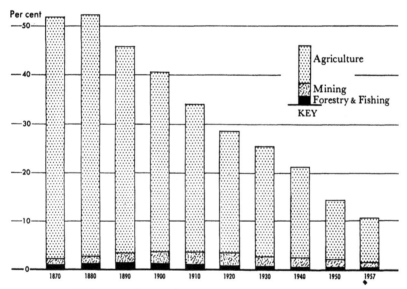

Figure 33. U.S. extractive workers as a percentage of all workers, 1870–1957

which affect the division of final and intermediate product demand between the more resource-intensive and less resource-intensive goods and services; and (3) changes in labor cost per unit of extractive output relative to nonextractive. If society, because of very favorable parametric change and income increase, shifts away from the more resource-intensive products to those that are less intensive, the percentage of the labor force engaged in extraction would fall, even if resource quality were declining and labor cost per unit of extractive output were rising. Indeed, substitutions away from increasingly costly extractive products would be fostered, as has occurred in lumber. If capital and purchased inputs (including imports) replace labor in the extractive sector to a greater degree than in the nonextractive, the proportion of extractive to nonextractive labor in the United States would decline simultaneously with a fall in the quality of resources.

Historically, the behavior of the extractive labor indicator has been dominated by three powerful trends during the period we examined. One, the steady introduction of labor-saving machinery and materials, has reduced labor per unit of output, extractive included. The second, the great relative growth of demand for nonagricultural goods and services, has reabsorbed the great bulk of the labor thus saved. The third is the decline that has occurred in net U.S. exports of extractive products. Whatever forces of resource scarcity might have operated to increase unit resource conversion cost during this period, their influence on the ratio of extractive to nonextractive labor would have been overwhelmed by these three trends. It is typical for the labor force of preindustrial countries to engage predominantly in extractive activity—especially agriculture. And it is typical for the three trends listed above to characterize industrial countries. For the United States and other advanced countries, statistical evidence for nearly a century past contradicts the view that, because of increasing resource scarcity, the work force increasingly becomes occupied in extractive industry.

A variation on the same theme could be that it is the proportion of society's total capital employed in the extractive sector, and not labor, that will rise because of increasing resource scarcity. This is subject to the same criticism as described for the labor input. And, similarly, total capital in the extractive sector today is a smaller proportion of total capital than formerly, as shown in Figure 34.

The extractive labor and the extractive capital percentages are not significant as indicators of increasing scarcity for still another reason. The percentages might decline because the extractive sector had economized both labor and capital by substituting inputs of materials purchased from the nonextractive sector.

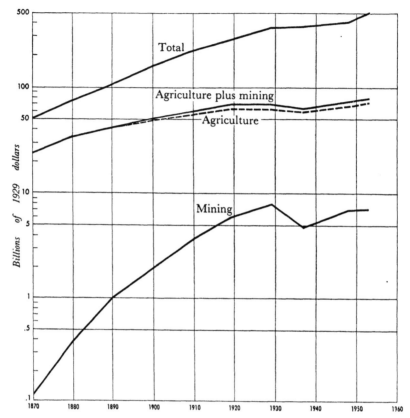

Figure 34. Capital goods in the U.S. private domestic economy and in agriculture and mining, 1869–1953

Value of Extractive Output Relative to GNP

A variant of the preceding indicators of resource scarcity is that the value of extractive activity will rise as a portion of GNP because of scarcity.

The gross value of extractive output relative to value of national product has declined substantially and steadily from 1870 to the present. In 1870, the extractive share was nearly 50 per cent. By the turn of the century, it had fallen to 32 per cent; and, by 1919, to 23 per cent. In 1957, the figure was 13 per cent, and still trending downward. Figure 35 presents a time series of the ratio of extractive output to national output at approximately decade intervals. The average rate of decline in the ratio is indicated by the straight line trend on the semilogarithmic scale. It is roughly 14 per cent per decade.

A comparison of the gross value of extractive output to gross national product overstates extractive values. The former includes, but the latter excludes, purchases of producing units from each other. A more appropriate representation of the ratio of extractive output to total output, therefore, may be obtained by use of value-added data. This eliminates double counting from the measure of extractive output, and makes it consistent with the valuation of national product (GNP). While the use of value-added data for extractive output overcomes double counting, they are, unfortunately, of somewhat inferior statistical quality. Figure 35 shows the extractive output ratio computed on the alternative basis of value added relative

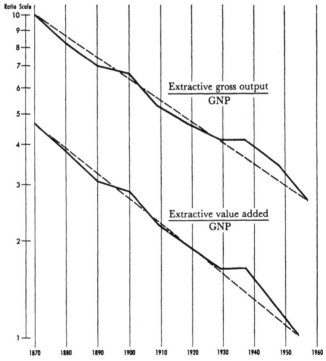

Figure 35. U.S. extractive output relative to gross national product, 1870–1957

to gross national product. As expected, the extractive output ratio is less in the latter case. It is about 44 per cent in 1870; declines to 27 per cent by 1900; to 18 per cent by 1919; and to 10 per cent in 1954. The time trends are very similar in both series. Extractive output, in terms of value added, which once constituted a major share of national output, has declined steadily and substantially in relative importance. Table 9 shows the declines by decades in value of output and value added.

TABLE 9. Rates of Decline in Extractive Output Relative to Gross National Product, 1870–1957

| Decade | Percentage decline from beginning of decade | |
	Value of output (1)	Value added (2)
1870	—	—
1880	18	19
1890	16	18
1900	6	7
1909	22 [a]	25 [a]
1919	12	14
1929	12	13
1937	− 4 [a]	0
1948	18 [a]	22 [a]
1957	24 [a]	29 [a]

[a] Decade rate.

The above data relate to domestic output rather than to domestic consumption of extractive goods. The conception of extractive goods as absorbing an increasing portion of the nation's productive capability because of scarcity might be confined to extractive goods consumed domestically. In this view, exports of extractive goods should be excluded from the above data, and imports of such goods should be included. This error is not too serious, however. Despite the fact that U.S. net exports of extractive goods shifted from a positive to a negative figure, as described earlier in Chapter 8, the above findings are not modified when extractive goods consumption is substituted for extractive output. Table 10 shows how the extractive output ratio is changed by taking into account the decline in net exports of extractive products. The consumption percentage declines more slowly than the output ratio. At present, the two percentages are nearly identical.

In summary: (1) However measured, the ratio of extractive output to national output has declined persistently and substantially since 1870. (2) Extractive output is still large enough relative to national economic activity to justify concern over tendencies to significant advances in unit cost, if such should soon begin to occur. But this is far less true today than formerly, when extractive output was relatively much more important. (3) Assuming unit costs of extractive products at 50 per cent higher than actual, but output of

TABLE 10. Ratio of Gross Value of Extractive Goods to Gross National Product, 1870–1957 [a]

| Year | Percentage of national product value | | Ratio of (2) to (1) |
	Extractive production (1)	Extractive consumption (2)	
1870	49	45	0.92
1900	32	28	0.87
1929	20	21	1.05
1957	13	14	1.08

[a] Valued in 1954 prices.

extractive products at the actual amount, the real value of GNP would have been lower in 1870 by 26 per cent; in 1900, by 19 per cent; in 1929, by 12 per cent; and in 1957, by 6 per cent.

The basic explanation for our findings in this section—that the extractive to nonextractive ratio, however measured, has declined or remained constant—is that in the approximate century since 1870 the product mix and output per capita of the United States have changed from those of a preindustrial to an industrial society. These influences were so profound that they completely outweighed whatever influence could have been exerted by changes in unit costs of extractive relative to nonextractive goods.

Evidence of Resource Economizing

SUBSTITUTIONS

A familiar proposition is that a growing economy tends to substitute labor and capital for natural resources if the unit cost and price of resources rise under the influence of scarcity. Therefore, it might be contended that declines in the ratio of resources to extractive labor-capital or to extractive output will indicate increasing scarcity. In a parametrically progressive situation, changes in the product mix and shifts of the production function would alter relative input requirements in various ways. Hence, a decline in the ratio of resources to other inputs would, to a considerable extent, reflect parametric changes and not necessarily indicate increasing resource scarcity.

The switch from net exports to net imports of raw materials that occurred about the time of World War II has sometimes been cited as an example of economizing that indicates increasing resource scarcity. In an otherwise changeless world, an increasing ratio of net imports of raw materials to output of the extractive sector would betoken a shift in international comparative advantage with respect to extractive output, and be taken as circumstantial evidence of increasing resource scarcity. But, in a changing world, it could reflect any number of other possible reasons for alteration of the structure of comparative advantages. Among these are: discovery abroad of new and better resource reserves, or improvement of transport facilities; technological progress that rendered foreign supplies competitive with domestic; a change in the structure of domestic or foreign demand; increase in intermediate goods exports with a proportionate decline of raw material exports; an increase of productivity in domestic nonextractive industry relative to extractive; a relative rise in extractive relative to nonextractive wages (or taxes) in the home country; a relative increase in the degree of monopoly in the extractive sector (with no offsetting increase in protective tariffs and quotas); and so on. In brief, an increase in the ratio of net imports of extractive goods to domestically produced goods will reflect a change in the position of the importing country relative to that of the foreign country. But such an increase will not necessarily indicate that resource quality has fallen in either country; it could have improved in both. To say that increasing relative imports of extractive products show that resources are becoming absolutely scarcer in the importing country is to overlook the fact that comparative advantage is a sufficient basis for mutually beneficial trade.

INCREASES IN ECONOMIC RENT

Another frequently proposed indicator of increasing resource scarcity is increasing economic rent. The usefulness of rent from this standpoint depends partly on empirical and partly on theoretical considerations. If the world conformed to the specifications of our parametrically invariant, Ricardian no-depletion model initially developed in Chapter 5, where unhomogeneous resources were assumed to be free goods, increases in economic rent would reflect increasing resource scarcity, and nothing else. Assume standard resources, R, to be the highest quality ever available historically. Then their rent would always equal marginal resource conversion cost for R_u of marginal quality, and would be a precise index of the increase in scarcity that had occurred from the beginning of man's economic history.

By now, however, we have recognized that there will be many types of R; therefore, there will be many different figures for standard rent; and, for institutional reasons, unhomogeneous resources (including those at the margin) command a reservation price in private enterprise societies. Rent will now contain a pecuniary element that reflects, but does not measure, increasing scarcity; and there will be no single figure for rent—it will be different on each type of resource. As scarcity increases, rents will increase; and rents will also change as the result of changes in interest rates, relative demands, and expectations concerning future resource availability. Under these conditions, advances in rent on unhomogeneous resources are an ambiguous indicator of increases in scarcity.

Rent would be a useful indicator of increasing scarcity in a Ricardian no-depletion world where the resource conversion path stayed put, and the process of growth involved nothing more complicated than a systematic traversal of the path. But in a world of depletion, of variable reservation prices and degrees of reservation, and especially of sociotechnical change, this is no longer so. The conversion path changes shape and position, with the result that quality differences among resources, their rank in the quality spectrum, and, therefore, the rent that they earn vary irregularly over time. Rents on different resources will disappear, decrease, or increase as a result of the depletion and reordering of resources discussed in Chapter 5, of changes in resource economizing behavior, or of changes in the technical or social parameters that determine the rank of resources in order of quality. Because of these changes in the resource quality spectrum which are induced by sociotechnical change, depletion, and so on, economic rent is a nonoperational concept in the modern world. The changes cause capital gains and losses and a variety of income elements to be blended with economic rent and make its determination impossible.

Urban land is a case of particular interest. Let us assume that rent per unit of urban land is high and increasing in the United States, even if income earned on the cost of improvements is deducted. Does this signify increasing natural resource scarcity? We think not. The phenomenon of urban rent does not reflect a quantitative scarcity of land on which to build; there is still an ample supply of building space in the United States. Further, increasing urban rent does not reflect a declining absolute quality (increasing resource conversion cost) of marginal land under the impact of growth. It reflects, on the contrary, the absolute *increase* in economic quality of urban land due to its advancing productivity. Man's propensity to build where he has already built—his liking for crowds, together with the existence of economies of concentration—has raised the price of land in metropolitan areas. It is not its intrinsic physical and locational qualities that advance the value of urban land, but the fact that it is where people are congregating in ever-increasing numbers, together with the economies which the combination of sociotechnical advance and agglomeration create. Urban rents thus reflect the economic advantages of agglomeration, not disadvantages imposed by nature.

As the demand rises from growth and technical advance, the labor-capital intensity of urban product increases and urban product is supplied at an ever-mounting aggregate labor-capital cost, but a declining unit cost. The marginal productivity of strategically located blocks of land increases under these conditions, and rents rise. Urban rents have risen primarily because labor-capital cost per unit of urban product has fallen. Thus, urban rent, though an indicator of relative economic scarcity, is not an indicator of natural resource scarcity. Increase in urban rent accompanies a declining cost trend for national product, opposite to that postulated by classical growth doctrine of increasing resource scarcity and increasing rent.

We conclude that increasing economic rent would not be an indicator of increasing resource scarcity in our sense, even if it could be measured. Specifically, increases in urban land rent do not signify an imminent cost-increasing shortage of either land or natural resources in general.

Direct Measurement of Changing Resource Quality

For the problem of measuring possible decline in the quality of resources as more of them are brought into use, an obvious idea is to try to compile an inventory of resource availability according to classes of economic quality. This was a major proposal of the Conservation Movement at the turn of the century, and of two important national conferences held in the early 1900's. It has been a favorite proposal of conservation groups ever since, and it has had support from economists as well. For example, the President's Materials Policy Commission strongly recommended such an inventory, and at certain points made estimates of specific resource availabilities classified by grade.[1] The thought is that if, in such an inventory, it were found that unused resources were of inferior economic quality to those used (quality being measured in terms of the cost of producing a unit of E), it could be said that economic scarcity is present and increasing. The idea has some obvious merits, and some not so obvious defects; it is more complex than would at first appear.

A major defect of the inventory idea is its built-in tendency to characterize unused resources as inferior to those in use. This is because estimates of cost inferred from physical properties necessarily employ existing sociotechnical knowledge. That is, the implementation of the proposal assumes that presently known resources will be used to

[1] *Resources for Freedom,* "The Outlook for Key Commodities," Vol. II (Washington: GPO, 1952), pp. 138–67, *passim.*

produce presently known products by presently known techniques for the present economy. There is no alternative. How can one appraise the quality of unknown resources? Or the quality of resource inputs for unknown products? Or the costs entailed by unknown techniques, social arrangements, and tastes? Because these are truly unknown, the inventory can only be a test of whether economic enterprise is using least-cost resources at the present time. Thus, the inventory will divulge only the extent to which resources are being used in order of economic quality, given the existing products, available technology, and other parameters. Since there is certainly a tendency for the economy to follow this economically rational use pattern, the inventory will tend to confirm that, with some exceptions, marginal resources are inferior to intramarginal ones, and that unused resources are inferior to marginal ones. But this is because the inventory tends to be cast in a framework of static knowledge, products, techniques, and institutions.

This suggests that inventories of resources based on their intrinsic physical properties would be most useful for the particular extractive subsectors—if such there be—that are relatively insulated from parametric change. Examples are rather harder to give than might at first be imagined. Forests for saw timber come to mind; in general, unused U.S. forests are of lower saw-timber quality than those in use. But then we recall major exceptions; some of our finest forests are, in fact, without access roads, largely for institutional reasons related to government ownership. The economic order of use would change with change in the institutional parameter. We recall that agriculture has taken over and holds large amounts of land which would be of high quality for growing timber, and which many conservationists recommend be returned to forestry. This is quite feasible, provided the time horizon is as much as a couple of generations. How, admitting the possibility of parametric change, should the ordered array be laid out—if we allow for the reforestation of idle farm land? As we think of a descending economic quality gradient for lumber, we also wonder —in view of displacement of saw timber by metal, masonry, plastics, and new types of timber products—whether additional forest lands would be economical and used in the distant future even if they were of a quality equal, or superior, to present marginal supplies. With regard to the other major element in forestry, we recall very recent advances in pulping technology which are reordering the array of pulpwood supplies.

Agricultural growth also is a possibility for simulating the conditions of a static model. But perturbing thoughts arise here, too, to make us doubt that the static framework is a fair representation of reality over a long period. We remember that U.S. cropland is no more extensive than fifty years ago, yet crop output is much higher and acreage is believed to be excessive. In some cases, land in the soil bank is not inferior to land in production. The natural physical properties of land have declined in importance with increases in irrigation, chemical fertilizer, and scientific farming (including antibiotics for livestock). Land in the western and plains states, which in former inventories would have been described as submarginal, is now intra-marginal, and the reverse has occurred for New York and New England cropland and much cotton acreage in the South. The view that a current inventory would describe scarcity over time in a changing economy is not convincing. Past inventories would have proved wrong.

The case of minerals has some interesting possibilities for the proposition that natural resource inventories can, by providing an array in order of declining concentration of currently usable and accessible mineral content, indicate the phenomenon of increasing scarcity in a dynamic economy. The situation in iron ore was very promising for this hypothesis some years ago, when the Mesabi Range began to approach exhaustion of its high-grade iron ore. But recent discoveries in Venezuela, Labrador, and Canada have badly shaken the validity of a declining-quality inventory which might have been made then. Further, while it was thought in the 1940's that a unit of pig iron or steel would cost more if it had to be produced from 35 per cent taconite than from 60 per cent hematite, this no longer seems to be the case in the 1960's as a result of recent advances in technology. The use of a resource inventory arrayed in order of declining quality once appeared reasonable for copper. The fact, however, is that incremental supplies have not been coming from the declining quality spectrum that would have appeared in an inventory drawn up at, say, the beginning of the century. The copper ore inventory would have down-rated the porphyries and foreign sources which have become primary supplies for the United States.

We doubt that the cases of coal, oil, or gas are suitable for inventory in the way discussed. Western coals are much cheaper to mine than many eastern ones, and it is only distance and a stable or declining demand for coal in the first instance which keeps them out of larger use. The unused oil and gas fields in the continental shelf, the Dakotas, Canada, Latin America, and the Middle East are not all inferior to the Pennsylvania, Texas, and California oil and gas deposits now in use.

Further, from our resource viewpoint, we may be missing an essential element of the dynamic economy if the mineral fuels are considered individually. If we view the energy resources as an aggregate, man's successive use has been wood, manure, peat, coal, oil, gas, uranium, and boron (and, in the future, possibly deuterium from the sea). This is the actual order of use. Does this suggest that, in the march of time and parametric change, supplies of fuel have been progressively met by utilizing the fuels of higher economic quality first and then moving to those of lower economic quality? What would an inventory of fuels have shown in 1850 or 1900 concerning scarcity?

We have just implicitly asked, for energy resources, what it is that should be economically ordered to reveal an increasing scarcity. The same question should be asked for all resources. The use of physical properties to arrive at an economic ordering is clearly possible only when the product is specified as a particular physical thing—for example, coal. Even here, the desirable properties have changed— anthracite is no longer the preferred coal. If, realistically, we view the resource quality spectrum in terms of the economic services for which society calls, the notion of economic ordering becomes immensely difficult. The ordering of resources, it would seem, should be done according to broad use categories such as food, heat, materials for clothing, construction materials. But this means that if economic growth and parametric change bring in new products to serve these functions, such as nylon for cotton, it can turn out that formerly inferior resource properties become superior ones. With hindsight, for example, we observe that an economically inferior resource (agricultural land) was being used to obtain fibers by producing cotton, while superior resources for getting nylon (mineral fuels) were unused and not even listed in the clothing materials inventory.

The study of properties and qualities of resources formerly used, now in use, and now available for use is obviously useful. As increments to knowledge concerning the natural environment, they provide a base for more intelligent behavior than would be possible in their absence. But the idea that static inventories of resources display the dynamic scarcity of natural resources should be viewed as overly simplistic.

Removal of Technological Change

We have not attempted to determine what would have happened to the cost of extractive output as a whole in the absence of those sociotechnical changes that have caused it to decline in absolute terms, and prevented it from increasing in relative terms. Such a calculation might be based on the assumption that we could have had the population and the GNP of the 1950's with the extractive techniques and product mix of the 1870's. Since the growth that has occurred was in large part a consequence of sociotechnical change, a test that attempted to remove the effect of the latter on the cost of extractive output, while leaving the former unchanged, would be ambiguous. Or such a test might attempt to remove all effects of sociotechnical change, including those on growth of output and population and the composition of the national product mix.[2] If validly performed, it would yield a static cost function. Under neither assumption would there be an empirical test of the dynamic scarcity hypothesis in a changing world.

Our two tests of changing resource quality, presented in Chapters 8 and 9, involved efforts to measure changes in the unit cost of extractive output that might be attributed to the influence of increasing resource scarcity. In the present chapter, we have reviewed a number of alternative tests or, rather, indicators—some of which did not directly involve the concept of cost. We have found many more sources of ambiguity in these partial scarcity indicators considered in this chapter than in our unit cost measures of the two preceding

[2] For a useful review and discussion of pitfalls and difficulties, see Evsey Domar, "On the Measurement of Technological Change," *Economic Journal,* Vol. 71 (December 1961).

chapters. This does not mean that the partial indicators are useless. Each has potential value as a signal of some kind of change, or of its absence. Taken together, they contribute to a broadened understanding of the resource problem. But no one of them, nor all of them together, signifies the presence or absence of resource scarcity as well as did the cost data in Chapters 8 and 9.

PART IV

WELFARE IN A PROGRESSIVE WORLD

Chapter 11

SELF-GENERATING TECHNOLOGICAL CHANGE

AN ATTEMPT to define the hypothesis of increasing resource scarcity for a parametrically variant world and to test it in a variety of ways for the United States over nearly a century of rapid economic growth was undertaken in Part III. In the aggregate, the results of the various tests were overwhelmingly negative. Labor-capital cost per unit of gross national product fell rapidly, without retardation, over the entire period; and there was no observable tendency for the cost of extractive output as such to fall more slowly, as might have been expected if resource scarcity had been increasing. In terms of our models, resource conversion cost—as represented by the unit cost of extractive output—declined throughout the period. When particular extractive sectors were examined separately, only the cost of forest output was found to have risen over the period as a whole. The question arises how to interpret these results, or analogous results that could be expected from studies of other industrial countries, both over the past century and into the predictable future. The question at issue is whether the cost-reducing forces can keep up with, or ahead of, those that tend to increase costs.

Knowledge and Technological Progress

There has been a certain tendency to regard technological advance as a chancy phenomenon, a bit of luck that is sure to run out sooner or later (with the ever-present implication that it will be sooner). Economists, until recently, at least, have been prone to regard the stock of knowledge as relatively fixed. Innovation has not been a built-in element in their models. To some, it has even seemed that

235

there were limits to the possibilities of technological advance, analogous to those for natural resources. Marshall, for example, conceived the law of diminishing returns to be a historical law that had been only temporarily set aside by the industrial revolution and the opening up of new lands. He regarded the law as almost inoperative in Great Britain at the beginning of the twentieth century, but thought that "after a generation or two it may again be a powerful influence here and nearly all over the world. . . . The world is really a very small place," he continued,

> . . . and there is not room in it for the opening up of rich new resources during many decades at as rapid a rate as has prevailed during the last three or four. When new countries begin to need most of their own food and other raw produce, improvements in the transport will count for little. From that time onward the pressure of the Law of Diminishing Returns can be opposed only by further improvements in production; *and improvements in production must themselves gradually show a diminishing return.*[1]

The view that improvements must show a diminishing return is implicit in the thought of those who regard more optimistic opinion as "cornucopian." Yet a strong case can be made for the view that the cumulation of knowledge and technological progress is automatic and self-reproductive in modern economies, and obeys a law of increasing returns. Every cost-reducing innovation opens up possibilities of application in so many new directions that the stock of knowledge, far from being depleted by new developments, may even expand geometrically.[2] Technological progress, instead of being the adventitious consequence of lucky and highly improbable discoveries, appears to obey what Myrdal has called the "principle of circular and cumulative causation,"[3] namely, that change tends to induce further change in the same direction.

[1] *Memorials of Alfred Marshall*, A. C. Pigou, ed. (1925), p. 326, as cited in A. J. Youngson, *Possibilities of Economic Progress* (London: Cambridge University Press, 1959), p. 33. Italics added.

[2] There is, perhaps, more question concerning increasing returns to knowledge in the biological than in the physical sciences. Many biologists appear to believe that there are definite limits to the possibilities of genetic improvement. But this may only be because the art of manipulating genetic structures biochemically has not yet been mastered.

[3] Gunnar Myrdal, *Economic Theory and Underdeveloped Regions* (London: Gerald Duckworth and Co. Ltd., 1957), Chapter 2. (Also published under title *Rich Lands and Poor*, in New York by Harper, 1957.)

The scientific advances in the late nineteenth and the twentieth centuries are genuine "breakthroughs" of mammoth significance; the world today is very different from that of Malthus. In Malthus' time, the major part of national output originated on the land—food, natural fibers for clothing, wood for construction and furniture. Increased output of these goods largely depended upon uncontrolled natural processes—sunlight, rainfall, temperature—impinging upon surface resources. "Fixed" agricultural and forest land was therefore inevitably viewed as an ultimate barrier to expansion of such output. The usable acres seemed clearly limited, even under optimistic assumptions of fertilization and reclamation. The land coefficient—the input of land acreage required per unit of output—at best could be reduced only slowly, if at all. And there seemed to be bounds beyond which reduction could not proceed. A limit to the number of plants a field could bear or the number of animals it could support seemed certain, and the potentialities of further improvement through breeding were not visualized.

Moreover, the ability to obtain an increase in final product services from a given quantity of raw materials was limited by the manner in which the materials were processed and fabricated. The gifts of nature, retrieved from field and forest, were subjected only to gross mechanical transformations: grain separated from husk and hide from meat; timber sawed and shaped; fibers combed, twisted, and woven. The opportunities for substitutions and increased efficiency were limited in such a technology, and wide avenues of escape from the confines of nature were not imagined.

Industrial development in the nineteenth century altered this view of affairs in only one important respect. It introduced mechanical energy on a large scale into the processes of extracting, modifying, and forming materials. Human labor was displaced and economized; labor cost per unit of output was reduced. But technological innovations, that led economists increasingly to the view that manufacturing was subject to a law of increasing returns, made growing drafts on the limited supplies of organic and fossil fuels; [4] accelerated the depletion of traditional sources of metallic ores; and reinforced the view that raw produce was subject to a law of diminishing returns. The social

---

[4] William Stanley Jevons' monograph, *The Coal Question* (1863), reflected the growing awareness and concern.

implications of this doctrine excited the American Conservationists at the turn of the century. Concerned with policy rather than analysis, the Conservation Movement stressed the conflict between a rapacious industrialism and a parsimonious nature, and sought ways of ameliorating the impact of the one upon the other.

These earlier, simplistic views of a world divided into two economic sectors—one progressive, but recessive, the other regressive and dominant—have continued to govern economic thinking down to the present time. Yet they, and the analogies by which the classical law of diminishing returns is "demonstrated" to be approximately descriptive of today's long-term growth potentiality, border on the archaic. The transformation of materials into final goods has become increasingly a matter of chemical processing. It is more and more rare for materials to be transformed into final products solely by mechanical means. The natural resource building blocks are now to a large extent atoms and molecules. Nature's input should now be conceived as units of mass and energy, not acres and tons. Now the problem is more one of manipulating the available store of iron, magnesium, aluminum, carbon, hydrogen, and oxygen atoms, even electrons. This has major economic significance. It changes radically the natural resources factor of production for societies that have access to modern technology and capital.

Further, it is important that the newer technologies utilize very extensive, frequently ubiquitous, resources. As we have noted, such plateaus of virtually constant physical properties constitute an important qualification to the Ricardian hypothesis of monotonic decline of resource quality. Moreover, as plateaus become broader and the quantities of usable resource substance become absolutely greater, society gains time for further advance. The gain of time in our modern world assures, in turn, a further gain of experience and knowledge—and that gain then yields further plateaus. Generally speaking, the low-grade resource materials are more abundant than high-grade, simply because it required special geological conditions to produce high concentrations of relatively pure substance. This greater abundance, it should be understood, applies not only to the gross resource material—for example, sea water—but to the absolute content of usable substance. A hundred years ago, it would have been impossible to list some of these assets, and it would have seemed fanciful to mention others. The fact is that the technology of low-concentrate resources is in its infancy, and one may be confident that effort to discover replacements for depleting resources will uncover potentialities yet undreamed of.

This phenomenon, we suggest, is far from trivial in importance. One of the vastest plateaus of all, the sea, is not simply a great stock of resource substance but, as noted earlier, a continually augmenting stock. Advancing ocean technology could conceivably lead to a "steady state" equilibrium of a great circular flow process analogous to, but far more complex than, the carbon dioxide cycle. Equally important are the energy plateaus already created by atomic fission and eventually, perhaps, to result from nuclear fusion and solar energy devices. Once energy becomes available in unlimited quantities at constant cost, the processing of large quantities of low-grade resource material presumably can be undertaken at constant cost without further technological advance, and at declining cost with technological advance and capital accumulation. Hence, the physicist's concept of "available energy" constitutes a plateau of virtually limitless extent,[5] and one whose availability will tend to reduce virtually all other resource conversion processes to a constant-cost basis as well.

The import of the foregoing observations is that the problem of economic growth should not be viewed as a matter of diminishing returns staved off by a series of lucky discoveries. Viewed in the large, scientific advance and technological applications are not, and have not been, a matter of chance. Development of a method for fixation of atmospheric nitrogen was an inevitable eventual consequence of the application of the new chemical technology, with its wide-ranging potentialities, to a problem singled out for priority attention at least as early as 1890, and countless other examples could be given. The demands made upon the natural resource environment by economic growth will create problems aplenty, and we must not expect all of them to be solved simultaneously. They will be attacked, as they appear, seriatim. The differential impact of scarcity, of the

---

[5] Defined in the *Scientific Encyclopedia* (3rd ed.; Princeton: D. Van Nostrand, 1958), p. 150, as follows: "AVAILABLE ENERGY which can be converted into mechanical work by means at human disposal. While incalculable quantities of energy exist all about us, only an insignificant fraction of it is in such form that human inventiveness has been able to utilize it for the performance of work."

growth elasticities of supplies and demands, will dictate the path of sociotechnical progress, selecting the more urgent problems for immediate attention and leaving the less pressing ones to be dealt with later.

The process of growth thus generates antidotes to a general increase of resource scarcity. Technological and many other advances are causally integrated with the growth process. To the extent that there is an actual or anticipated tendency for labor-capital cost to increase in one industry or another, there is inducement to devise and introduce ways of avoiding the cost squeeze. Induced resource-saving technology includes all ways of reducing waste, increasing the efficient recovery of scrap, extending the life of durable products, reducing the resource content of existing products, developing less resource-intensive new products, increasing the efficiency of engines and processes, and so on. These economies affect the labor-capital cost of output only indirectly. Their immediate effect is to reduce the amount of the particular extractive output formerly required per unit of nonextractive output. Absolute or relative reduction in the labor-capital cost of social output then follows upon adjustments in the extractive sector, where a movement down the resource conversion path in the direction of increased resource quality—or a retardation of the rate of growth-induced expansion along the path—will either reduce resource conversion cost or moderate its rate of increase.

One of the most striking and productive developments of the period of the industrial revolution has been the relatively increased capital intensity of the production process—that is, the increase in the ratio of capital to labor. A corresponding development has characterized the household economy. Both producers' and consumers' capital are resource intensive. Not only do they embody mineral resources but they are energy-using to a high degree. Installed horsepower per capita in the United States has increased astronomically since the middle of the nineteenth century. Since such horsepower directly uses energy, and indirectly (via the machines that embody it) uses materials, this increase would seem to imply a roughly proportional rise in the demand for both fuels and structural materials (especially metals). It has not done so, however, as a result of a huge increase in the efficiency of obtaining work from energy sources, and equally spectacular reductions in the bulk of machines and buildings per unit of output.

In other words, resource-saving improvements were induced and have played a major role in reducing both the initial cost of capital equipment and the current cost of capital-intensive (and energy-intensive) output.

The prospect of increasing resource scarcity also fosters research, exploration, and discovery of new or alternative resources of equal or superior quality. Firms need to develop techniques for discovering new reserves of high-quality resources or exploiting those of lower quality in order to stay in business. Major iron and steel companies, as a result of research and exploration initiated well in advance of the foreseen exhaustion of Lake Superior reserves, developed processes for beneficiating taconite and began to develop iron ore resources in foreign countries. Petroleum companies have developed technology for discovering and tapping oil sources in deep formations and offshore waters, and they have devised increasingly efficient modes of transport to industrial centers from more distant regions in the Middle East and Latin America.

Nor is scarcity-induced innovation confined to private firms. Since at least the Renaissance, governments have been concerned about resources and have taken measures to improve their availability. Some have directly encouraged exploration: the voyages of discovery, for example. Others have fostered technological change—through research and experiment in agriculture, mining, forestry, and fishing. Or they have created incentives for the private sector to innovate by providing favorable purchase contracts, financial assistance, tax preferences, and other subsidies. Along with this has gone facilitative institutional change: the establishment of special government agencies to promote discovery and efficiency in agriculture, forestry, and mining. Even the Conservation Movement in the United States, and analogous efforts elsewhere, were in part responses induced by concern over anticipated cost increases; and they may have directly and indirectly altered the sociotechnical framework in a cost-reducing manner.

Increased per capita incomes and associated changes in the structure of the final consumer product mix also help to explain certain innovations, chiefly in the form of product modifications and introductions, which operate to reduce the pull of growth on the resource base. According to Engel's law, as individual incomes rise, expenditures and preferences shift from relatively crude and basic necessities to more highly processed commodities. The increase in the services component of the final product mix is a related manifestation. These phenomena could not have occurred on the scale they have in the industrial nations without an increase in the differentiation of consumer goods to match the increase in the number of rungs in the ladder of income distribution. The social structures and income distributions of preindustrial societies are typically dualistic, with the relatively undifferentiated masses living at or near a land-intensive subsistence level, and the elite living in luxury. There being little or no middle class, no set of variously differentiated middle income groups, the available product mix in a premodern society consisted of what classical economists used to call necessaries and luxuries. The complex product mix of our modern industrial societies developed from one like this, and it may have been a condition for the proliferation of income levels that there should be a proliferation of products. When Adam Smith said that the division of labor depends on the extent of the market, he was making a plea for freedom and extension of international trade. But he might also have said that a differentiation of job opportunities and income levels (the other side of the division of labor) depends upon the differentiation of products. Malthus recognized this and used it as an argument in his confused efforts to controvert Say's law.[6]

Allyn Young's contention that the "persisting search for markets," and particularly for potential markets, has played the leading role in economic evolution is relevant in this context.[7] Inventors, patent holders, resource owners, and manufacturers undertake in various ways to

---

[6] Consider the following from Malthus, *Principles of Political Economy* (New York: Augustus M. Kelley, 1951): "That an efficient taste for luxuries and conveniences . . . is a plant of slow growth, the history of human society sufficiently shows; and that it is a most important error to take for granted, that mankind will produce and consume all that they have the power to produce and consume . . ." (pp. 320–21). "Something else seems necessary to call [the powers of production] fully into action. This is . . . a distribution of produce, and . . . an *adaptation of this produce* to the wants of those who are to consume it . . ." (p. 361; italics added). "The distribution, which I mean, is not so readily accomplished. It is that which effects the *best adaptation* of the supplies of produce, both in quantity and quality, *to the actual tastes and wants of the consumers, and creates new tastes and wants . . .*" (p. 371; italics added).

[7] Allyn Young, "Increasing Returns and Economic Progress," *Economic Journal*, Vol. 38 (December 1928), p. 536.

steer final demand toward products that utilize new, abundant, and cheap raw materials. This is one reason why product innovation implies materials innovation. Another is that traditional materials sometimes are unsuited to the technical requirements of new products, or are unavailable in suitable quantities or costs at the new centers of manufacture. Therefore, new materials will be sought or developed. More important, perhaps, will be the effort to provide mass purchasers with product services analogous to those enjoyed by the well-to-do at prices suited to the pocketbooks of the potential buyers. This leads, naturally, to a search for new and inexpensive materials, with the result that the resource base is enlarged but resource conversion cost is not increased (and may even be decreased).

Thus sociotechnical change, to an important degree, has been the consequence of stimuli arising out of the growth process itself and of responses made possible by the cumulation of knowledge.

A Possible Neo-Ricardian Hypothesis

Growth, depletion, and sociotechnical change continually alter the resource spectrum and, by so doing, confront man with a never-ending stream of new problems, with an ever-present need for adjustment. When certain problems are solved imperfectly, unit costs increase and we have local diminishing returns. If the problems are solved well, as they typically have been in the modern world, we avert diminishing returns and often bring within our horizon goals that once were beyond our reach.[8] For this, there is need not only for continual adjustment and progress in the technology of production but also in social organization. Once the techniques of breaking nature's codes and

---

[8] Within the broad characterization of the relation of resources to economic growth there is ample scope for variation in space and time. Regions and eras differ in the nature of the problems they face; in the knowledge, ingenuity, and wisdom available to overcome them; and in the cost of doing so. The mobilities of all these inputs, contrasted with the immobility of resources *in situ,* provide the means for reducing, or wholly overcoming, the relative disadvantages imposed by local variations in natural resources per se. But see Anthony Scott, "The Development of the Extractive Industries," *Canadian Journal of Economics and Political Science,* Vol. 28 (February 1962), for a suggestion that modern technology increasingly has the effect of destroying immobilities and therefore awarding advantages to the regions that possess capital, people, and skills, rather than to those with a "rich" natural endowment.

applying the knowledge to overcome her intransigence have been acquired—and they already have been to a remarkable degree—the threat of increased costs and the fact of changing wants stimulate search for the means of escape, whether by private or public action.[9]

In short, the resource problem is one of continual accommodation and adjustment to an ever-changing economic resource quality spectrum. The physical properties of the natural resource base impose a series of initial constraints on the growth and progress of mankind, but the resource spectrum undergoes kaleidoscopic change through time. Continual enlargement of the scope of substitutability—the result of man's technological ingenuity and organizational wisdom—offers those who are nimble a multitude of opportunities for escape.[10] The fact of constraint does not disappear, it merely changes character. New constraints replace the old, new scarcities generate new offsets.

The proposed reformulation of the Ricardian hypothesis, then, is that the character of the resource base presents man with a never-ending stream of problems but imposes a far less rigid and certain physical obstacle to a continual increase in the return to effort than economists have been wont to believe. That man will face a series of particular scarcities as the result of growth is a foregone conclusion; that these will impose general scarcity—increasing cost—is not a legitimate corollary. The twentieth century's discovery of the uniformity of energy and matter has increased the possibilities of substitution to an unimaginable degree, and placed at man's disposal an indefinitely large number of alternatives from which to choose. To suppose that these alternatives must eventually become so restricted,

[9] It is true that sociotechnical progress is not costless, but it is also doubtful that its cost can confidently be assigned a rising trend in either the near or distant future. It is also relevant that research is both labor intensive and enjoyable. There is, therefore, some question whether an increasing aggregate outlay on it should fully be regarded as a social cost. People need some form of activity, as Marshall emphasized, and research may therefore be both a low-cost output and a highly productive input. Perhaps all "work" in Utopia will be done by machines, while men occupy themselves with figuring out ways to get it done—cheaply.

[10] For some speculations concerning present constraints and possible escapes, see Richard L. Meier, *Science and Economic Development* (New York: Wiley, 1956), and Paul W. McGann, "Technological Progress and Minerals," in *Natural Resources and Economic Growth* (Baltimore: The Johns Hopkins Press for Resources for the Future, 1961). Joseph L. Fisher, in *Natural Resources and Economic Growth* (*op. cit.*), contributes a number of pointed observations concerning the character of substitution possibilities, as does Scott, *op. cit.*

relative to man's wants, that increasing cost will be inescapable, is not justified by the evidence. An absolute limit to the possibilities of escape may exist, but it cannot be defined or specified. The finite limits of the globe, so real in their unqueried simplicity, lose definition under examination.

This is so, even of living space. It is true, as we recognized in Chapter 3, that extrapolation of existing rates of population growth for only a few hundreds of years raises the specter of "standing room only" as the eventual fate of the human race. But there is danger in this exercise. It often implies, when coupled with a sense of current urban overcrowding, that the eventuality is close at hand, despite the abundance of unoccupied land and the technological possibilities for utilizing space above and below the ground and on the seas. It also implies skepticism concerning modern man's ability to learn within the time available how to regulate family size as required for the welfare of mankind as a whole. Yet many primitive societies have avoided population pressure by devising appropriate mores for the regulation of male and female behavior. Progressive societies, it seems probable, will not be found wanting in this respect.

In general, it should be expected that societies will attempt to control their population numbers when the social gains of such action —or the costs of unlimited expansion—pose a clear threat to social welfare. Population growth may or may not become a problem in societies already industrialized, but it is a current threat to growth and welfare in many of the nonindustrial regions of the world, as we note in Chapter 12, and some of the less developed nations, taking cognizance of this, have instituted programs designed to slow up the rate of increase. The case of Egypt is particularly interesting, for it reflects a change within the space of a few years from refusal to acknowledge the existence of a population problem to a policy of initiating serious efforts to deal with it. Responsiveness to evidence of the adverse effects of population growth is thus an actual and potential fact of the modern world.

Even though its presence be recognized, however, the problem cannot be solved easily. The difficulties are mainly social. We already possess useful contraceptive technology, and can expect it to improve, but it is hard to bring about the changes in national customs, value standards, norms of behavior, and social relations that will lead to reduced rates of population growth. And if a need should be felt to develop and put into effect a world-wide policy for stabilization of population, special difficulties would be encountered. It would not be easy to allocate responsibilities for stabilization among nations, with their different degrees of "population pressure," their unlike economic potentialities, their variant ideologies and political aspirations; or to decide how the appropriate institutional arrangements should vary with cultural differences—religious doctrine, status of women, age and frequency of marriage, degree of urbanization, level of living, and so on. There has been a minimum of social experience, and very little research concerning the cultural and social aspects of the problem. Time is not unlimited, but there seems to be no present reason to believe that it is too short for the necessary lessons to be learned and for effective action to be taken wherever and whenever the need is great enough to be recognized. In the matter of population growth, as in that of diminishing returns, man's ingenuity and wisdom are the crucial factors.

All that can be asserted confidently, therefore, concerning the struggle of man against nature is that it endures as a continuing reality; that problems increase in complexity; but that no empirically supportable prediction of the outcome can be made. Output per capita, as measured by any suitable indexes at our disposal, may conceivably increase into the indefinite future, and eventual overcrowding is by no means a foregone conclusion.

Obligation to Future Generations

Belief in the threat of diminishing returns, and in an obligation to future generations, have been major premises of conservationist thought in the present century. We have just stated the reasons for our belief that the first of these premises is no longer appropriate as a basis for policy. Now, in the light of this judgment, we examine the second.

These empirical and ethical premises led the leaders of the Conservation Movement to believe, as indicated in Chapter 4, that natural resources should be physically "conserved" by all available means, for otherwise the future would be impoverished. Renewable resources should not be drawn down, but should be used at the highest possible level of sustained physical yield; nonrenewable resources should be used only after renewable resources were fully employed—water power before coal, for example; physical "waste" should be reduced wherever it was found; current production should be constrained, if need be, to retard the depletion of nonrenewable resources. So far as necessary to achieve these objectives, the economic freedom of private property owners, producers, and consumers—specifically, freedom to engage in those short-sighted, self-interested behavior patterns which destroy resources or deplete them rapidly under laissez faire—should be restricted in favor of government regulation or ownership.

The foregoing prescriptions for physical conservation of natural resources are not appropriate, however, for meeting the premised obligation to the future. First, reservation of resources is a form of investment—that is, a present sacrifice in favor of a presumably more valuable future gain. The level of resource reservation that will yield the maximum economic return to the present generation—if economic gain is the objective—must be determined on the basis of economic, not physical yield, principles. Resource reservation, on current calculations, if not economically meritorious, will reduce the economic value of output over the time period taken as relevant for the calculation and may, by curbing research and capital formation, have a perverse effect on future output and welfare. It is by no means necessary to reduce production today in order to increase production tomorrow. If, instead, current production is maintained, and consumption is reduced in favor of research and investment, future production will be increased. Higher production today, if it also means more research and investment today, thus will serve the economic interest of future generations better than reservation of resources and lower current production.

Second, the Conservationists' premise that the economic heritage will shrink in value unless natural resources are "conserved," is wrong for a progressive world. The opposite is true. In the United States, for example, the economic magnitude of the estate each generation passes on—the income per capita the next generation enjoys—has been approximately double that which it received, over the period for which data exist. Resource reservation to protect the interest of future generations is therefore unnecessary. There is no need for a future-oriented ethical principle to replace or supplement the economic calculations that lead modern man to accumulate primarily for the benefit of those now living. The reason, of course, is that the legacy of economically valuable assets which each generation passes on consists only in part of the natural environment. The more important components of the inheritance are knowledge, technology, capital instruments, economic institutions. These, far more than natural resources, are the determinants of real income per capita. Even with respect to natural resource wealth alone, as Edmund Jones remarked at the White House Conference of Governors, which dealt with conservation in 1908, "we shall add far more to our natural resources by developing our ability to increase them than we can ever do by mere processes of saving." [11]

Third, in advanced societies it is not true, as commonly alleged, that the time perspective for making calculations is distorted in favor of the present; that too brief a period is employed for the purpose of determining whether an investment is worthwhile; that, unless a moral obligation to distant generations is recognized, a self-interested bias will tempt current generations to consume the "natural capital" to which future generations allegedly have equal right—will lead them to squander the estate that should be available for the use of man throughout eternity. Nor is it true, as Pigou and others have contended, that including the welfare of future generations in a contemporary economic calculus would necessarily imply a social rate of time discount lower than the private rate.[12] The process of discounting is one of determining the value of future income relative to present income, *to the present generation*. It is keyed to the welfare of those now living, not to that of future generations. If it were desired that the welfare of future generations be taken into account, it should be done by attempting to determine the value *to them* of alternative prospective incomes, not the discounted value of the alter-

[11] Quoted by Thomas B. Nolan in *Perspectives on Conservation: Essays on America's Natural Resources,* Henry Jarrett, ed. (Baltimore: The Johns Hopkins Press for Resources for the Future, 1958), p. 54, where it is also noted that Andrew Carnegie expressed similar sentiments. Nolan's paper, "The Inexhaustible Resource of Technology," is a useful summary of the case for science.

[12] For a discussion of the social rate of time preference in relation to resource conservation, see Anthony Scott, *Natural Resources: The Economics of Conservation* (Toronto: University of Toronto Press, 1955), pp. 88 and 93, and references there cited.

natives to us; and then applying an ethical standard, not an economic calculus, to resolve any conflict between the outcomes of economic welfare for the several generations involved. Juggling the interest rate might or might not be appropriate.

But, while the use of ethical principles to mediate the competing claims of different generations would have clear relevance in a Ricardian world, where today's depletion curtails tomorrow's production, it has little if any relevance in a progressive world, where efforts to serve the interests of the present also serve those of the future. If those now living devote themselves to improving society's productive power, and also its capacity to reach decisions concerning the use of that power that will increasingly benefit themselves and their children, the value of the social heritage will grow continually. To increase current real income, physical capital is accumulated. To satisfy his curiosity, man adds to society's intellectual capital. To enrich its own life, each generation strives to improve the health and education of its children, thereby augmenting society's human capital. And, in consequence of efforts to improve society's functioning as a productive enterprise, economic institutions and standards are rendered more effective. By devoting itself to improving the lot of the living, therefore, each generation, whether recognizing a future-oriented obligation to do so or not, transmits a more productive world to those who follow.

But one point needs to be stressed. A more productive world is not necessarily a better world. Currently rational calculations suffice, in a progressive society, to serve the economic interests of the future as well as the present; but the ways in which these calculations are reached and applied at any given time—the current value standards and decision-making procedures—need not be taken as incapable of betterment. On the contrary, we regard these standards and procedures as capable of never-ending improvement, and as a necessary object of continuing attention from generation to generation. Indeed, given the present and prospective states of science and technology, the question of how and to what ends we shall use our knowledge and productive power acquires a special importance. The value of the total social heritage, including values and institutions, not the economic heritage only, is the appropriate object of attention.

Our view, in sum, is that, in order to discharge our obligation to future generations—to recognize their right to at least as good a set of opportunities as we enjoy—we must ignore the element of time and shift our attention to progress. Instead of trying to create a better intertemporal distribution of welfare by deliberately transferring productive capacity and output from the present to the future, instead of essaying the impossible task of determining the ethically optimal amount of such transfer, we should concentrate on devising and introducing sociotechnical innovations that will increase total welfare—economic welfare plus everything else that determines the quality of life as a whole. No generation can anticipate the conditions to be faced by generations in the distant future, or how they will choose to deal with them. But every generation should be able, on the basis of accumulated human experience, to arrive at a rational judgment concerning the sorts of conditions and consequences that constitute a better life for itself and its children. Emphasis on economic and social progress in the present is a much improved alternative to preoccupation with an undefinable and nonoperational moral obligation to reserve natural resources for the economic benefit of future generations —though preservation of wild and scenic features of the natural environment for our own aesthetic benefit will presumably be appreciated by our successors.

What we are saying is exceedingly simple: our debt to future generations will be discharged to the extent that we maintain a high rate of quantitative and qualitative progress, to the extent that we alter—in a direction favorable to human welfare generally—the conditions that determine the choices open to men when they are free to choose. Already, we have argued, the heritage of knowledge, equipment, and economic institutions that the industrial nations are able to transmit to future generations is sufficient to overcome the potentially adverse effects of continual and unavoidable shift to natural resources with properties which, on the basis of past technologies and products, would have been economically inferior. The industrial nations have learned, in short, how to maintain technological progress, to avoid quantitative diminishing returns. An open question is whether they have also learned how to maintain social progress, to continue improving the quality of life, to avoid qualitative diminishing returns. Even more open is the question whether these nations, in cooperation with those that have not yet become industrialized, will be able to assure both quantitative and qualitative progress for mankind throughout the world. Thus interpreted, our obligation to future generations poses difficult problems—problems that touch the sensitive core of our value standards, our methods of calculating aggregate benefits and costs, and our decision-making procedures. We explore some of these problems briefly, as they relate to natural resources, in the concluding chapter.

Chapter 12

NATURAL RESOURCES AND
THE QUALITY OF LIFE

MODERN societies have evolved economic institutions and procedures which respond to signals of cost and demand by introducing resource-saving or cost-reducing innovations and substitutions. The prospect, therefore, is that economic welfare, as measured by indexes of output per unit of input, will continue to increase. But what of the other aspects of welfare? If, along with the achievement of increasing returns, the distribution of income becomes inequitable; or market processes become more imperfect in their allocation of benefits and costs; or the quality of the available product mix changes unfavorably; or there is a net reduction in the intangible satisfactions derived from the appearance of the environment; or in any other way the social framework becomes less desirable—if any or all of these types of changes should occur there might be a consensus that total welfare had not increased along with economic welfare, that the quality of life had, in some significant respect, been impaired.

This type of question has occurred to many of those who have seriously considered natural resource questions. As we observed in Chapter 3, John Stuart Mill looked forward to population stabilization from concern over what would happen to the quality of life ". . . with every rood of land brought into cultivation, which is capable of growing food for human beings . . . and scarcely a place left where a wild shrub or flower could grow without being eradicated as a weed in the name of improved agriculture." A number of conservationists, both in the original Movement and today, have argued strongly for control of natural resource use in order, on the basis of their value standards, to prevent damage to the quality of life from the process of economic growth. We saw, for example, that the leaders of the Conservation Movement believed that monopoly and in-

252

dustrialism, with consequent neglect of the public interest and impairment of the values of rural life, were related to man's efforts to exploit the natural resource environment. One need not subscribe to these earlier views to recognize that the contest between man and nature, especially man's efforts to overcome nature's limitations, may have many undesirable consequences if conscious and timely efforts are not made to avoid them. Increasingly, for these and other reasons, contemporary social scientists have been calling attention to the possibility of conflict between the materialistic aspects of continuing economic growth and the achievement of a high quality of life.[1]

Modern societies may be less able to counteract adverse qualitative change, or take advantage of opportunities to improve the quality of life, than they are to circumvent increases in the economic scarcity of natural resources. Political and other social decision-making processes are available, but their operations are more cumbersome and less assured than technical and market processes. The problems of qualitative evaluation are more difficult, especially where they require joint evaluation of consequences for large numbers of people; they are a social rather than a private value problem. Cases of this kind arise with particular frequency as a result of the impact on natural resources of economic growth, depletion, population expansion, and technological change.

We identify several such cases of impact which have emerged during the past generation: urban agglomeration; waste disposal and pol-

[1] By way of illustration, we quote two such observations, one by an American political scientist, the other by a British economist. (1) "Welfare: faring well, well-being. How well are we going to fare in the new society without poverty and hunger? In many ways, pretty badly. In many ways, our standard of living, our well-being, is very likely going to be much worse than that of our grandparents . . . Utopia may be a pretty frustrating, irritating, inconvenient, unpleasant, disagreeable place, a place of ill-fare rather than welfare." Robert A. Dahl, "The Role of Government in Individual and Social Welfare," an unpublished manuscript (New Haven, 1956). (2) "While accepting, therefore, 'an expansion of the area of choice' as synonymous with an increase of welfare for the individual, and as an unexceptional norm of policy, it requires an alarming degree of complacency to believe that a rising standard of living as commonly understood is the certain instrument of an expanding horizon of opportunities. Obviously the growth of material prosperity, and its dispersion among the populace, entails—by definition, we might say—more goods, and new kinds of goods, among the mass of the people. But it is scarcely less obvious today that the concomitant subtopiaisation of society involves a continual erosion of opportunities, at least for a sensitive minority." E. J. Mishan, "A Survey of Welfare Economics, 1939–1959," *Economic Journal*, Vol. 70 (June 1960), pp. 255–56.

lution; changes in income distribution, particularly in relation to distressed areas; water supply; land use; international relations with underdeveloped nations. These illustrate the need for social analysis and decisions, beyond simple acceptance of the results produced by the operation of existing economic and other institutions.

Social Problems Related to Natural Resources

Urbanization has been a striking feature of economic growth in the United States and other major countries, including those just beginning the process of industrialization. To a large extent, this results from the economies of scale and the consequently higher productivity that is characteristic of urban agglomerations. Stated otherwise, agglomeration is one of the conditions which has resulted from, and contributed to, man's efforts to reduce costs and increase income. But it is also one that is coming under increasing question for its possible negative effects on the quality of life. As cities grow, there are the accompanying phenomena of urban sprawl, traffic congestion, blighted areas, pollution of water supplies and atmosphere. Even increased mental tension, juvenile delinquency, and crime have been among the alleged consequences of agglomeration. Such effects, to the extent that they occur, imply a need for analysis and possibly for decision-making procedures beyond those now available.

Consider, in particular, the earthy and undramatic problems of waste disposal in urban centers and of pollution in general. These clearly require policy decisions at the societal level. But it was not always so. Families in sparsely settled regions were once free to dispose of their waste on the basis of self-interest; they did not adversely affect the environment of others. The habit so formed persisted when cities came into being. Progressive cities then proscribed use of the streets as sewers, and substituted direct discharge into rivers, lakes, and oceans. In terms of local interest this is reasonable—sewage treatment is expensive. But it is becoming anachronistic for large communities to determine their methods of disposal independently. The problem has been greatly augmented by the growth of industrialization. The wastes of modern industry have reached huge volume. In terms of individual interest, industrial firms—paper mills, chemical plants, refineries, and so on—find economy in downstream disposal of untreated waste and heat, but this reduces and often destroys the value of the streams for individual use, recreation, and other purposes. In terms of their interest, it is equally reasonable for great metropolitan centers to claim pre-emptive rights to regional waters for waste disposal, as when Chicago reduces water levels in the Great Lakes to flush its sewage down the Mississippi River.

The problem in industrial societies has been extended beyond discharge of wastes into water. The atmosphere has increasingly become a waste trap. Multiple deaths have been caused (as at Donora, Pennsylvania); and whole communities have been subjected to distress, and possibly damage to health (as in Los Angeles), or seriously inconvenienced (as in Pittsburgh and London). Four of the world's leading nations have found it necessary, each according to its own calculus of benefits and costs, to increase world-wide radioactive fall-out.

Less dramatically—and less urgently in relation to health—land, too, is despoiled by waste and debris. Most striking are the lands denuded of plant and animal life by noxious smelter gases and the like. Lesser forms of disfigurement, the unplanned by-product of efforts by firms and individuals to minimize costs, include the mountains of mine tailings, the urban dumps and scrap piles, and the vacant lots and highway margins strewn with bottles, cans, and other rubbish, which our value standards and institutions have thus far condoned.

True, the problem of waste disposal, once a problem solely for individual decision, is coming to be recognized as a problem requiring the application of social decision processes, but only slowly. There is a lag in social cognizance and a reluctance to assume new responsibilities. The consequences of continuing practices are not widely appreciated; or they are not deemed sufficiently disadvantageous to warrant action; or the institutional arrangements required for effective evaluation and decision do not exist. Often, as in the case of radioactive fall-out, all three reasons operate simultaneously.

Social problems concerning water have been created by growth. Most advanced societies are faced with such problems. Some are related to pollution. Others are those of providing adequate supplies at reasonable cost, and allocating supplies among competing claimants. Owing to lack of data, water was not included in our investigation of the cost of extractive output in the United States, but it is reasonably certain that the costs have increased and may increase further.

Water, of course, is a resource for which, in many uses, there is no available substitute. But it is also a resource which, until now, has been virtually a free good, and has been used with corresponding lavishness in modern societies. Already the provision of water at a nominal charge is ceasing to be appropriate in the arid American Southwest, where rapid population growth, due largely to immigration, has begun to strain available water supplies. In the course of time, provision of water at nominal charges could also become impractical in more humid regions.

There is a possibility, of course, that private and public research on desalinization and other methods of augmenting water supplies will rob the problem of some of its importance and urgency. But it is also likely that important changes will have to be made in institutional arrangements concerning water, and perhaps in value standards. One possibility is adoption of the price system as a device for rationing the use of water whenever its increased availability is subject to increasing cost. Another possibility is to change value standards concerning the use of water—to foster and develop a resource-saving ethic so far as water is concerned.

Land use, in our society, is often regarded as solely the owner's business. There is a degree of social decision-making, but the extent of planning for the use of land is extremely variable among the larger urban areas, is frequently absent in the smaller ones, and is virtually nonexistent elsewhere. It is legitimate to ask whether the present system is producing the kind of physical environment we want for ourselves and our children; and, if it is not, whether we want to pay the price, in dollars and restrictions, for better surroundings.

This question is often treated as if the only standards of value involved were entirely individual—matters of personal preference for urban parks and tree-lined avenues versus bare and narrow streets; for the outdoors versus the bustle of city life; for hunting and fishing versus nonpredatory modes of recreation; for the preservation of nature in the wild versus the creation of man-made harmonies or discordances. Regarded from the individual point of view it is true that these are matters of personal predilection. But the fact is that our preferences were largely built into us by the preceding generation, and that individuals as such have very limited opportunity to shape their environments. This suggests that the maintenance of a wide variety of alternative choices has social value, is likely to provide a larger number of people, in both the present and future, with environments permitting a more satisfactory quality of life than more restricted choice would do. It may often be difficult to obtain consensus on how to amend the environment in a particular case, especially if the decision caters to local and perhaps transitory interests, but there should be a possibility of substantial agreement on such general and durable goals as provision of widely accessible recreational opportunities, elimination of obsolete and ugly structures, preservation of the unusual, and so on. The chances of consensus should be further increased by knowledge of the effects of environmental conditions on physical and mental health.

The problem of the availability of recreational areas, which is likely to become more acute as the work week shortens and vacations lengthen, can surely be approached more deliberately and objectively than has been our custom. Similarly, the strand of conservationist thought which is concerned with parks, wildlife, and preservation of the natural biological environment generally reflects recognition that such resources have a unique and irreplaceable contribution to make to the quality of modern life. If society deems specific characteristics of the environment worth preserving, they must be saved from irreversible destruction. We say "irreversible" because, even though later generations could restore what earlier had been destroyed, often this could be done only with lavish outlays of time, trouble, and economic inputs. The future can reconstruct selected aspects of the past, and sometimes may do so at quite reasonable cost, but frequently the cost will be very high indeed.

The major problem of social interest in land use concerns the procedures for balancing benefits and costs. In many situations, institutional obstacles prevent this question from being faced. There are few adequate mechanisms for reaching community decisions concerning the physical environment, for matching the intangible benefits of a quiet and pleasing outlook to the tangible costs of acquiring it. Part of the problem is lack of a value consensus, for unless there is wide agreement that provision of pleasant surroundings, and replacement of monotony with variety, are good for everybody, the allocation of costs on an acceptable basis is difficult. Given better knowledge of consequences, however, and availability of enough alternative environments, existence of personal idiosyncrasy in matters of taste can be wholly consistent with the development of a new value consensus concerning the aesthetics and other noneconomic features of land use —a consensus conducive to an improved quality of life.

Natural resources, because of their high specificity and immobility, exert a particularly important influence on the geographic distribution of income, a circumstance stressed by the leaders of the Conservation Movement (who acquired some of their views from Henry George). In a Ricardian world the influence would be predictable: a concentration of income in the owners of agricultural land. In a modern world of technological change, owners or developers of other types of resources sometimes benefit—often, as in the case of Oklahoma and Texas oil fields, or real estate in a rapidly expanding metropolis, to an extreme degree. But sometimes they suffer serious losses, as in the case of Pennsylvania anthracite. More important, it is not only the owners and developers of natural resources that gain or lose, but entire communities and regions. Prosperity has accrued to broad sections of the Gulf States as the result of petroleum and other mineral reserves, but much of West Virginia is a distressed area. The cutting of forests has created and then stranded many communities. Agriculture provides numerous examples of regional distress resulting from the impact of growth. Social decision-making with respect to agriculture has been extensive. The dust bowl of the 1930's, for example, led to adoption of the federal Soil Conservation program. But solutions have sometimes brought forth new problems. Partly in consequence of publicly initiated and financed research and extension services, increases in productivity since the 1930's have exceeded the growth of demand for agricultural staples. Thus, growth and technological change, in a variety of combinations and circumstances, have created substantial shifts of income distribution, have been responsible for the creation of distressed areas, and have led to social decisions in the form of government interventions in markets, income distribution, and research.

The modern natural resource problem in these cases, it appears, is not diminishing returns, but social adjustment to a variety of adverse indirect effects of technological change and economic growth.

International arrangements concerning the use of natural resources, or for dealing with the consequences of such use, present a number of increasingly important and difficult problems. Radioactive fall-out, already mentioned, may cease in time to constitute a menace, but the development of large numbers of atomic power plants will raise problems of the disposal of dangerous wastes. Radical climatological control, already envisioned by meteorologists, holds great potential for improving social welfare. It also poses serious problems of social control. If used by particular nations for their individual benefit, the damage to other nations could be substantial. In extreme form, used as a weapon, the manipulation of ice caps could match the destructive potential of nuclear war. The use of man-made space satellites for weather prediction, and especially for the establishment of world-wide communications channels, is another area that transcends the interests of particular nations. The exploration of the moon and space have potential implications that are not parochial.

There is also a set of less dramatic international problems centering around world trade and investment in extractive products in less developed countries. One is the division of nations into two groups—the industrial countries, and the less industrialized, mainly raw material producing countries. During the past generation or two, technological advances and economic policies in the industrial countries may have worked against the interests of the less industrialized countries more often than in their favor. Synthetic fibers, rubbers, resins, detergents, dyestuffs, nitrates, and other chemicals have adversely affected the producers of natural products in underdeveloped areas. Increased agricultural productivity in the industrial countries, coupled with policies designed to protect their producers from adverse price effects, have disturbed world markets, again to the disadvantage of low-income nations. The protection of other domestic producers—as in U.S. petroleum and other minerals—has also denied low-cost producers in the raw materials countries ready access to industrial markets.

The prospect is possibly for further shifts, due to research, investment, and market dominance, which would favor the industrial countries. The case of iron ore, mentioned in the preceding chapter, is instructive. Technological research is making the abundant North American taconites competitive with traditional ores; and this could adversely affect the Latin American and African countries which expected to advance toward industrialization by transforming exhaustible natural assets into valuable man-made wealth. In this case perhaps, and probably in others, the tendency of technological advance to make natural resources more homogeneous, which we have noted in earlier chapters, reduces the actual or potential value of high-quality natural resources that once were essential for industry. Since the unexploited reserves of rich mineral resources are located mainly in the less industrialized countries, these countries are harmed, not helped, by such technological developments. It is possible that, on a broad criterion of social welfare, and probably also in the long-run interests of the industrial countries themselves, this problem requires social analysis and action.

Population growth is the most pervasive, persistent, and pressing of all the influences affecting quality of life in the poorer countries, mainly because its high rate retards the rate of growth of per capita income. The problem is not one of increasing natural resource scarcity and consequent diminishing returns, but of ability to achieve and maintain a desired rate of economic growth. In the well-to-do nations, as noted in Chapter 11, population growth presents no immediate threat to welfare, and if or when it does it will be manifest as deterioration in the quality of life due to overcrowding, not as an inadequate rate of growth of material welfare. In the poorer nations, now urgently seeking economic growth and development, the difficulty is primarily a severe shortage of capital per head, which is needed to exploit technological advance. At current rates of population increase, they cannot achieve the rate of capital formation, and the accompanying measure of technological progress, which are required for the rate of economic growth to which they newly aspire. Coale and Hoover, for example, have estimated that in India the growth of per capita output could be more than doubled in the next two generations from the single influence of a 50 per cent reduction in fertility rates and its effect on population numbers, age distribution, and capital formation.[2] To achieve such a goal is painful and difficult, no less for being the consequence of institutional and technical

---

[2] A. J. Coale and E. M. Hoover, *Population Growth and Economic Development in Low Income Countries* (Princeton: Princeton University Press, 1958).

conditions, than if it were the result of an inexorable law of increasing resource scarcity. To the extent, therefore, that scientific and social assistance is wanted by the underdeveloped nations which already have family planning programs, or subsequently establish them, they should be able to obtain it. Indeed, it is a valid question whether the industrial nations, and such international agencies as the World Health Organization and United Nations Educational, Scientific and Cultural Organization, should not help to initiate a basic and long-term program of study and research designed to make responsible planning of family size effective and acceptable. Such investigations, designed primarily to help the poorer countries meet their current pressing problems, would have the further advantage of helping the world society to consider how to limit its population when and if this should become a recognized social problem.

Reasons for Emergence of These Social Problems

The problems we have just identified, and others like them, have arisen because favorable technological changes, and the growth of output and population which they have made possible, have brought about certain unfavorable changes in other parameters of our existence. Undesirable conditions have been created which it would be very costly for individuals and private enterprises to correct, or which exceed their capacity to act. Such conditions, therefore, constitute social problems which, if not solved, deteriorate the quality of life.

The rate at which social problems arise, and their complexity, have increased with technological progress. Scientific advance, so rapid over the past century and a half, has increasingly become the strategic determinant of the influence of natural resources on the trend of social welfare over time. In advanced countries, it has freed man of the need to be concerned about diminishing returns but it has brought new problems in its wake.

The innovations that have increased productivity have vastly multiplied the alternatives among which, as producers and consumers, we are compelled to choose. Choice itself has thus become a problem, and therefore the mechanisms by which choices are made. The increasing division of labor that characterizes technological progress persistently increases economic and social interdependence, so that the number of persons affected by any given decision expands steadily. Economies of scale, also, are a notable feature of modern industrial societies. The resulting concentrations of productive capital in huge enterprises, and of people in urban areas, lend a special importance to many decisions with respect to natural resources. The method and extent to which some resources are developed and produced is determined in a relatively few corporate and governmental offices; and the mere fact of population density creates the increasingly difficult problems of waste disposal and pollution. Government increasingly has had to accept responsibility to mediate conflicts between interdependent interests, or to exercise its authority to solve problems that arise. But the procedures by which government evaluates alternatives and reaches decisions often lead to actions that are ill-conceived, poorly analyzed, insufficiently considered, and irrationally decided.

The capacity of scientific progress to create new problems for society, it appears, has outrun the capacity of social progress to solve them. Because of the lag of social innovation, it is possible to be concerned with whether man has learned how to avoid something comparable to diminishing returns in the quality of life, a point on which Mill was optimistic. The dynamic, accelerative character of technological change seems to suggest that expansion in the number of social and individual choices available to us is an endlessly cumulative prospect. But our calculus of decision-making and our social value standards are not much changed from Mill's day. And, unlike Mill, we do not look forward to a stationary state, with endless time to contemplate and devise a steady, costless improvement in the quality of life. There is, therefore, a question of whether requisite changes in our mechanisms of choice will keep pace with the dynamic development of the scope of choice. The classical economists saw the process of growth as subject to limitations, and we agree. But they saw the limitations as residing in nature, and we see them as residing more in man. The consequential problems may be old but their form and urgency are new.

Need for Improved Social Evaluation and Decision-Making Procedures

Great social progress, it is true, has occurred without collective concern over society's direction. A market system, as observed in Chapter 11, tends to generate changes in sociotechnical parameters, to modify its own conditions of operation, to produce a stream of innovations which help to provide escape from diminishing returns. If we are prepared either to forego making judgments concerning the total welfare value of market-generated decisions which change the conditions that determine how we work and live, or to adopt the postulate that such decisions always promote total welfare, the question of subjecting them to independent evaluation does not arise. If we are not prepared to take either of these steps, there is need to look beyond the "automatic" processes by which changes in sociotechnical conditions are brought about, and to consider whether in some respects social decisions beyond the market place—in addition to those already institutionalized—are necessary to prevent deterioration in the quality of life. We believe that there is need to look beyond the automatic processes, and to do so in a manner, and to a degree, somewhat different from current practice. The question is whether, if market decisions were supplemented, perhaps guided, to a greater extent than at present, by social decisions reached on the basis of social value judgments and analyses, this might not forestall some of the adverse effects on the parameters that determine the quality of life—effects which often accompany technological advance. In social benefit-cost analysis, so called, an attempt is made to estimate corrections to be applied to market results, and to recommend social action. This technique, however, treats only external economies and diseconomies, and only a part of these. A broader approach is needed. In particular, account especially needs to be taken of adverse parametric change, and methods for preventing or ameliorating the change need to be devised.

Adherents of the doctrine of consumer sovereignty may object that, although man has the power to make social decisions broader than those of the usual social benefit-cost analysis, he has not the right to do so.[3] This is a value judgment. It implies that the shape of welfare, generation to generation, will be better under absolute consumer sovereignty, with its limited horizons, its given sociotechnical parameters, and its individual-oriented decision processes, than if analysis and action are extended to include changes in sociotechnical parameters within their scope. Of course, the effectiveness of market mechanisms in permitting individuals to attain their chosen positions, or close approximations thereto, should not be lightly interfered with. This is our major means in a free society to achieve allocative efficiency within any given parametric framework. What we are saying is that we also regard the quality of the framework, and especially its rate and direction of change, as important. By its very all-embracing nature, moreover, the framework is a matter of political and social, as well as economic, concern to each individual, and thus a matter for societal decision. Standards of social value, in addition to private value, must be applied.

Society, it must be recognized, is not only a competitive but also a cooperative enterprise. Although ultimate ends are, in considerable measure, individual, cooperation is one of the ways of attaining individually valued ends more efficiently than in its absence. But it is quite impossible to maintain effective cooperation if each of the cooperators is concerned solely with his personal ends.[4] The means for their attainment involve other cooperators—some very close to him, as in family or business firm, some so remote as to belong to a different nation and culture. Since no individual or subgroup can possibly control all the conditions to which he or it is subject, the consequences of action must be, and are, evaluated to some degree in terms of their value for others. Otherwise the system of cooperation would break down, and all would lose.

[3] We say "may object" because the fundamental issue—evaluation of the parameters of choice—has been neglected. It is difficult to build a theory of welfare optimization if the parameters of choice are themselves among the items to be chosen. But if they are taken as given one must be a historical determinist to maintain that they are the best attainable at any given point in time.

[4] Chester Barnard, in his classic monograph on the theory of administration, puts the matter this way: "Cooperation compels changes in the motives of individuals which otherwise would not take place. So far as these changes are in a direction favorable to the cooperative system they are resources to it. So far as they are in a direction unfavorable to cooperation, they are detriments to it or limitations of it." *The Functions of the Executive* (Cambridge: Harvard University Press, 1938), p. 40.

Thus social value judgments have as their reference point what is good for mankind in general.[5] This does not require us to make subjective, interpersonal comparisons, to decide what is good for others in their individual capacities. Rather, it requires us to find out, objectively, what promotes the biological, psychic, and social health of the human animal—to determine the appropriate parameters for the fruitful exercise of freedom. Value judgments viewed collectively, the value consensus of a society, are the distillation of experience of what has been good for mankind. And, like all experience, this is capable of penetration and interpretation by the methods of science.[6] There is nothing odd in the familiar notion that the conditions of biological and psychic health are subject to empirical investigation, or that the assignment of a high social valuation to the attainment of such conditions is desirable. Modern societies promote such values where they do not exist. Much of what we do through the agencies of government and private association is based on the assumption that values are not wholly relative and ephemeral—that there are absolute, or at least long-enduring, needs and wants for which provision ought to be assured.

The problem with respect to much of the social framework is more difficult, however, than for health. The ill effects of agglomeration, for example, and the benefits of an environment with less ugliness and noise, are perhaps observed only by a minority. Water shortages and smog-laden air make an impression when they actually occur, but as mere potentialities they excite little serious concern. Distressed

[5] That is, value standards are not wholly relative. Many, as G. C. Homans has observed, have universal or near universal validity. Thus, he writes, "Social assumptions [value premises] stand because a large number of people accept them and for no other reason. . . . Some may be unconscious assumptions *of all human behavior.* In their emphasis on cultural relativity, the anthropologists have almost—not quite—forgotten that *there may be some premises held by all mankind." The Human Group* (New York: Harcourt Brace, 1950), p. 128. Italics added.

[6] Compare Emery Castle in "Criteria and Planning for Optimum Use," a paper given at the 1961 Annual Meeting of the American Association for the Advancement of Science: "The resolution of value conflicts will result from the 'hammering' out of policies which will differ only incrementally from those we now have. In this process empirical information will be of use; by their nature it is possible to achieve agreement on empirical propositions. . . . The acceptance of any given set of values represents an assumption with respect to the desirability of those values. It may well be that if the consequences of a given set of values were clearly understood they would no longer be accepted by the society."

areas are often regarded as unavoidable features of a private enterprise society. The acts of one's own sovereign state are usually but little questioned, regardless of the unintentioned bad consequences they sometimes have for others. Population growth as a social problem is avoided in legislative halls. Yet the more extensive, pervasive, and persistent adverse consequences of the ways in which we handle natural resources are capable of analysis and, presumably, of prevention by acceptable means. To recognize the possibilities is the first step. Our skill at analysis and social innovation will then determine how well we shall succeed.

In short, one may accept the desirability of increasing the opportunities for individual choice (itself a value judgment), while maintaining that a series of social judgments is necessary to define the limits of individual freedom in accordance with the criterion of what is good for mankind in general, or for society as a cooperative enterprise; and recognizing as a corollary of this proposition the implicit involvement of social value questions whenever there is the possibility of change in the conditions that define what can be done.

The difficulty, of course, is that, of all social processes, the most mysterious and the least subject to guidance are those by which value standards are formed and changed. But the formation and modification of a social value consensus is obviously a legitimate and a crucial object of concern. We think it would be desirable to act on the assumption that it is, in fact, possible to apply a more objective methodology to our value problems than we have been accustomed to believe. Man's relations to nature, we could well remember, were once regarded as governed by uncontrollable natural forces. Science, indeed, had just crossed the threshold to objectivity when the classical economists wrote; and this is why they held its potential in such low esteem. We may hope that we may be on the threshold of a similar transition to greater objectivity with respect to man's relations to man, which in our time has become crucial for handling man's relationship to the natural environment.

APPENDICES

A. GRAPHIC SUPPLEMENT

B. NOTE ON STATISTICS

GRAPHIC SUPPLEMENT *

Resource Conversion Function and Path

THE resource conversion function introduced in Chapter 5 may be visualized as a three-dimensional surface with R on the vertical axis, and R_u, $L_r + C_r$, on the horizontal axis, as in Figure A-1. The origin in this representation is in the center foreground and the surface rises as it recedes into the background. We are not, however, interested in the entire resource conversion surface. Since labor-capital is the only real cost element, it will suffice to find the particular path along the conversion surface where $L_r + C_r$ is a *minimum* for each amount of R made available. What we have labeled "path on surface" is the one we seek—the resource conversion path.

As noted in the text, the quantity of R_u is unimportant. It is therefore convenient to assume that the physical amount of R_u per unit of R is constant. If we express this physical relationship (along the conversion path) as $R/R_u = g$, this means that g is a constant ($g \gtrless 1$). The simplifying assumption employed (when necessary) for graphic purposes, is that $g = 1$; that is, that $R_u = R$ in physical magnitude for all points on the conversion path. But any other relationship, not necessarily constant, would be possible.

To simplify the graphical presentation in the text we employed a projection of the conversion path on the plane of R and $L_r + C_r$. In so doing, we lose no information concerning R_u. The assumption that $g = 1$ means that we can read both R_u and R from the initial scale on the R-axis. But no matter what the value of g, and whether constant or not, a single axis will serve. Given the scale for R, the R_u equiva-

* The assistance of Wolfgang Schoellkopf in preparing this appendix, including especially the figures, is gratefully acknowledged.
269

lents can also be shown along the vertical axis, whether g is constant or variable. An assumption that $g = 1$ means that the projection of the conversion path on the R, R_u plane will be a 45° line.

The unimportance of the magnitude of R_u for the Ricardian case points up the danger of confusing mere changes in the physical properties of a unit of resources (such as an acre) with true declines in economic quality. One may, for example, imagine a "pseudo-

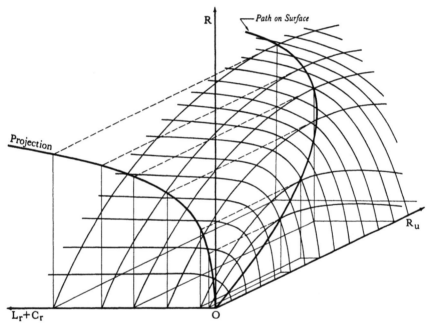

Figure A-1. Resource conversion function

Ricardian" case, in which there are changes in physical properties and in the quantities of resources used per unit of output, but none in economic quality. Thus, as one shifts from rich but heavy land to poorer but more friable soil, it may be possible to obtain the same output per unit of $L + C$ by using more of the latter land. The resource conversion relation in physical terms would then be simply $R = gR_u$ (g greater than 1), and the conversion path would coincide with the R-axis, but with a scale change. If this solution is substituted into the standard social production function the only modification is an increase in the number of units of resources per unit of output and per unit of labor-capital. The effect is similar to that of substituting acres for hectares.

Economizing Converted Resources

Use of the curvilinear grids, as in Figure 6 in Chapter 5, permits the relation of production with unhomogeneous resources to production with homogeneous resources to be shown explicitly. This is brought out in Figure A-2. Consider point c on X_8. The aggregate

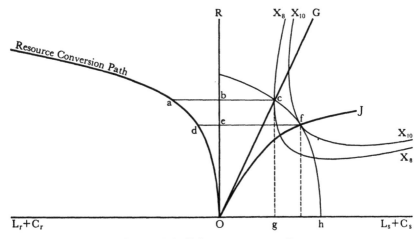

Figure A-2. Cost effects of declining resource quality

amount of labor-capital required to produce X_8 of output with Ob units of R is bc $(= Og)$. With a corresponding number of units of unhomogeneous resources, R_u, an additional amount of labor-capital equal to ab is required. That is, output X_8 now requires ac $(= Oh)$ units of $L + C$, divided into ab units of $L_r + C_r$ and bc units of $L_s + C_s$. Average real cost of output has increased correspondingly. Neither the amount of $L_s + C_s$ nor its marginal productivity has been changed by the switch from homogeneous to unhomogeneous resources. Point c, however, is not an optimal use of $(ab + bc)$ units of $L + C$ in the Ricardian case. By moving down the curvilinear grid to f the same amount of aggregate labor-capital df $(= Oh)$ can yield X_{10} of output. At this point, $L_r + C_r$ has been reduced to de and

$L_s + C_s$ has been increased to ef. This means that, because of the decline in economic quality of resources and the need to apply $L_r + C_r$ to get R, there will be a substitution of $L_s + C_s$ for R (and thereby for $L_r + C_r$) in the standard production function. In other words, owing to the rising cost of converting unhomogeneous resources it becomes economical to use less R. (Alternatively, the same output as before, X_s, can be produced with less than df of $L + C$.) On these assumptions, with Oh labor-capital available social output is a maximum at f, and similarly at every point on a Ricardian expansion path, for the given amounts of aggregate $L + C$ and the given conditions of resource availability.

The adjustment just described has another meaning. At output X_s, with Ob units of R and bc units of $L_s + C_s$, the marginal product of R is zero. Consequently, if the corresponding substitute amounts of R_u and $L_r + C_r$ were employed, the marginal product of $L_r + C_r$ would also be zero. The adjustment process described above, which reduced resource use to the equivalent of Oe units of R, raises the marginal product of R, and therefore of $L_r + C_r$, above what they were at c. Conversely, it reduces the marginal product of $L_s + C_s$ below its value at c. Since f, on path OJ, is a point of tangency between a production contour and a grid, total and average output are maximal for the given amount of aggregate labor-capital ($= Oh$), and the marginal products of the two types of labor-capital are equal at that point. This is true of every point along OJ, and is the defining characteristic of the path. The final result is that the labor-capital cost per unit of output at f is lower than at c.

Utopian and Malthusian Depletion Effects

The Utopian and Malthusian cases are illustrated in Figures A-3, A-4, and A-5. All assumptions are the same as in the first part of Chapter 5, except for the fact of resource depletion, introduced in the second part of the chapter, which is conceived as "eating away" the resource axis and, therefore, as shifting the expansion paths downward. The Utopian case is represented by the expansion path OJ on Figure A-3. There the path slides downward in a southwesterly direction through the origin as resources, extinguished through use, are simultaneously replaced by others of identical quality. In this limiting case, it makes no difference whether output is constant or expanding. Resource depletion has no real effect of any kind.

For the Malthusian case, where the resources available are of constant but fixed initial quantity, we define the point E on Figures A-4 and A-5 as the maximum point attainable on the *static* expansion path OE, given an original resource endowment of b and no depletion. Here, E has the same meaning as in Figure 5 of the text. So long as there were still unused resources, output would expand along the path OE, as in the Utopian case. Eventually the forces of growth, pushing expansion out along OE, and the forces of resource depletion, progressively reducing the available stock, would bring the society to the situation represented by E_o, where there are no more unused resources to bring into use as replacements for those lost through depletion. The precise location of this point would depend, of course, on the time path of output through all previous history as well as on the size of the initial stock of resources. Thus, E is never reached. Scarcity begins to be felt at point E_o, which is the maximum point attainable given the initial resource endowment, b, the fact of depletion, and a certain growth history. Resource extinction has the effect of reducing available resources to b_o, b_1, b_2 . . . (at times t_o, t_1, t_2 . . .) and of progressively lowering the resource-limit kink from E to E_o, E_1, E_2. . . . The cumulation of output progressively reduces the original endowment. For purposes of Figures A-4 and A-5, we have assumed that 20 per cent of the resources in use at the beginning of each time period are depleted during each period. Hence, the absolute amount of depletion per unit time becomes successively smaller.

Once point E_o had been reached, the society could follow two basic paths, or variations thereof. One, with constant labor-capital, would be the output contraction path, $E_of_1f_2$ . . . , on which each point (as on the other paths here considered) is conceived to be dated. This is shown on Figure A-4. Depletion makes it impossible for output to be stationary at E_o, assuming labor-capital to be constant at F. The other basic path, shown on Figure A-5, would be that in which labor-capital increases just fast enough to maintain output con-

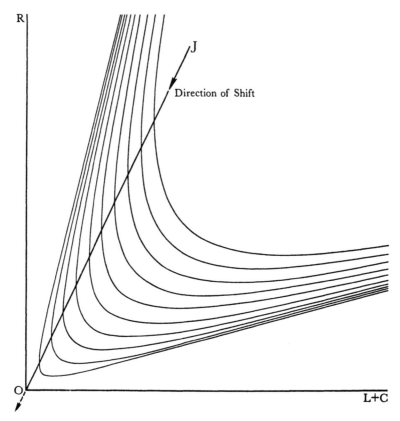

Figure A-3. Extinction effect: Utopian case

stant (for a time), as along the constant-output path, $E_0 g_1 g_2$. . . . Beyond g_3, no rate of growth of labor-capital is high enough to maintain output constant.

Given our initial assumptions in Chapter 5, there was only one optimal expansion path for each of the static models, regardless of the rate of growth of labor-capital. In the present depletion models there is a different optimal expansion path for each rate of growth of labor-capital (and each depletion rate).

A mental image somewhat similar to that represented by Figures A-4 and A-5 is, we think, implicit in some of the public concern cited in Chapter 2. The frightening feature of depletion in a parametrically invariant economy is that, even if $L + C$ did not increase, economic scarcity would develop and output per capita would decline. The original Malthusians could hope for escape from the dilemma of scarcity by means of moral checks to population increase. But a Malthusian who regards depletion as of overriding importance has not even this hope.

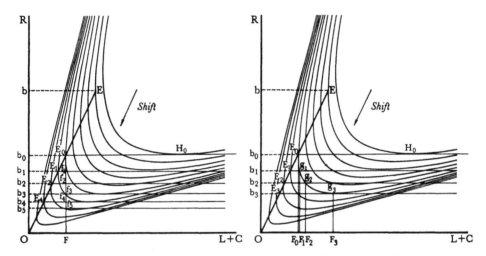

Figure A-4. Extinction effect: Malthusian scarcity, labor-capital constant

Figure A-5. Extinction effect: Malthusian scarcity, output constant

Alternative Reactions to Depletion in the Ricardian Case

The effect of depletion on the resource conversion path was described in the text. Here we consider certain possible reactions of an economic system such as that described by the production contours of Figure 6. Three basic reaction patterns can be distinguished for the Ricardian depletion case. Two of these correspond to the Malthusian constant labor-capital and constant output cases of Figures A-4 and A-5. The third is a special case of extreme rigidity of socio-technical organization in which output is held constant without re-allocating inputs.

The third reaction is the simplest to represent. This case is shown on Figure A-6. The assumption is that both output and the use of standard resources, R, are held constant. The resource conversion path is successively shortened by equal amounts of R_u. Under the present assumption, the R_u units cut off during any period of time possess the highest "quality index" of those in use at that time. (See Chapter 5.) The conversion paths, grids, and expansion paths shift together. To maintain production at E the society uses constant amounts of R and $L_s + C_s$, but because the quality of R_u falls, successively larger amounts of $L_r + C_r$ are required.

Leaving open for the moment the question of how the point E was reached in the first place, it is clear that E is not an efficient production point at t_1, t_2, and t_3. Too much R is being used, and thus too much of the available $L + C$ is being used to convert R_u into R.

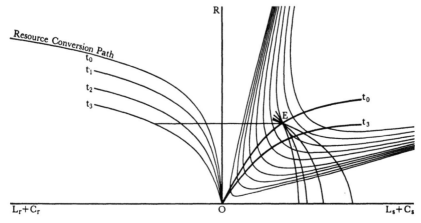

Figure A-6. Extinction effect: Ricardian scarcity

By reducing the use of R and R_u, and economizing on $L_r + C_r$, output could be held constant at an optimal level with smaller additions of $L + C$.

This optimally constant output case is shown in Figure A-7. If labor-capital grows at a rate that is just sufficient, with continuing optimal reallocation, to offset the effects of resource depletion, output will remain constant, and will trace out the path $E \ldots g_n$. For output to remain invariant, it must be noted, labor-capital must increase not only by the amount of $L_s + C_s$ indicated by the increasing distance between the R-axis and the path $E \ldots g_n$ but also by the amount of $L_r + C_r$ indicated by the increasing distance between the R-axis and the relevant resource conversion path. Since ever-smaller amounts of standard resources are used as they become more expensive,

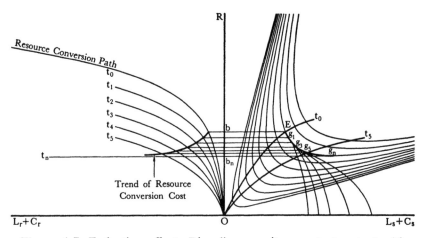

Figure A-7. Extinction effect: Ricardian scarcity, constant output with optimal reallocation

$L_r + C_r$ increases more slowly than in the previous case; and, in addition, the absolute amount of depletion per unit time becomes smaller. This case degenerates in the limit to a situation like that of Figure A-6, where production can be maintained only by holding R and $L_s + C_s$ constant without reallocations, and employing sharply increasing amounts of $L_r + C_r$ for resource conversion.

There remains the case in which labor-capital is maintained constant, shown in Figure A-8. As resources deplete and $L + C$ is kept

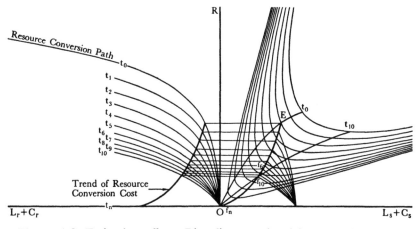

Figure A-8. Extinction effect: Ricardian scarcity, labor-capital constant

constant, smaller and smaller amounts of resources are used, and the absolute amount of depletion steadily declines. At the same time, the $L_r + C_r$ conversion cost also increases steadily, due to declining quality, as can be seen along the trend of resource conversion cost. Under these conditions, depletion forces output to follow the contraction path $E \ldots f_n$. The rate of contraction is greater than in Malthusian Figure A-4 because here resource quality is declining. Should resources deplete to a level corresponding virtually to the point t_n, the full amount of the available $L + C$ would be required to convert resources and none would be available to put the converted resources to use. A positive output could then occur only if hitherto constant labor-capital should begin to grow.

It is clear that, depending on circumstances, a given society may, under conditions of Ricardian depletion, attain a rate of growth of labor-capital that either exceeds or falls short of that necessary to maintain constant total output. If the process of resource depletion is very slow, it follows that the time rate of growth of labor-capital required to maintain output unchanged is also very small. On the other hand, if the depletion rate is high, it may be impossible for society to generate labor-capital fast enough to maintain constant output. It is now easy to see how society must have reached point E. It did so by attaining a rate of growth of labor-capital that was large in relation to the rate of resource depletion.

NOTE ON STATISTICS *

THE empirical data used in testing our hypotheses are derived chiefly from the related RFF volume, *Trends in Natural Resource Commodities* by Neal Potter and Francis T. Christy, Jr.[1] Since Potter and Christy do not include estimates of capital inputs, these data, together with the relative weighting factors for capital and labor, are taken from *Productivity Trends in the United States Economy* by John W. Kendrick.[2]

Our labor inputs are employment—"persons engaged" for the most part. Man-hours are more frequently used as a measure of productivity or real cost, but were found unsatisfactory by Potter and Christy because of lack of data, and because decreased hours per man and increased skills of labor tend to offset each other when employment data are used.[3] Man-hour data cover only a much shorter period of time and fewer industries than employment data; they are particularly unsatisfactory in the cases of farming and fishing, in which most of the workers live on the job and punch no time-clocks.

The weighting of outputs from 1870 to 1957 is by 1954 unit prices, except where otherwise specified. This gives each unit of each commodity the relative value which the market placed on it in 1954.

Similarly, the price indexes for the period 1870–1957 are weighted by the outputs of the principal resource commodities in 1954, thus reflecting the relative importance of each type of domestic output in that year. They thus omit commodities obtained only by imports,

---

* The assistance of Neal Potter in preparing this note is gratefully acknowledged.

[1] Baltimore: The Johns Hopkins Press for Resources for the Future, 1962.

[2] Princeton University Press for National Bureau of Economic Research, 1961.

[3] *Op. cit.,* p. 61.

such as tin, natural rubber, and coffee, and give relatively little weight
to some commodities produced in large quantities only in the earlier
years, such as firewood and anthracite. Commodities produced in
large quantities in 1954 (such as oranges and natural gas) are, on
the other hand, given heavy weight. Minor commodities which would
not significantly affect the movement of our indexes were omitted
from the computation of the indexes.

Our deflator, for calculating the price indexes of extractive *relative*
to nonextractive goods, is the "GNP deflator" calculated by the Department of Commerce [4] and Kendrick [5] adjusted by subtraction of a
linked extractive price index. This extractive index was computed by
chaining indexes with 1902, 1929, and 1954 output weights [6] with
links at 1914 and 1939. Weights were made proportional to value
added in the extractive industries as compared to that in all industries
—or more simply, extractive net output relative to gross national
product. An adjustment in these weights was made for each decade
(more or less) and the resulting 11-year nonextractive indexes were
then linked for the 87-year period.

The nonextractive output series is GNP in 1954 prices (Department of Commerce series as extended to 1870 by Potter and Christy)
less extractive output (value added) in 1954 prices, as estimated by
Potter and Christy.

The labor and capital inputs for the nonextractive sector were
similarly derived by subtraction of the extractive series from the
totals for the GNP. For labor, the employment estimates of Potter
and Christy yielded the required data directly. In the case of capital,
Kendrick's study provided data for the national total and for farms
and mines; to these we added allowances for the forest and fishing
industries based on the employment in these industries as compared
to that in the other extractive industries. The relative weights used
for combining the nonextractive labor and capital into a single input
were those given by Kendrick for all nonfarm industries.

We ran an extended series of data tests, using different weights;
Kendrick output and labor input data, to the extent available, in place
of Potter-Christy; alternative general price indexes for the economy

[4] U.S. Department of Commerce, *U.S. Income and Output*, 1958 Supplement
(Washington: GPO, 1958).
[5] *Op. cit.*, Tables A-IIa and A-IIb.
[6] Potter and Christy, *op. cit.*, Table EP-1.

as a whole; and other quantitative variations. The trend results were similar to those presented here in Chapters 8 and 9, and our interpretations and conclusions would not have been affected by using alternative data, where these were available and of good quality.

INDEX

For Product Safety Concerns and Information please contact our EU representative GPSR@taylorandfrancis.com
Taylor & Francis Verlag GmbH, Kaufingerstraße 24, 80331 München, Germany

www.ingramcontent.com/pod-product-compliance
Ingram Content Group UK Ltd.
Pitfield, Milton Keynes, MK11 3LW, UK
UKHW021117180425
457613UK00005B/124